MW00610382

RECOLLECTIONS

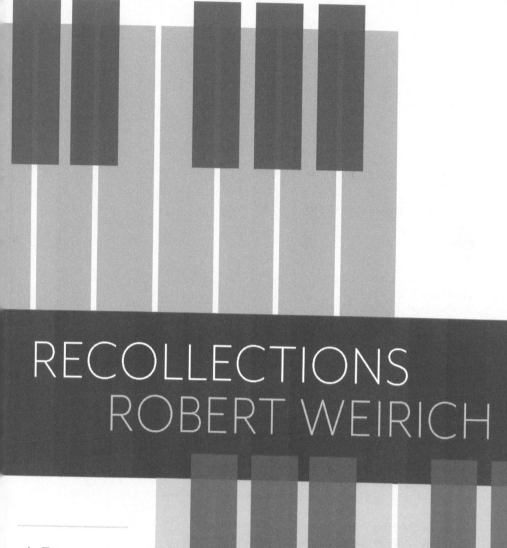

RECOLLECTIONS
ROBERT WEIRICH

A Pianist's
Essays on
Teaching,
Performing,
and Living

© 2023 by The Frances Clark Center

Piano Education Press
The Frances Clark Center
90 Main Street, P.O. Box 651
Kingston, NJ 08528

All rights reserved. This book or any portion thereof may not be reproduced or used in any manner whatsoever without the express written permission of the publisher except for the use of brief quotations in a book review.

Permission to reprint "The View from the Second Floor" and "Out of the Woods" columns was granted in an agreement between The Instrumentalist Publishing Company and The Frances Clark Center for Keyboard Pedagogy dated September 11, 2008.

"More Evidence" by Mary Oliver. Reprinted by the permission of The Charlotte Sheedy Literary Agency as agent for the author. Copyright © 2010 by Mary Oliver with permission of Bill Reichblum.

"Messenger" by Mary Oliver. Reprinted by the permission of The Charlotte Sheedy Literary Agency as agent for the author. Copyright © 2006, 2010 by Mary Oliver with permission of Bill Reichblum.

"Zen and the Art of Piano Study." Copyright © 1982 *Fanfare Alumni Magazine*, Northwestern University School of Music. Used by permission.

"The Education of the Performer." Copyright © 1985 The Instrumentalist Publishing Company. Used by permission.

"Thirty-Seven Years of Giving: A Thanksgiving to Donald Currier." Copyright © 1989 *Yale School of Music Alumni Magazine*. Used by Permission.

"Report on the 2013 American Pianists Association Awards Finals." Copyright © 2013 *International Piano Magazine* and the Mark Allen Group. Used by Permission.

ISBN-13: 978-1-7377237-5-2

To my students—with thanks for lessons you gave me.

Music: what so many sentences aspire to be.

—*Mary Oliver*

Contents

Foreword
By Mark Wait

For the better part of five decades, Robert Weirich has been one of the nation's prominent concert pianists and teachers. His range of achievements is daunting: he has held faculty positions at distinguished conservatories and universities, given master classes and lectures at national conferences, and played numerous concerts at leading venues throughout the country.

As if that weren't enough to give the rest of us an inferiority complex, Weirich is also an experienced composer, conductor, and artistic administrator. And in this book, he reminds us of another dazzling skill. Readers of *Clavier* and *Clavier Companion* know that he is a writer of uncommon eloquence and wisdom. His columns in those magazines have helped guide an entire generation of teachers and aspiring musicians since 1984.

This marvelous book collects many of those columns and provides narrative continuity to give them a new context. Instead of reading them one at a time, as we might examine individual pieces of a mosaic, now we see the entire picture, a coherent musical philosophy that continues to evolve.

The book you are holding could be called *The Making of a Musician's Life*. It is an inspiring memoir, a musical and intellectual autobiography. Here we find themes we will all recognize—the importance of various teachers over a lifetime of learning, encounters and events (planned or not) that change our lives. Many of us will be especially grateful to Weirich for his loving attention to his earliest teachers.

But this book is much more than a memoir or a collection, for it recounts the changing musical and cultural landscape of the past half century. Weirich has a broad vision, and he casts a wide net. We hear his thoughts, always carefully considered and often provocative, on artistic and educational values and the place of the arts in our society.

In all these issues, Weirich holds up a mirror to our cultural institutions—and to himself, for some of his views and opinions have changed during his fascinating and multifaceted career. We share his struggles as he considers the future of an art form to which he has dedicated his life.

This is a remarkable book by a singular artist, and it speaks to all who love the arts. It reminds us why we love music—and how fortunate we are to have Robert Weirich in our midst.

—Mark Wait, dean and professor emeritus
at the Blair School of Music,
Vanderbilt University

I

■ Beginnings

AT THE PIANO

The old upright player piano sat in the corner of Grandma's living room. She lived next to us along a red-brick road in a farmhouse built in the 1800s. All around were the fields of my Grandpa's farm on top of a northeast Ohio hill. The five miles we had to drive to get to the town where my father worked in the steel mill seemed to take forever. My other grandparents lived in town, but they didn't have a piano.

No one still alive in the farm family had ever played the piano, and its player mechanism had long since stopped working. The keys still worked, though, and whenever we visited, that piano had magnetic powers over me.

At first those odd knobs and levers inside the fallboard of the player piano became the controls of my rocket ship; these were the days of the Space Race. Slide the left lever and the engines came to life. Slide the lever on the right and, *vroom*, liftoff! Pump the pedals to control the speed, just like Dad's car. We were off to the moon.

Occasionally I would "play" the piano, hitting whatever keys fell under my hands and fingers, and my sister would "dance" to the music. Things could get loud, and Mom would shout, "Stop pounding that piano!"

One day the town side of the family had a reunion of sorts in a house I'd never been in. I knew what that big thing in the corner was, though—a piano! Various cousins took turns making noise, and Stanley, a year older than me, said with pride, "I can play 'Silent Night.'" With one finger, he plunked out the opening on the black keys, starting on D-flat. Just four notes repeated, "Silent Night, Holy Night," but he carefully showed me which keys did the trick. The first key was the lower note in the group of two black notes. I paid attention.

Back at the farm, when we went for our next visit, I tried to play "Silent Night" and found the correct keys easily—but where was the next key? The rest of that song had to be in there somewhere. Since Stanley had used the black keys, I started my search there. "*All* is calm." I found the note for "All" pretty quickly, my ear being the guide. The other notes I tried simply sounded wrong. I didn't know its name, but the right note was A-flat, sitting in the middle of the group of three black notes just to the right of the two black keys.

The next note took a while to find. "All is *calm*," I thought. "Where is *calm*?" I tried all the black keys, but nothing sounded right. So I ventured onto the white notes. "Sing it. Where is calm? Eureka! That white key just to the left of the three blacks sounds right!" Once *calm* was out of the way, the next few lines came easily. Back to the obvious black keys rising from the whites so visibly!

That tactic got me through to the line "Sleep in *heav*-en-ly peace." Where was that high sound for *heaven*? "Sing it again. Keep trying until you match that note. Aha! It's the white key just to the right of the three black ones." I plunked my way to the end, simply finding the notes that sounded right. It was fun. I liked it even more than playing Buck Rogers.

My ear must have known its way around "Silent Night" because my immediate family sang a lot. All those trips into town could be dull, so we sang songs. Five miles back then took a while. We sang Christmas carols. Folk songs. We attended church services every week, where there was congregational singing. I remember sitting next to my father as he sang bass, feeling his body vibrate with the low notes. I sang along as soon as I could. In short, the ear that helped me find the right keys to depress on the piano had been long in developing. I was blissfully unaware that it was happening until I needed it.[1]

After "learning" "Silent Night," I figured out "Hark, the Herald Angels Sing" and "Auld Lang Syne." All this was with one finger, but it

---

1. There is a remarkable book by Harriet Ayer Seymour from 1910 recommending that *all* musical training be ear-based. It is called *How to Think Music*, well worth reading. I also recommend a novel by Richard Powers called *The Time of Our Singing*, fictional but thought-provoking. It contains some of the most beautiful writing about music that I have ever encountered.

worked. My parents took notice, and before I knew it, Grandma's old upright had moved into our dining room. I was to have piano lessons with Mrs. Getz, a lady who lived on the road into town. We passed her house every time we made the trip. I was in the second grade. The lessons cost $1.75 for a half hour.

While it may seem impossible, in the first lesson I learned that my fingers had numbers, starting from the thumb (1) to the pinky (5); that counting involved quarter notes and half notes; how there were two clefs in the grand staff (treble and bass); and how the lines and spaces were named and remembered ("*All Cows Eat Grass*," and so forth). I also learned a song by rote called "Peter, Peter, Pumpkin Eater" that used both hands. My method book's first piece used only the note middle C, played first by the right hand and then by the left—"one-two, one-two, one-two," and so forth. I may be conflating a couple early lessons, but I don't think so. Mrs. Getz got things done!

I started lessons in November at the age of seven. My mother attended the lessons and sat with me while I practiced. The time at the piano did not feel like work, with Mom sitting at my elbow and our pet cat purring contentedly on her lap. I must have progressed quickly, because when it was announced to my grade school that all the students taking piano lessons could play in a recital that March, someone (me? Mom? Mrs. Getz?) leapt at the chance. I learned by heart "The Skaters' Waltz" and remember that the most traumatic thing about the process was being taught to bow. (I even cried!) At the recital, I must have been unbearably cute. The audience of parents and friends loved it.

* * *

As all this unfolded in rural Ohio, something called the Cold War hung vaguely in the air. Everyone was deathly afraid of the Bomb. Sputnik won the Space Race, but our side scored one at the piano, when in 1958, a tall Texan named Van Cliburn won first prize in something called the Tchaikovsky Competition in Moscow. I knew this from *TV Guide*, which advertised his long-playing record of the winning piece. I also noticed a show on occasional Sunday afternoons called *Young People's Concerts*, featuring the New York Philharmonic and its conductor, a galvanizing young American named Leonard Bernstein. The first one aired on January 18, 1958, barely two months after my piano lessons had begun. I think I saw it.

Midcentury America was optimistic about a lot of things then, including music. Public-school music instruction thrived. The itinerant vocal teacher who circulated among the grade schools in my Ohio district taught our class songs by ear. The township raised the ante when all the students in my small, rural elementary school's fourth grade were offered free flutophones. Once a week, the district's band director would come around, and the regular teacher gave him class time to teach us to play that simple melody instrument. Later that year came the invitation to take lessons on a real instrument—a clarinet, flute, or trumpet being the most popular. Parents paid a small fee and could rent the instruments before purchase. The students were immediately put into a ragtag grade school band. They loved it.

Since I already played the piano, I wasn't allowed another instrument. However, every one of my classrooms had an old upright piano stationed at the front, so I often played it at recess. When my friends started learning their instruments, I would try to accompany them on the piano. Their sheet music threw me, though. When they played a written C from their sheet music, it sounded B-flat. So rather than complain, I just transposed and found chords to accompany. I didn't know this was supposed to be difficult. "Mary Had a Little Lamb" is easy in any key, isn't it?

AT THE TYPEWRITER

I give all this background to set the stage for the essays I wrote between 1984 and 2018. Until 2003 these appeared in *Clavier* magazine, published by The Instrumentalist Publishing Company based in Northfield, Illinois. Founded in 1946 by Traugott Rohner, their first magazine was *The Instrumentalist*, a journal for the growing field of public-school music educators. By 1957 it had grown from a bimonthly printed only during the school year to eleven issues per year. The company started *Clavier* in 1962, riding the wave of interest in all things pianistic.

I wrote two different columns for *Clavier*. The first was called *The View from the Second Floor* and ran on a fairly regular basis until 1993. I taught on the piano faculty of nearby Northwestern University and was acquainted with the magazine's then editor, Barbara Kreader. She liked a longer piece I had written called "Another Look at the Competition Syndrome," and buoyed by her endorsement, we discussed a monthly column written from the standpoint of a university teacher. The magazine's content ranged from interviews with famous concert pianists to helpful hints for beginners. I reasoned that all pianists, be they teachers or performers, might be interested in the musings of a thoughtful correspondent from the trenches of the college world, a place and time that so meaningfully sets the tone for the future. As pianists we shared a love of the instrument and its music as we fought the good fight of making it as professionals. Surely there were messages that needed expression. So off we went.

For a variety of reasons, I changed the name of the column in 1993 to *Out of the Woods*. First of all, the second-floor metaphor was no longer truth in advertising. I resigned from university teaching that year, again for many reasons, not the least of which was burnout. In the meantime, I was living in upstate New York in a rustic setting, so the new title was as honest as any. You can read more about this on pages 10–11. I returned to university teaching two years later in 1995 and continued *Out of the Woods* until 2003, when I was elected president of the College Music Society. The two-year term required bimonthly writing from me, and this, coupled with increased teaching and administrative duties in my university position in Kansas City, led to the decision to retire the *Clavier* column.

Fast-forward to 2009. *Clavier* ceased publication entirely, selling its name and back issue content to the Frances Clark Center, based in Princeton, New Jersey. The Center published a magazine for teachers called *Keyboard Companion*, founded in 1990 by the late Richard Chronister, the chief organizer of the National Conference on Keyboard Pedagogy. With the acquisition of *Clavier*, the Center decided to merge *Keyboard Companion* and *Clavier* into a new magazine called *Clavier Companion*. The editor, Pete Jutras, and I had known each other since he was a student in the piano literature class I taught for one year at the Eastman School of Music in the early '90s. In his phone call inviting me to pen a column for the new magazine, he promised not to mess with my style. Furthermore, he only wanted three columns per year. How could I say no? *Winds of Change* is the result, written from 2009 until my retirement from university teaching in 2018.

The columns were essentially essays, by their nature momentary bursts, little explosions of personal insights shared with readers I could only imagine. The term comes from the French *essayer*, "to attempt" or "try," and indeed these essays are attempts at saying something that mattered deeply to my interior world when they were written. Time passed between essays, sometimes a month, sometimes a couple of years. Time has certainly passed since the 1950s, my childhood, to these days of retirement. Rediscovering the essays, I recognize each as an attempt to shine a light down a path, uncertain where it might lead. Those moments are now past, yet rereading many of them today, I recognize their prescience. As the winds of change blow, we are not out of the woods yet. The essays are presented here under subject groupings rather than chronologically. I precede them with an introduction or prelude written with the wisdom of hindsight to set the stage. Interludes may connect chronologically disparate pieces, and a postlude may follow to offer a final word. These thoughts span forty years. It is only now that I can draw lines one to another, to make the connections that have lurked there all these years. I hope the reader finds the journey rewarding.

PRELUDE TO THE FIRST COLUMN

Clavier prefaced the first *View from the Second Floor* with the following statement under the heading "About Pianists."

Beginning with this issue, *Clavier* introduces "About Pianists," a monthly column designed to provoke thought, strike a responsive chord, vent professional frustrations, or amuse. Allowing for a broad range of topics that do not fit easily into the regular table of contents, it is hoped that this column will stimulate letters and comments that may find their way into future columns. *The View from the Second Floor* introduces the first of three regular columnists, Robert Weirich, who will be sharing his perspectives as a pianist on the music faculty at Northwestern. Weirich received his formal training at the Oberlin Conservatory and the Yale University School of Music; his teachers included Emil Danenberg, Donald Currier, and Claude Frank. A winner in the first Rockefeller Foundation Competition for Excellence in the Performance of American Music, he is currently the Chairman of Piano at Northwestern University's School of Music.

1

The View from the Second Floor

SEPTEMBER 1984

Whenever I go to my studio at the university, I climb two flights of well-worn stairs that creak with every step. At the top of the second flight is room 218, my place of work for the past five years, and the scene of a lot of future work as well, if the gods of tenure are kind. The room itself has a fourteen-foot ceiling and three windows that look out over the street and a triangular patch of grass and trees called Oldberg Park. Arne Oldberg was a predecessor of mine, having chaired the piano department for forty-four years back in the days when that kind of longevity in a school was not out of the ordinary. Now the park separates the music building from a row of shops and restaurants. Just thirty yards from my hub of musical activity, you can purchase the *New York Times*, have your shirts laundered, and gain unwanted pounds at J. K. Sweets, as tempting a mecca for individuals with a sweet tooth as ever opened its doors.

As I gaze out over the park, my back is to the door of the studio, and on the other side of that door, students are frantically engaged in pursuing their musical education. In September new faces look about for signs that others are as frightened as they. By January everyone knows each other and is aware that the pace of life here is fast and furious. Practice, study, occasional breaks are followed by more practice, more study, few breaks. The stairs positively groan under the weight of feet changing classes. One floor above me, the practice rooms are going full tilt from 7:00 a.m. to 11:00 p.m. With so much going on all around me, I have to force myself to look out the window sometimes. Too often the frantic pace leads to an unwanted isolation and a lack of perspective as to our real purpose.

From the outside, the school is the epitome of the ivory tower—too many talented people in one place trying to outdo one another. From the inside, it is often a lonely place—in the effort to learn and improve, it's easy to lose track of the basics, to forget from whence we came. For example, college students usually have no memory of the learning process they had as a child. They forget the simplicity and wonder. College teachers are just as prone to forgetting their way, falling into the internal politics of the school or losing sight of their place in the larger scheme of music education. When I look out my window, I remember that the students who may come to me in ten years are right now out beyond that park somewhere, studying piano with an independent music teacher who allows them to delight in the freshness of learning before it gets hard. When I look out my window, I remember that the music world is much larger than the building whose stairs I climb every day.

While my views are from the perspective of a university teacher, I hope they will touch a recessed nerve in all pianists, appealing to the unspoken bond that unites us in the pursuit of our assigned muse. As musicians in the broadest sense, we have more in common than not. A concert artist rediscovering a Chopin nocturne is not unlike a child who first learns that a soft, caressing sound can be beautiful. Independent music teachers should take heart that I, as a college teacher, am constantly reminding my students to observe rests or that G major has only one sharp. Similarly, convincing the eight-year-old powerhouse that there is life in pianissimo is just as artistic a kind of teaching as that which I would attempt with a twenty-year-old playing the Schumann "Arabeske" for the first time.

Musicians are busy people; we often don't have time to think about the obvious but unremembered things. I am certainly capable of forgetting a good many basic tenets on a day when the phone is ringing every five minutes and all my students have the flu and are asking to reschedule their lessons later in the week.

In my five years of looking out the window, I've learned that sometimes it is particularly difficult to see anything. There are times of year when the weather is nasty and the accumulated winter is caked onto the glass; everything you see is either gray or melting. These are the times that we are often afraid to look, falling in upon ourselves, remembering only our failures. It is cold and dismal outside the window, and the hall outside the studio door is swept with a chilling, forbidding draft. Inside, the room is positively frigid. These are the times that we usually stop looking, fearing that there is nothing to see.

These are the times when it is most important to look.

2

Out of the Woods

Just as Dorothy in Oz discerned she was no longer in Kansas, the observant among you will note this is no longer *The View from the Second Floor*. After confessing in the November issue my indefinite withdrawal from university teaching, it seems only right to retire the venerable title of the old column as well. Upon publication, I received several notes from readers sending good wishes upon my retirement from writing for *Clavier*.

No such luck, dear friends. Anyone who spends even a moment on a soapbox realizes that one will relinquish said platform reluctantly, if at all. The *View* began in 1984 as the musings of a young, recently promoted associate professor who was confident of finding answers to every question. Topics emerged from whatever happened in the studio, in committee meetings, in the hallways, and in my head as I grappled with any of these. By putting something down on paper, I was forced to deal with each issue and usually committed to doing something about it after the act of writing.

Looking back over old columns, I can trace my gradual loss of innocence and the growing realization that answers may not always be easy to define. Nine years of writing the *View* left me feeling cornered, hemmed in by the unspoken expectations of the pedagogical party line. Headquartered on the second floor—my metaphor for advanced-level teaching in academia—I was supposed to know it all, and reading articles in other keyboard journals left no doubt that the piano teaching profession teems with certainty.

In my own work, though, the more I learned, the less I realized I knew. The harder I worked, the less I seemed to accomplish. The more I succeeded, the less each new success meant. I needed to get off the second floor.

So, I've gone into the woods.

The literal truth of that is that right now I live in the woods. My nearest full-time neighbor is at least a quarter mile away. Trees surround the house—lots of trees—and a stream runs down from the western fields past our house on the way to a lake that lies just to the east. I am learning the names of trees, and I've planted several that are new to the neighborhood. In the spring, I want to learn to name the birds by their calls. A friend about a mile up the lake has an ear that can distinguish the songs of most all the feathered natives in these parts. This column now comes to you from out of the woods.

I don't want to stay here forever, though. The metaphorical forest that I've entered is dark, threatening, inhabited by the gremlins that are my doubts. All our paths occasionally run through a forest; the thick trees block out the light, the temperature drops, and shadows flicker in the gloom. It's scary in there. We have two choices: go in, knowing full well something disastrous could happen, or don't go in, in which case we may remain safe but stuck exactly where we are—forever. The point is to get through the woods, confronting and defeating the demons.

Stephen Sondheim said all this much better in his work for the musical theater *Into the Woods*, inspired by Bruno Bettelheim's book on fairy tales and mythology, *The Uses of Enchantment*. The plot involves two trips into the woods by a cast of characters ranging from Cinderella to Jack of beanstalk fame. The trip in the first act is an innocent romp, symbolic of a person's coming of age. The second act trip is more serious: this time a couple of the best characters die in the woods. One of my problems is I know which trip I'm making. In both acts, the words to the song go "Into the woods, Out of the woods, and Home before dark." Yes, let's hope.

Finally, there is the forest-and-trees aspect to entering and successfully exiting the woods, as in the old saw about not being able to see the one for the other. I've already confessed elsewhere to confusion about how the many branches of our profession flow blindly along, following the paths of least resistance. This is why so many symphony orchestras program down to match the interests of a mass audience rather than enlarging the number of listeners through education. I question why so many public schools cut music from the curriculum despite the wealth of evidence that music study has so many positive effects on every aspect of a student's life. I wonder why independent piano teachers operate alone as tiny, part-time voices in a vast wilderness when performing arts organizations of all kinds could work with the local teachers cooperatively. All branches of music—performing, teaching, composition, publishing, instrumental sales—suffer more today than when I started writing a column nine years ago.

As someone who believes strongly in music's power to bring beauty into the life of a home, a community, and a nation, I think we need to work together to help our profession find its way out of the woods. This new column dedicates itself to that task.

3

Winds of Change

JANUARY 2009

Within days of this new magazine's release, the forty-fourth president of the United States will take office. The Constitution remains the same—legislative, executive, and judicial branches continue to operate as they have since George Washington's inauguration in 1789. No one would deny, though, that the man taking office in 2009 represents a fundamental change to the way this nation does business. Barack Obama ran on a platform of change. "Yes, we can!" chanted the crowds at his rallies. His call to arms—"We are the people we've been waiting for"—empowered more than one generation to throw off their complacency and become involved in the political process. As a result, we stand at the threshold of a new age—no one can predict what will happen, but whatever comes about is likely to be significantly different from the past.

It may be a long way from the halls of power to the practice rooms of our music schools or the studios of our independent teachers, but change is coming to our world. In fact, it has already arrived. You are holding at least one piece of evidence in your hands: *Clavier* magazine is no more—long live *Clavier Companion*.

As someone who wrote regularly for *Clavier* for nineteen years (1984–2003), let me offer a eulogy. Here was a special-interest magazine aimed at amateurs, performers, teachers, and students of the piano (*and* organ—how's that for change?). The editors recognized that these categories often represented different readers. Thus, the content aimed at something for everyone—an interview with a famous artist; a discussion or comparison of different interpretive possibilities in a repertoire standard; a new score offered for intermediate students; a pedagogic pep talk for beginning teachers; reviews of new publications, books, recordings; and rounding out each issue, a practical teaching tip from Frances Clark, the doyenne of progressive, enlightened piano teachers.

Over time, things changed: the amateur pianist is a dying breed, as are magazines aimed at a diverse readership. In search of subscribers, *Clavier* aimed increasingly at the piano pedagogy world—to some extent, that's where the advertising dollars were. Unfortunately, as year followed year, retired teachers gave up their subscriptions and new teachers, for whatever reason, didn't subscribe. The numbers dwindled. Fewer readers meant fewer advertisers. A venerable institution closed its doors.

Well, not exactly. *Clavier Companion*, the newly minted merger of the once-general *Clavier* and the even more pedagogically focused *Keyboard Companion*, stands on a threshold of its own, peering into the future, hoping it has one. So do its readers, because to a large extent the magazine's success or failure is the canary in the coal mine of our own.

There is a lot at stake here, more than any one of us can control. Print media of all kinds are struggling for existence given the revolutionary impact of the internet. If the *New York Times* is suffering, how can a little piano magazine survive? Quick answer: The *Times* has a fantastic website with extra material that can't be found in the print edition. It also emails subscribers the daily headlines. It has made itself even more ubiquitous—fewer people may buy the print edition, but the *New York Times* isn't losing its impact on society. (PS: *Clavier* didn't even have a website until a few years ago.)

I'd like to think that *Clavier Companion* can have an impact on society, but it can only do so by engaging a broader readership than either *Clavier* or *Keyboard Companion*. Somehow, it has to energize its readers to be the advance guard of change in our profession.

We don't need to change, you say? That's what *Clavier* said for too long, and then it was too late. We're quite comfortable in our little niche market, you say. Yes, I can relate to that—I'm busy enough and make a decent living. I've been haunted my entire career, though, by the fear that what I do is irrelevant. In 2006 I went through my old *Clavier* columns, hoping there was a book there somewhere. The only convincing theme I could find was my own quest to understand the place of "classical music" in modern, American society. Each column explored a question I basically tried to answer for myself and, by extension, for others in the profession who read them: as makers (practitioners and teachers) of classical music, how do we belong to *this* society—what is our role?

Over the years as I performed or taught throughout the country, people told me how much the columns meant to them. I guess there were others worrying about extinction. It seems there's still a need for a column like this, but this time around, I warn you that I'll not be content crafting swan songs to a noble yet superfluous pursuit. I am reminded of a recent bumper sticker: "If you are happy with the status quo, you haven't been paying attention."

Intentional change in any profession is initiated first through a shared sense of urgency. If the pipe in the basement has burst and you have two feet of water climbing the stairs, you immediately call the plumber. In our profession, we may not yet be wading around in hip boots, but how long have we ignored the leaks?

I think it's up to us, the ones trying to make sense of our role in this society, to call the plumber, and guess what, we are the plumber we've been waiting for (and our name is *not* Joe[1])! If recitals are boring, we need to change the way we present them. If our intermediate students want to stop lessons when they hit their teens, we need to find a way to enliven music study for them. It's not rocket science or even piano pedagogy—it's about connecting with others at the most basic level.

The Pulitzer Prize–winning author Thomas Friedman's latest book, *Hot, Flat, and Crowded: Why We Need a Green Revolution—and How It Can Renew America*, contains a most apropos Chinese proverb: "When the wind changes directions, there are those who build walls and those who build windmills."

From my vantage point, I believe our profession has built too many walls around what we do. (Can you think of anything more exclusionary than a piano competition?) It's time to build windmills. Let's work *with* the wind rather than resist it.

---

1. Joe the Plumber was a meme of the losing side in the presidential election of 2008.

II

▪ Foundations

The essays in the first section were meant to invite *Clavier* readers to reflect, remember, and perhaps renew their commitment to music study. Whether it be the memory of changing classes in a crowded hallway, taking time away from the hubbub of constant work, or finding faith in a new start, these momentary illuminations sought to soothe, encourage, and perhaps inspire.

Over the years, *Clavier* readers have asked me how I came to writing. Partially, it was a love of words. I adored grade school spelling bees. Two high school English teachers were grammatical taskmasters, failing a paper if it contained a comma splice. Mostly, I loved to read. The early possessor of a library card, I borrowed Steinbeck as often as long-playing classical recordings. As a teenager, my parents enrolled me for testing at a local vocational school to see what career suited me best. My father had high hopes for engineering. I remember a barrage of tests on two Saturday afternoons, asking questions about what I most liked to do, what mattered most to this young student. When the answers were tallied, I was told I was in the ninety-eighth percentile in music. The surprise at the time was learning that I was in the ninety-ninth percentile for reading and writing.

Before I started writing for *Clavier*, I wrote two "think pieces" that I now see as cornerstones to my approach to music and teaching. Both were requested by the Northwestern School of Music for different occasions. I'm not sure why they trusted a young, untenured faculty member with these assignments, but, never one to turn down a challenge, I agreed to the requests.

The first piece appeared in the tenth anniversary edition of *Fanfare*, the alumni magazine. Contributions came from professors from different departments: music education, jazz, theory, music criticism, and large ensembles. To recognize the many performance majors, I was asked to write about what goes on in private lessons. The somewhat touchy-feely result, "Zen and the Art of Piano Study," was probably not what the powers that be expected, but it gave me an opportunity to delve into the long-term psychological/philosophical journey that anyone undertakes when pursuing a life in performance. The title still embarrasses me, obviously borrowed from Robert Pirsig's novel from the '70s about a motorcycle trip in the West, but it rang true then and continues to seem right.

The piece has not been read widely, so including it in this compilation also seems right. I've reread it several times over the years and realize that the thoughts therein are foundational to all I have done since. There are immature things about it, but my teaching and performance have been guided by these inner beliefs.

The second piece, "The Education of the Performer," evolved from a speech I was asked to give to a group of donors at a reception following an afternoon performance at Pick-Staiger Concert Hall (where I played Beethoven's third piano concerto). The assignment was to engage the donors in how the performance program's educational goals were met. "Zen" did not seem appropriate, so I concentrated on five areas of training every performance major underwent: (1) sensitivity to sound, (2) complete physical control, (3) complete intellectual command, (4) complete emotional response, and (5) communicative projection. My remarks to the audience served as the basis for a three-part series of essays that followed the very first *View from the Second Floor*. The publisher Jim Rohner then requested I combine the three essays into one long article that appeared in *The Instrumentalist* in May of 1985, the end of my first year of writing for the organization.

These thoughts still seem foundational to applied music teaching in many schools. Despite their somewhat dated tone, I share them here. What can I say? I was young and trying to sound smarter than I was!

4

Zen and the Art of Piano Study

Fanfare Alumni Magazine
Northwestern University School of Music
1981

The most recent *Directory of Music Faculties* published by the College Music Society lists 3,895 teachers of piano in American institutions of higher learning. A full-time professor of piano at a conservatory or university school of music is likely to teach twelve to twenty students, ranging from freshman through doctoral students. Other full-time faculty in college music departments may teach piano in addition to music theory or history, and thus have fewer private students, as few as two or as many as ten, usually undergraduates. Some teach only as part-time piano instructors but may have as many students as full-time professors. It is impossible to know how many piano majors are presently working on degrees in the United States, but just to give the discussion a tentative focus, however arbitrary, let us assign a conservative average of eight students to each of the 3,895 teachers. We arrive at an estimate of 31,160 piano students studying each year in the American university system. This does not account for serious pianists studying with independent teachers unaffiliated with a school.

If a quarter of these students graduates annually, we find 7,790 pianists stumbling into a severely limited job market. Those 3,895 teachers already have the college market sewn up, and very few of them are willing to throw away their own security to give the young a chance. In recent years, as few as twenty-five college teaching positions have been announced annually—no cornucopia of opportunity there. The pianists planning on conquering Carnegie would do well to check the 1980 *Musical America Directory of the Performing Arts* that lists 439 "concert pianists" in its index. It is again an outright guess, but I would say that perhaps eighty of them make a living primarily from concert engagements. Of those, only eighteen are under the age of thirty-five.

What's going on here? Why are so many healthy, multitalented young people with dozens of options spending thousands of dollars and the best years of their lives in pursuit of an education that has little practical significance in these days of supply-side economics? Who is leading whom down the primrose path?

Rhetorical though these questions may be, they deserve answers. There is considerably more going on here than meets either the eye or the ear. The primrose paths of yesteryear have long since been grown over by poison ivy and bramble bushes. Students are constantly warned that they cannot expect a career handed to them upon graduation. They know it isn't easy; four to eight years of music study in college, university, or conservatory guarantees nothing. The question then remains: Why?

Most students arriving as freshman piano majors have already had some success as soloists. They have enjoyed special attention from their peers, from other adults, and especially from their parents. The classmates have been awed by the *Fantaisie-Impromptu* at the senior class talent show. Adults, teachers in particular, have encouraged the young musician since childhood, allowing him entry into the adult world through his music. The parents have doled out money, chauffeured him to countless lessons, suffered through attacks of nerves and stage fright (their own as well as the child's), and been proud as only parents can be. However, chances are good that our young Rubinstein has no idea why he wants to study piano in college. So far, it has simply felt good. The "Pathétique" Sonata and "Malagueña" are pretty much interchangeable.

The scene changes rapidly in that first September. The freshman is confronted with the serious upper-class piano majors who normally practice five to six hours a day and have nothing but disdain for sophomoric show-offs. He is aware of their ears listening to him in stern judgment through the practice room walls. The first lesson with the new teacher is also traumatic—our young friend leaves the studio, loaded down with incomprehensible works from four or five stylistic periods and enough technical exercises to put a gymnast in traction. He wonders if all his previous training has been inadequate.

The question quickly arises, "What am I doing here?" It is a very difficult, unavoidable question that must eventually be answered. There are, of course, numerous responses, but I believe they can be narrowed down to three basic answers.

The first seemingly simple answer is the most difficult to admit: "Get me out of here—this isn't for me!" Its meaning is self-explanatory, but the implications are broad, and unfortunately many students feel that they have failed, even though they often go on to great success in other fields.

Another answer is "I don't know what I'm doing here, but as long as no one forces the issue, maybe I can muddle through." Alas, this is a fairly common response, and it only delays the eventual coming to terms with the real situation. The implications of avoidance deserve more attention than can be given in this article. Suffice it to say that the faculty has a great responsibility to deal head-on with this response whatever means are at their disposal. Not doing so can prevent the student from learning anything of lasting value.

The third answer is again somewhat simplistic: "I'll show *them* I can do it!" This answer is masochistic, childish, and altogether necessary if one is to go on.

Playing the piano well is as difficult a chore as any of the many complex tasks humankind has invented in thousands of years of civilization. Physiological control of the fingers, hands, wrists, and arms must be complete. A good deal of the rest of the body is involved as well. The infinity of scale patterns, arpeggios, contrapuntal combinations, and chord configurations concocted by composers of the past three hundred years must literally be at one's fingertips. (There are 479,001,600 different combinations of the chromatic scale alone.) Each composer worthy of that title has built an aesthetic world complete unto itself, which must be totally assimilated by the performer if he is to project the music successfully. Finally, the sheer quantity of piano music is enough to occupy the pianist for several lifetimes. A list of the standard repertoire put together for a literature class contains over 870 different works. This number is staggering, since it contains only the *standard* repertory. And while it contains many short works, such as the nineteen nocturnes of Chopin, it also includes the thirty-two sonatas of Beethoven, many of which are monumental works.

So, the student struggles. He works long into the night in the practice room. He juggles practice time with other coursework, with a dining hall job to help pay the tuition bill, and with a semblance of a social life during a stage in his personal development when such interaction is of paramount importance. He gets through the first public performance without falling off the stage or doing too much damage to Brahms.

He continues to practice. He performs as an accompanist and begins to make music with others. He performs in juries that are graded by the faculty. He receives little encouragement or attention as in the old days before college, but he is determined to prove something, and he is getting better. At any moment in this progression, the student can still answer "This isn't for me" and move on to the greener pastures of prelaw. At every step of the way in music, expectations rise rather than relax. Each performance should be better than the last, each confrontation with a composer's spirit closer to the ideal. If the student is still a piano major in the junior year, chances are good that he will graduate as a piano major.

The hours in the practice room bring on a subtle change in the student's motivation. The childish answer "I'll show them" begins to give way to "I am showing myself." The question, too, is no longer "What am I doing here?" but rather "Why am I so obsessed with playing the piano?" The transformed question and answer blend into one: "What am I showing *myself*?"

To answer this, we must take a closer look at the nature of music itself. Most people know of the historical conventions of the Classical and Romantic stylistic periods. The music written between 1750 and 1820 by such composers as Haydn and Mozart is usually thought of in terms of its economical, carefully proportioned form—hence, classical. However, between 1820 and 1900, composers like Schumann, Liszt, and Tchaikovsky were more concerned with the emotion inherent in music, with spontaneity and tonal opulence—in a word, romantic. In our dualistic society, classicism is opposed to romanticism, just as science is opposed to art or intellect is opposed to feelings. We have been stuck in this way of thinking since the ancient Greeks invented Apollo and Dionysus.

Would any scientist claim that there is no art in his work? Is any artist unaware of the science inherent in art? Although the terms *classical* and *romantic* are useful in discussing certain aspects of music, the truth in a larger sense is that all music is both classical and romantic *at the same time*. The underlying form of the classical coexists with the spontaneous, romantic beauty of the moment. Music is a reconciliation of two modes of seeing the world. It is intellect and emotion simultaneously.

Music has another elusive characteristic that is extremely important. Among all the arts, only music and drama unfold in time. At the conclusion of a composition, when the work has been revealed in its artistic entirety, the beginning is long past, possibly forgotten. In fact, *every* moment of the piece is in the past, and the present contains only the final chord. How does one apprehend a sense of the whole?

Music is a realization of the past, present, and future, all occurring simultaneously. Every note of a composition (each note representing the present) implies every other note, both past and future. This is a philosophical concept that has appealed to both Occidental and Oriental thinkers throughout the ages. Saint Augustine wrote:

> For if there be time past and time to come, fain would I know where they be...yet this much I know, that wheresoever they now be, they are not there future or past, but present.[1]

In Eastern thought, the yoga system of *sphotavada* (sound metaphysics) conceives of all manifestations of the universe, both mind and matter, as consisting of sounds of varying concentration, frequency, and wavelength. The four categories of sound are interesting to consider: *Vaikhari*, the sound produced plucking a string; *Madhyama*, the transition between heard sound and its inner vibration; *Pashyanti*, the sound heard

---

1. *Confessions XI, xi, xviii*. See also T. S. Eliot, *Burnt Norton*.

only by the spiritually awakened aspirant; and finally *Para* (from the Sanskrit word meaning "transcendental" or "beyond"), which lies deeper than ordinary silence—it is the inner sound that is experienced as the unrealized root-sound, or sound potential.[2]

Even in Western music, the sound carries the listener from present moment to present moment, hinting at both the past and future of the composition along the way. "The past cannot remember the past. The future cannot generate the future. The cutting edge of this instant right here and now is always nothing less than the totality of everything there is."[3] Classical truth and romantic beauty come together in an eternal present that transcends time and place.

Meanwhile, our student is still practicing, probably not consciously aware of any of this, and much more concerned with getting through his senior recital than with philosophical implications. Still, he starts to notice that the highly emotional Liszt Sonata he is working on has an underlying form that gives the virtuoso abandon an additional and far more profound meaning. He struggles with the excruciatingly slow tempo of the second movement of Beethoven's Sonata Op. 10, No. 3. Each bar takes between six and seven seconds to play, and there is a four-bar phrase at the end of the exposition that takes nearly half a minute with a *ritardando*. Yet, when it works, it is as if it were conceived in one instant. He begins a contemporary piece that at first seems impossibly frustrating, but it soon takes on a logic and beauty of its own that carries him relentlessly forward. He finds that he spends nine hours at the piano one day and is astounded that he is more happy than exhausted. The greater the challenge, the more rewarding the work becomes.

If things are going well (and it should be noted that this still implies no outside recognition of the student's work), the aspirant becomes aware of an answer to the question "What am I showing myself?" He is showing himself his Self, if you will. He begins to know himself. The daily focusing of physical, mental, and spiritual energies in one direction causes the student to probe ever deeper into himself to find

---

2. Ajit Mookerjee, *Yoga Art*, 26–27.

3. Robert M. Pirsig, *Zen and the Art of Motorcycle Maintenance*, 283.

greater stamina, more intellectual discipline, and a truer response to his own humanity. This probing can be painful—how many twenty-year-olds from late twentieth-century Middle America can enter Beethoven's world without a struggle? The pitched battle is a necessary prelude to artistry. Mozart's *Die Zauberflöte* and Wagner's *Die Meistersinger* are both concerned with the ordeal of this inner conflict and are wonderful lessons, musically and philosophically, to the young supplicant. Artistry must be deeply desired and fought for with great determination.

What began as a way of securing attention and admiration has become a quest for an ideal realization of the composer's work. One attempts to achieve a complete union of the Self with the Music. One must know the Self and the Music completely, and, as difficult as that is, a union is even more difficult. We are speaking metaphorically of the pursuit of satori in Zen, of Poincaré's harmony,[4] of something similar to Plato's Good. (It is interesting to ponder the fact that our words *god* and *good* come from the same old English root, *gōd*; the old High German word is similarly *got*.) More precise than Plato's Good is the ancient Greek concept of *arête*, which predates Apollo and Dionysus and can be translated as excellence or duty to Self. This in turn is an almost exact translation of the Sanskrit word *dharma*, the One of the Hindus. Each individual is capable of a union, and therefore capable of an ideal performance, but no two performances will ever be alike, since no two individuals are alike. Even two ideal performances by the same individual will be different since that person's existence will be different at different times. There is an infinity of possibilities.

It does not matter to the musician that the union is seldom, if ever, achieved. What matters is the attempt, which is the very process of music making.

If the student realizes any of this, however subliminally, during the course of his education, he will be forever richer. Even if at this apparently advanced stage he decides to change fields, he is still richer for his experience with music. The concept of *arête* can be found in many areas of endeavor—the chef who prepares the gourmet meal you order

---

4. Jules Henri Poincaré (1854–1912) was a French astronomer, physicist, mathematician, and philosopher.

at a fine restaurant, the architect who designed the building in which you enjoy being, the mechanic for whom your car purrs contentedly. All know something of *arête*. However, for everyone who knows, there are hundreds who know nothing of it or care nothing for it. It is a concept that is valuable in everything from ditchdigging to neurosurgery, but it is not easily taught. Music allows its teaching.

If the student stays in music but achieves neither fame nor fortune, that too doesn't matter. With each partial success comes the realization that the union still beckons and is even more worth seeking. It is at least a lifetime's work.

I died for beauty, but was scarce
Adjusted in the tomb,
When one who died for truth was lain
In an adjoining room.

He questioned softly why I failed?
"For beauty," I replied.
"And I for truth, — the two are one;
We brethren are," he said.

And so, as kinsmen, met a night,
We talked between the rooms,
Until the moss had reached our lips,
And covered up our names.

—Emily Dickinson (ca. 1862)

5

The Education of the Performer

The Instrumentalist Magazine

MAY 1985

Faculties everywhere spend a lot of time in committee meetings discussing "the Program." We endlessly revise and modify requirements in the hope of devising a curriculum of study that will turn every one of our students into first-class musicians. How many juries should they play? How many recitals? How many years in a major ensemble? Should we require this class or strongly recommend that one? We have these meetings year after year trying to find one program that will work for every student. By now most faculties know this is impossible, but we keep trying. Perhaps, one day, we'll get it right.

A performance study program is an especially tough nut to crack. We can assign technical exercises to improve the fingers. We can teach courses in music history and theory. We can put the students through performance requirements in which they show how much the technical exercises and courses in history and theory have helped. Unfortunately, none of this guarantees that first-rate performers will emerge from the system. Even talented students can go through such a program and not know what it is to be responsible, expressive, and artistic.

We need to examine the nature of the performer and the training needed to create one. We have the capacity in the American university system to give performing students a great deal more than they presently receive, if we are willing to challenge conventional notions a bit.

Every performer needs the following assets:

1. Sensitivity to sound ("a good ear")
2. Complete physical control ("a good technique")
3. Complete intellectual command ("head")
4. Complete emotional response ("heart")
5. Communicative projection ("personality")

Musicians communicate their thoughts and feelings through the sound they create. They must have extraordinary sensitivity to the evocative powers of sound—the ability to conjure up tangible images through intangible auditory impulses. They must personally identify with the sound so that performer and sound are literally inseparable. When you think of the truly great artists, the first thing that comes to mind is their sound. Artists like Stoltzman, Rampal, and Horowitz each have a sound when they play that immediately identifies them. During the days that Heifetz, Piatigorsky, and Rubinstein played together as a trio, it was said that people felt great pleasure just hearing them tune. How can we promote this?

Technical control is in large part physical. A pianist must exercise complete control over fingers, hands, arms, shoulders, torso, posterior, and feet. Even that is a partial list. Scale practice is the tip of the iceberg for any student musician in coming to grips with the physical aspects of playing their instruments. What we are really talking about is the physical ability to produce that intangible sound, and to do it with each note we play. Are we teaching this?

Intellectually, performers must coherently organize an entire composition, relating each note in the piece to every other note while understanding the place of the composition in the sweeping panorama of history. Performers should be able to memorize—an intellectual and physical feat. If their performances are to be of lasting value, an analytical persuasion is necessary. Many child prodigies fall by the wayside because they are not able to analyze the music or what they are doing; they are simply good imitators. To simultaneously achieve that almost mystical sound, understand the physical necessities required, and conceptually hold together the entire composition is quite a challenge. The flimsy, dull, irrational mind is not up to the task. Are we training the mind as a whole?

Performers should also be capable of great emotional response. They react to the music only when it touches something they can hold on to, cherish, remember in dark times—in short, something they can love. Response also suggests responsibility. Performers are responsible for touching in others that which music touches in them. A great performance is one in which the listener comes away feeling exalted by the beauty of the music and renewed by the emotional truths that the music holds. Performers are the intermediaries through which this takes place. Can this be taught in a program?

Finally, performers must have the desire and ability to project all the above to an audience while living with their own rapid pulse, rushing adrenaline, and fear of repudiation that goes with the act of performance. There is a great deal at stake and the pressure is sometimes overwhelming. Yet it is in the act of performance that all of one's strivings come together; the sound, the body, the mind, and the heart are all united in the attempt to touch. How is this taught?

If music making is to be an imaginative, humanistically integrated pursuit, music education itself must be at least as inventive, designed for the whole being.

Teaching a student musician to listen to sound involves training the ear to concentrate with an intensity bordering on the maniacal. The ear must become a magnet for every aspect of the sound produced: the attack, the sustaining quality, the decay, the joining of one pitch to the next, the blending of the voices of a chord, the movement of one harmony to the next. Learning this sensitivity to sound should involve more than a couple of ear-training classes taught by a graduate assistant. What about a class that cleans out the ears of the students? Immerse them in things they have not heard before, like electronic music, African music, or John Cage's music of chance. What about a class that trains them to ascertain pitch and duration to a more exact degree than we presently require? Many pianists have no idea of intonation, and they should. How about requiring at least one term of composition? The putting together of notes and harmonies is an extraordinary lesson in the nature and power of sound. No less an authority than Schnabel advised his students to spend some time every day putting notes on paper. What about the ubiquitous requirement of playing in a large ensemble? Many schools require four years of constant membership in a band, orchestra, or chorus, but all too often the requirement is an excuse for putting bodies on stage. Ensemble instruction should be, among other things, a workshop in sound. Four years buried in the back of the clarinet section is no guarantee that the weaker student will improve.

The study of instrumental technique takes place in the studio, but there is more to playing a scale than moving one finger after another. Is an anatomy class designed for musicians out of the question? Actors take movement classes. Is there a musical equivalent? The dreaded "phys ed" classes of high school days failed because they concentrated on brawn rather than brain. If students understood why they were studying a pursuit such as yoga, swimming, or gymnastics, might it not affect the physical aspects of their playing? Inner balance, the smooth transition of muscle groups, and the sequence of preparation, execution, and recovery are as much a part of instrumental technique as they are a description of the ideal tennis stroke. Yet we do not encourage this kind of thinking.

We are probably most successful in our present system of education in the realm of training the intellect. We have theory courses that teach form and analysis. We have history courses that fill out the students' understanding of the events surrounding a composer and his work. What we do not have is a way of integrating these courses into the fundamental experience of performing. Is it time for the applied teacher to teach an occasional class in analysis, showing that it is indeed important to know where the recapitulation begins? Is it time for the classroom teacher to visit an occasional lesson to see that the esteemed artist-teacher doesn't fill up fifty minutes talking about the color of the sunset in the coda? At long last, might we have learned that it takes more than music courses to train the mind? For too many years, we have given short shrift to the role of foreign language study, mathematics, logic, art history, literary criticism, and philosophy in the music curriculum. The present ratio of one liberal arts course per term to three or four in music is not necessarily the best. What about intellectual recreation? How many students at your school know how to play chess?

The rhetorical questions raised have answers, which you may have supplied along the way. But the most important questions are: What can we do about any of this? Whose responsibility is it?

I would suggest that the applied teacher and the conductor have the most power to affect change. They are the people who see the students regularly on a one-to-one basis. They have the most influence, for better or worse. The students are not likely to be open to the fullness of the musical experience unless these two crucial figures encourage and lead the way. If the adviser does not suggest foreign language study, the applied teacher should. If the conductor cannot demonstrate what is meant by listening with magnetic ears, how can a student be expected to pick it up in any other class? No matter how much thought is given to a curriculum, integrated or otherwise, the private teacher and the conductor have the lion's share of responsibility for the musical education of the students—an awesome and frightening fact.

We must now deal with the qualities of a performer that are most difficult to teach: the capacity to respond emotionally to music, and the ability to communicate that response to an audience. Indeed, our usual procedure is to avoid dealing with these matters altogether, falling back on the old explanation of "They either have it or they don't." Talent surely helps, but that is not enough.

The fact that few musicians agree on the role of emotion in music is already an impediment. The pendulum has swung throughout music history, ranging from the Apollonian elegance of the Classics to the Dionysian excitement of the Romantics. In our own century, we have had both; composers as diametrically opposed as Stravinsky and Rachmaninoff were alive and working as contemporaries. The fact remains, however, that most teachers active today were trained in the period that favored neoclassicism and ultrarational serialism.[1] Composers like Boulez and Babbitt wanted nothing to do with emotion and said so. Conductors such as Toscanini made a religion out of fidelity to the score; it is a lesson that many have embraced. However, this reliance on the printed score does not help us get to an awareness of that which the music touches.

Sometimes I ask one of my piano students playing a Chopin Ballade what the composer is trying to say emotionally in a given passage. The usual response is embarrassment and then a halfhearted stab at, perhaps, "...Sadness?" It isn't long before we begin to discuss the meaning of the word *emotion*. Students are often even more uncomfortable with this, since many have the sense that emotion cannot be defined. It is a private

---

1. This was true in 1985; I'm not sure it is still the case. Music education changes as tastes change.

matter, hidden in the subconscious, and most people are happy to leave it there.

I ask them if Chopin had emotions.

"Of course," they say.

"How do you know?"

"Well, it's in the music!"

"How do you know?"

"Well, listen to this, you overintellectual professor! Hear that falling minor second? Listen to that resigned cadence!" Suddenly they play with conviction and true feeling.

I wish it were that easy. In this scenario, the student felt several emotions: embarrassment, indignation, fear, possibly defensiveness, and finally the resignation and melancholy of the music. He also felt the desire to communicate this last feeling, to touch another person with his own insights into human emotion. He cannot be taught to feel those emotions. However, he can be taught to recognize them. This awareness allows him the objectivity to consider the emotion openly, turning it this way and that to refine and focus its communicative potential.

Again, we can take a lesson from our friends in theater. Actors study Stanislavski and the "Method," which suggests that the performer study a character, be aware of the emotions of that character, and then "feel" those emotions by recalling an event from the actor's own past in which the same emotions were present. It is a practice that not only acknowledges the primacy of the emotional message of art but integrates the personal experiences of the performer with the work at hand.

The emotional content of music and the ability to communicate it are closely related. Both depend, in large part, on how much the fledgling performer loves his work. Again, this love cannot be taught, but the teacher can encourage it and help the student become aware of this love. Often, our work as educators can be thought of as a process of unlocking or tapping potential, not of building one block at a time. Of course, it is necessary to put certain pieces in place. Each of the performer's needs—the sensitivity to sound, the physical technique, the perceptual as well as conceptual capacities of the mind—can be built up methodically. All can be taught. Getting to that reservoir of artistry in every student is another matter. Finding it and helping the students to accept their capacity to feel and touch is perhaps the greatest and most rewarding task of the teacher.

We teach performance, but performance is not a product. We can't put it on a shelf and admire it. What we really teach is a way of living, a pursuit of life in which all sides of our being are put to use: sensory, physical, intellectual, and spiritual. Socrates implored his students, "Know thyself." Thomas Carlyle suggested, "Know thy work and do it." Performing is a remarkable synthesis; it is certainly work, and the study of performing is in a sense the growing awareness of Self and its abilities. The daily focusing of physical, mental, and spiritual energies in a concentrated direction causes the student to probe ever deeper into Self to find greater stamina, more intellectual discipline, and a truer response to his or her humanity. Even if the student does not make a living in music, the study of music has helped him know himself, and he will do whatever he does—his work—better because of that study.

III

■ On Becoming a Performer

It was a long way from figuring out "Silent Night" to playing at the White House during the Ford administration. Somehow, by age twenty-six I had become a performer. Not that I was famous, then or now, but a good part of my life was centered on trying to play the piano so well that others would want to hear me.

Unpacking that last sentence, we can explore three areas. "A good part of my life" suggests that succeeding meant a lot to me. No hobbies to speak of, although I occasionally tried to make myself into a gardener or a skier. Didn't party much. Travel usually meant getting to the next performance. "Trying to play the piano so well" admits that although I had talent, I still needed to practice—a lot. The desire to succeed at the highest level meant hours alone at the instrument, repeating things for that demanding audience of one. "That others would want to hear me" gets into the business side of performance, involving managers, presenters, conductors, and sponsors—a world of which I was blissfully ignorant. I thought if only I could play well enough, the performing world would invite me onto stages everywhere. By the time I figured it out, it was too late—I was middle-aged, busy as a teacher who nevertheless performed as often as I could.

Naive? Yes. Fatal? Absolutely not! I have had a rich life in music, as have many others whose names are not famous. As small as it is, the classical music world offers opportunities for those determined to make themselves indispensable. However, the rewards are not always concrete. The essays that follow sing of some of the glories, those intangible incentives.

As suggested in the earlier "Zen" essay, part of the desire to perform at a concert level comes from an internal need to "show them." It is related to that old maxim about pulling yourself up by the bootstraps. Alas, this is physically impossible, but American meritocracy promotes it, especially to the susceptible young. There is also the desire to overcome fear. Among other things, stage fright is the fear of failure. (The fancy word for this is *atychiphobia*!) Perfectionists are lifelong sufferers. On the good days, when you soar through a difficult piece or surmount the obstacle of playing for judges in a competition, you gain confidence, and the next time is easier. You feel stronger; you come closer to your imagined ideal. Beware, however, of perfectionism. No one can get there, despite trying.

I painted a sunny picture of my first lessons; recalling those memories still brings joy. There were also less rosy times, and in the interest of full disclosure, I'll share some of those. Once when I was no more than eight, I wrote a simple piece with a pencil on homemade staff paper. My mother chastised me and said I shouldn't be making things up. She may have meant well, but I didn't try to compose again until I went to college. Another mishap involved learning my first piece in six-eight time; I just couldn't figure out how the quarter notes should get two beats when I had learned that they only got one beat. My father, who played tuba in his high school band, was called in and became frustrated that I didn't get how in six-eight the eighth note got one beat and therefore a quarter got two. That brouhaha led to some tears. Another time, I played for the assembled family at our house and got a spank for taking the half-dollar my grandfather gave me. No wonder I later had troubles with the business side of music!

* * *

Growing up in music, though, encouraging things happen all the time. If it weren't for those shots of dopamine, we'd abandon the piano for something more rewarding. I never doubted I liked performing. There were those annual Moffitt Heights grade school recitals where I was the star. Around the fifth grade, the school principal asked me to play onstage every day while each class filed through the lunch line to pick up meals at the cafeteria window. That was the equivalent of a daily forty-minute recital experience (and yes, free Muzak, but I didn't care). There was an upright piano at church camp where I played pieces I knew, and if someone asked me for a popular tune of the moment that I didn't know, I'd try it anyway. The theme song to *Bonanza* was a big hit. At sixteen, I got to play *Rhapsody in Blue* with a local high school band and, a year later, the first movement of the Grieg Concerto with the Canton Symphony conducted by Michael Charry. In my last year before going off to Oberlin, I now see how my teacher, Daniel Winter, pointed me up the artistic mountain with his own veneration of such pieces as Beethoven's Op. 111 and Schubert's B-flat Sonata. Finally, there were the recordings I had been collecting with my two-dollars-every-two-weeks allowance—symphonies and tone poems, concertos, and solo playing by the likes of Fleisher, Horowitz, and Gould. These formative experiences validated my growing love for the art and my determination to stick with it.

Does one "decide" to become a performer? Chances are it will not be a cold, fact-based, rational judgment. One is constantly comparing pros and cons. It can be as simple as a physical feeling at the keyboard, and when the gods align to allow you an expressive, near-faultless performance, the happiness can last for weeks. The tough times (memory slips, inadequate technique for the difficulty of the piece) are discouraging, but the determined self-improver answers with "I can fix these things with more practice."

The essays that follow are love songs to the piano itself, to the feelings inspired by our connection to this glorious instrument, to great performers, on the future of virtuosity, and finally a speech I gave, full of attempted humor, at making a career in performance. Sometimes you just have to laugh.

6

In Praise of the Piano

The View from the Second Floor

OCTOBER 1989

Experts tell us that a piano has over ten thousand working parts. It is, without a doubt, a machine, one of the most complex of musical instruments. Unlike the violin or the flute, which are held, even cradled by the performer, the piano sits obstinately on the floor, confronting its executant, outweighing her by a significant margin. From the point at which the player's finger touches the key to the point at which the hammer strikes the string, all kinds of wooden, metal, and felt pieces swing into motion, distancing the player from the actual sound. As soon as the sound is made, it is beyond the player's control, irretrievably decaying into silence. As a musical instrument, it leaves a lot to be desired.

Yet if ten pianists in a row sit down at the same keyboard, the listener will hear ten different qualities of sound. If they were all to play the same piece, the listener will discriminate between ten different sonic varieties that defy verbal analysis. The same piece somehow isn't the same piece, and against all odds, this highly mechanical beast responds to ten unique artistic personalities. Even ten beginners have ten different sounds. It's nothing short of a miracle.

How to describe it? Some players have a crunch to their sound. Others defy gravity and send the tone floating up and away. Some create a meltingly fluid sound; others give each note the clarity of an etching. Some players have thick, plump sounds; others go for a sinewy muscularity. The best pianists can achieve all these—and dozens more. Most serious pianists can identify a Horowitz recording in about five seconds, just from the sound. Same with Glenn Gould. Of course an extremely personal style of playing is associated with both these pianists, but the sound alone is enough to identify them in a drop-the-needle game. The pianist produces the sound, but a well-regulated piano responds unerringly to the performer's wishes.

Not long ago, Alfred Brendel visited Peabody and talked about Schubert to a graduate seminar. As he spoke, he moved to an old and ailing classroom grand to demonstrate a point, and every pianist in the room cringed in embarrassment for what we feared our distinguished guest would hear. To everyone's amazement (perhaps even Brendel's), it sounded like Brendel playing Schubert. Even on a bad piano, everyone sounds different.

This is a delightful state of affairs. Here is an instrument that rewards the patient, listening player. It will whisper sweet nothings or strike with thunder and lightning. Furthermore, my sweet nothings will not sound like your sweet nothings. It is also an instrument that screams when mistreated and sounds thoroughly mechanical under the hands of a performer whose key punching takes precedence over his ears.

There is talk in the industry today that the piano is outdated, that composers aren't interested in writing piano music anymore, that young people find it boring. We are encouraged to look to the new electronic keyboard instruments as the way of the future. After all, with these modern miracles we can achieve any sound by flipping a couple switches or by connecting a computer to the keyboard. Want to sound like a violin? Great, just punch that button, crank up the potentiometer, and voilà—a violin. Only problem is, Billy's violin sounds just like Susie's. Yes, you can do a full orchestra on one of those babies, but it won't really sound like an orchestra, and my phony orchestra will sound just like your phony orchestra.

I'll take the piano as it is, thanks very much. To my mind, the new keyboards are a step backward: even the supposedly touch-sensitive ones are more like the harpsichord than the piano. I'm sure an electronic keyboard can be used with artistry and imagination (so can a harpsichord!), but it simply is not as personal as a piano. It only takes a millisecond to change the way two notes are connected on the piano: in an instant, a pianist can through sheer physical skill and musical artistry make the collective heart of an audience skip a beat. Turning a dial just isn't the same.

7

The Divine Madness

The View from the Second Floor

JANUARY 1993

When you play the piano, something happens that may well defy description. You might call it an awareness, a communion, even an enchantment. To know this feeling completely, one must experience it, but seduced by the late hour and a particularly good day of practicing, I want to try to write about it.

It can happen after many years of playing when you sit down and first touch the piano, finding a sonority that sustains forward into the silence. The keys are depressed, the flesh of the fingers finding the familiar contact with the keys. The arms move smoothly, floating effortlessly to the next sound. The body accustoms itself to the motions dictated by the preordained arrangement of black and white. You feel it happen with your whole being; the muscles align, the mind is alert, the spirit centers. When it happens during a performance, you feel that you can move mountains, that whatever gods there be have accepted you into their company.

There is, quite simply, a madness that descends when you play the piano. How else explain the dedication of its adherents to an instrument that takes up too much space, provides too little income, and promises complete fulfillment just around the bend of another day of practicing?

Like most pianists, I am convinced that this is a divine madness, a spell cast by a sorcerer of great power and wisdom. Perhaps the greatest reward of all is discovering the identity of that sorcerer.

Whatever happens can first be described as a feeling, an awareness that suffuses the body whenever it does something it has learned how to do—or discovered how to do—extremely well. It is the animal joy of motion, kinesthetic animation coursing through the limbs, the freedom of flight. It is not something you feel when starting lessons unless you are gifted with extraordinary technical facility. A student struggling with a scale isn't there yet. It can be discovered, though, at any age and does not depend on anatomical gifts. While youth's flexibility may facilitate its acquisition, more often than not impatience and inexperience combine to impede its revelation.

It is the sense that mind and body are one, that whatever the inner ear hears, the hands know how to find it. It is the connectedness of intention and result. For the truly gifted, it's achieving the end without even knowing how you got there.

The rest of us come to it after many years of knowing it exists but sensing as well that we've not yet experienced it. Each breakthrough excites us; the closer we get, the more we're sure that we have at last figured it out. Unfortunately, many of our certainties have a way of vanishing overnight or, conversely, of hardening into dogmatic concrete.

It is something that practice alone won't uncover. In fact, our most diligent, goal-oriented practice sometimes obfuscates the enchantment, and we perfect our discomfort, repeating for the umpteenth time the habits of our dis-ease.

This bewilderment goes beyond the body too. Where does singing originate? There is nothing physically inborn to cause our breath to pass over the vocal cords in such a way as to produce song, yet there is melody lurking in most human hearts. Our spoken language suggests that giving voice to that melody requires *expression*, literally something to "press out." This implies that making music is no easy task, not to be taken lightly, and that doing it involves digging down and bringing something out that would have been just as happy to stay inside.

But when everything is right, when the sounds happen just as you imagine them, when the instrument is an extension of your own being, there is no "pressing out," only liberation. There is no struggle, only euphoria. Somewhere above it all, the mind experiences the body finding its way through the phrases and sings along with the line pouring forth from that inner reservoir. There is no strain, only joy, and finally—surprise. How can this be happening? Where did that nuance come from?

It's addictive, this feeling. I suspect that people want to play the piano to experience, even fleetingly, true creative freedom. It may take forever, but that's not important. Every short-term goal, even if it is learning the E-flat scale for the next lesson, is part of the larger picture. If the task can be seen as unifying body and mind, seeking to release the inner song, it will prove fulfilling. The sorcerer will cast his spell, and eventually you discover—the sorcerer is you.

8

The Glory of Live Performance
The View from the Second Floor
APRIL 1986

Last night I heard a performance I will never forget. It was one of those times when from the first note you are transported into a musical realm that knows no argument, where everything seems right. Before the performance, you sit there waiting, knowing you are tired, that dinner disagreed with you, that it's been a long day. Then the music begins, and in that first instant, the fatigue vanishes, the mind focuses, and the heart opens to receive a timeless message bespeaking humanity's understanding of the universe. These are transcendent experiences, both joyful and chilling, exultant as well as humbling.

They happen so rarely. This column is in praise of the fact that they happen at all.

Last night the performer was Leon Fleisher. The music was the Bach Chaconne as transcribed by Brahms for the left hand alone. So profound was Fleisher's conception that three centuries were present in the moment of the performance. One heard the vast architecture of Bach's monumental structure vaulting heavenward, its foundations firmly rooted in the earth. One heard the achingly beautiful richness of Brahms exploring the high baritone range of the piano, remaining faithful to the gesture of the original yet adding a depth of expression that suggested the late intermezzi or, perhaps because of the key, the D minor piano concerto. Finally, one heard the present as revealed by Leon Fleisher, an artist of unique sensibility shaped by tremendous insight and personal courage. He is the Mahler of pianists.

One happily suspends critical judgment in a performance like this, but I forced myself to analyze the qualities that made it so uplifting. The sound was gargantuan, or so it seemed; the opening theme had the force of a pronouncement from on high, yet how could one hand on one piano be so strong? As the piece progressed, the sound had such a visceral impact that it seemed as though Fleisher were carving it from a vein of granite deep within the earth. As the first section inexorably grew, he found more sound, the rhythmic inevitability of each succeeding variation carrying one forward with an almost frightening intensity. Then came the second section in D major, the sound bathing the listener in a radiant warmth that was simultaneously soothing and ennobling. Here one listened rapturously to the subtlety of Fleisher's phrasing, wonderfully supple, always breathing. There was freedom, yet always in the service of that inevitable forward motion. For the second time in the performance, time stopped for me; I could hear in all directions at once, backward to the preceding variations, ahead to the inevitable musical goal, all contained within the eternal present. The rest of the performance was a blur—I know what happened, but it transcends words. By the clock, the whole thing took fourteen minutes or so; my experience of it was that it was both eternal and over in a moment. I know I wanted it to go on forever. It will do exactly that in my memory.

I have been extremely lucky in that about eleven months before this I heard another performance I'll never forget. On that occasion Claudio Arrau played the Liszt Sonata. The situations were completely different from last night's: the hall was much larger, I was farther from the stage, there were more people, and it was a Sunday afternoon. But again, the magic happened. Arrau has long been associated with the Liszt Sonata, and I have listened with pleasure many times to his recording of the work. Yet something happened that afternoon that made it a totally new experience for both the performer and the listener. From an already high level of understanding, Arrau broke through to an even more rarified vision of the work, and those present were privileged to witness an artistic veracity that had taken a lifetime to achieve. The sound in this case was not overpowering; in fact, it was rather weak. But it didn't matter—without going above a healthy *poco forte* to today's slammers, Arrau created a universe. The climax of the "second movement" was heartrending, emotionally draining and as powerful as any orchestra, yet in reality it was only a bit louder than *mezzo forte*. Pianistically the performance was amazing. The fugue flew by with a lightness and dexterity that would have been the envy of a pianist a quarter Arrau's age. The performance again became a blur after a certain point, but with the last enigmatic low B, Arrau seemed to snap his fingers and awake everyone from the trance that had been the piece. With that single note, the whole coalesced into a totality that is not only unforgettable but can never be repeated.

Such is the glory of live performance. It doesn't happen often, but when it does, it changes you. For that moment, music is a metaphor for creation, and through the interpreter we are allowed an understanding of our world that no scientific report, however profound, can give us. We had heard as one, which magnified the experience, and we needed only to look at each other as our eyes said it all. Did we really hear that? Were we present at Creation?

Exultant…and humbling.

9

The Horowitz Mystique

The View from the Second Floor

JANUARY 1990

On November 5, 1989, Vladimir Horowitz died. It takes some getting used to. No serious pianist alive today could ignore him. Most felt his influence. Some even imitated him—or tried. His recitals packed the largest halls. Everything he did made news—the musical press chronicled each nuance, while newspapers and television made his name known to more people worldwide than any other pianist in history.

His effect on pianists was so great that I predict many of us will remember years hence what we were doing when we heard the news of his passing. I was driving home from an afternoon recital I had given in Syracuse; National Public Radio led its second half-hour newscast with the story. Shock was followed by surprise, and then by disquiet as I remembered that I had played Schumann's "Arabeske" as an encore. It had given me more pleasure than anything else on the program, and of course it was one of Horowitz's trademarks. I shuddered a bit in the gathering autumn twilight, electronic voices emerging from the car speakers.

Pianists everywhere no doubt recalled their own memories of Horowitz, gifts garnered at private but significant moments. I was probably around thirteen years old when his first recording appeared after his long, self-imposed 1953 retirement from the stage. I was fairly naive at the time, but I was quite sure this was playing unlike any I had ever heard. He overwhelmed me the first time I heard him in person, around 1976 in Hartford. By this time, I was in my last year of graduate study at Yale, and you can be sure I had become more sophisticated since age thirteen. I couldn't wait to hear the legend, to see if he could possibly measure up to my expectations. He walked onstage, smaller than I had imagined; one could almost touch the crowd's excitement. He launched into Clementi's big C major sonata, and I recoiled from the clangor of what I took to be a truly lousy instrument. I spent that first *forte* phrase cursing my bad luck at hearing Horowitz saddled with an odious piano. Then he played the second phrase and dropped the dynamic to the most breathtaking *piano* I had ever heard. In less than ten seconds, he captivated me, and when the next *forte* came around, it seemed absolutely glorious.

Many of his firsts were front-page news: his first recital on network television, his first concerto performance since coming out of retirement, his return to the Soviet Union. Even his first Mozart concerto was a major event. He seems to have had an uncanny sense of publicity, a flair for dangling an irresistible carrot before a world that still cared enough to reach for it. More than any other pianist in recent memory, he made all kinds of people listen.

Horowitz and the public maintained a lifelong flirtation. Even in this day of shopping malls and fast food, perhaps especially in these days, people want something different, something special and exciting. He was one of the few classical artists to reach a public beyond the narrow field of classical music lovers. For its part, that public proved eager to lavish on Horowitz not only its attention but an ardor that reflected the pianist's own passionate music making. We put up with his eccentricities, both personal and professional, and perhaps even doted on them, because they, too, were something out of the ordinary. If his repertoire did not contain the twenty most requested concertos, it didn't matter, because what he did with a handful of pieces made you forget your own name, let alone the fact that he had never done Op. 111.

In prose that would bring a blush to a Fifty-Seventh Street press agent; the Associated Press's obituary mourned the death of "the 20th century's titan of the keyboard whose passing created a void than can never be filled." It's true: he was a titan, and there will never be another one like him. What he offered was—no other word will do—unique. His rewards were commensurate: fame, wealth, adoration, awe.

I mourn his passing, but I am grateful that he is irreplaceable. He proved that even today a pianist's life can make a difference.

10

The Greatest Generation?

The View from the Second Floor

FEBRUARY 1990

Several issues remain for consideration as we bid adieu to Vladimir Horowitz. To me his greatest legacy is that a pianist can still make a difference, even in today's postmodern, heroless world.

With luck, another pianist might rise to a position of similar influence and importance, unique in his/her own right. In an attempt to make a prediction about the next important pianist, it might help to look back on Horowitz's predecessors.

Here was a generation of giants. How else can one describe a time when Hofmann, Gieseking, Lhévinne, Cortot, Rachmaninoff, Schnabel, and Bartók were all active? Their combined accomplishment is almost overwhelming.

Bartók is recognized forty-five years after his death as one of the century's most important composers, comparable in stature to Beethoven or Brahms. That he was an excellent pianist is often overlooked, although David Yeomans's book *Bartók for Piano* has a revealing chapter on this topic. He performed traditional literature as well as his own works, and while his later life was devoted primarily to composition, he understood performing as few composers can today. Ours is the first generation in which composers do not perform and performers do not compose.

Rachmaninoff was well known and extremely popular as both pianist and composer. It's a pity if you are unfamiliar with Rachmaninoff's recordings; here was an artist of such towering attainment that even Horowitz pales somewhat in comparison. As a composer, he left three symphonies, four incredible piano concertos, the *Rhapsody on a Theme of Paganini*, two operas, important choral works, and numerous songs and piano pieces. Schumann would certainly have said, "Hats off, gentlemen...a genius."

Schnabel and Hofmann were also composers. Hofmann was the first classical pianist of note to make a recording; in 1887, at the age of eleven, he cut several cylinders at Edison's laboratory in New Jersey. He also directed the Curtis Institute for twelve years, wrote two books on piano playing, and left over one hundred compositions, many under the pseudonym Michel Dvorsky. Somehow he also found time to come up with seventy scientific and medical patents. Schnabel was at the forefront of the modern trend toward a more objective style of playing. His compositions, however, were quite daring, written in a Schoenbergian twelve-tone style. He was particularly influential as a teacher, and his students are among the present generation's most respected artists. His writings show a highly literate, civilized sensibility.

If we look back yet another generation, we find a truly formidable figure, namely Ferruccio Busoni. Here was a Renaissance man: a spellbinding pianist with a gargantuan repertoire; a prolific composer of some of the most avant-garde works of his time; a transcriber of numerous works of Bach and Liszt; a teacher of both piano and composition with full-time appointments in Finland and, later, Berlin; and an author of several essays on music, which reveal a profoundly philosophical mind. Busoni's character transcended uniqueness: his life and work were one, a continual quest toward a rebirth of the musical art. In his essay "The Realm of Music," he exhorted:

Come, follow me into the realm of music. Here is the barrier which separates the earthly from the eternal. Come, there is no end to the astonishment but yet we feel ourselves from the beginning at home. And now the *sound* makes itself manifest! Countless are its voices, compared with them is the whisper of a harp a fearful din, the blaring of a thousand trombones a mere chirrup. All melodies, heard and unheard, resonate together and at once...melodies of love and sorrow, of spring and winter, of melancholy and high spirits...are themselves the feeling of a million beings in a million epochs.

Heady stuff! Can you imagine Busoni writing a departmental memo? Even if the prose style is no longer fashionable, it's hard to imagine any other way of stating such beliefs. I admire his courage and stand in awe of his accomplishment.

Looking at these earlier generations of pianists forces us to acknowledge a frightening artistic depreciation. We toss the title *pianist* about proudly, but Schnabel's teacher Leschetizky once told him that he would never be a pianist because he was too much a musician. Most of these men were even more than that.

Perhaps specialization is partly to blame. There are more good pianists today than ever before, but as the level of playing improves, reaching that level requires more time. Less time is available to read, think, and live a full life. Today it is difficult to become a *Mensch*, let alone an *Übermensch*.

It's a perplexing issue and worth more thought. As far as predicting what the "next important pianist" might be like, I think we can be sure that this player will break the mold and defy the trend toward artistic depreciation. If not, there really won't be a "next important pianist."

11

Mountaintop Experiences

Winds of Change

November/December 2010

You may know the French phrase *plus ça change, plus c'est la même chose*: the more things change, the more they stay the same.

When I began this column not quite two years ago, my intention was to focus on the persistent winds that are blowing change through every corner of our profession. Some things don't change, though. One of those things is the subject of this essay: the need—indeed, the necessity—for the mountaintop experience.

These are rare—most of us live in the valleys or on the plains. What I'm thinking of are those occasional experiences that amaze us, take us beyond the mundane, maybe even change our lives. More specifically, I believe that musicians need mountaintop experiences *involving music*. This art with which we have the privilege of living every day can become—well—everyday. It's a struggle to avoid taking it for granted, especially when teaching little fingers to play. Let's face it: the earth can't move every time we play the piano or give a lesson. Days of routine blend into weeks and months and years, and unless a mountaintop experience intervenes to remind us just how extraordinary this stuff called music is, we can become—well—routine. Witnessing a concert or a master class that blows the dust off our habituated expectations can inspire us to rise above the ordinary. The breath of fresh Alpine air remains long after the visit to the peak itself.

Mountaintop experiences seldom come to you. By definition you have to seek them out. The effort required by the journey, usually a nuisance to your well-planned schedule and always more expensive than you can afford, is part of the deal. Pilgrimages aren't supposed to be easy. This is for your musical soul, after all; a little inconvenience is a small price to pay.

Finally, there is the need to find a mountain. Hills won't do—we need to get up where the air is rarefied, where the views stretch in every direction, and where we know with certainty that we aren't in Kansas anymore. At the top of the mountain, there could well be a wise man or woman, who shows you how to breathe the air, points out every detail of the view, and whose voice stays with you when you've gone home.

Over the past decade, I have attended workshops sponsored by the Weill Music Institute at Carnegie Hall given by Leon Fleisher on the late Schubert sonatas, four Mozart concerti, Beethoven sonatas, and most recently, Brahms chamber music with piano. Full disclosure: I came to know Mr. Fleisher as a colleague while teaching at Peabody twenty years ago, but I never studied with him, and of course I couldn't sit in on his classes back then while giving my own. I can still remember the effect his recording of the Brahms D Minor Concerto had on me as a teenager—"staggering" barely begins to describe it. That I would seek out such a figure in my own later years is not so surprising, I suppose. What is remarkable is that no matter how many times I heard Leon speak his beliefs and principles about music, I was moved to become a better musician myself. The matters he addressed in those classes on any given day are exactly the ones I need to ponder every day.

During the Brahms classes last May, the experience went beyond words when violinist Pamela Frank and cellist Yo-Yo Ma joined Fleisher one afternoon to coach four superb young ensembles. At one point, as Fleisher attempted to show the pianist how to change her sound as she responded to a phrase from the cellist, he looked over his shoulder to Frank and Ma and said, "Do you want to play this? Now?" Whereupon the two jumped for their instruments, sat down where the students had been, and the three read the entire movement, to the utter delight of students, auditors, and everyone within earshot of the room. This was unrehearsed, spontaneous, wildly-on-the-spot music making, as thrilling as anything I've heard in my life. No, it would never make it as a CD, and even as a concert performance would probably draw a negative review. But as an immediate, this-is-what-we-live-for expression of the life force, I cannot imagine anything more inspiring.

We were treated to three more impromptu reading sessions that afternoon. The final one is something I will never forget, and even as I type these words, tears flood my eyes as I remember the incredible beauty of their slow movement from the C minor piano quartet (the student violist playing along with the pros—now *that's* a mountaintop experience!). They all played as though their lives depended on it and as though this music were a condensation of everything that could be said about...well, that's why you had to be there! It was something that cannot be put into words.

I have a friend to thank for two other recent mountaintop experiences. Four years ago, he told me he was flying to Lucerne, Switzerland, to hear one performance of Mahler's Sixth Symphony, conducted by Claudio Abbado. My friend is a pianist and dean, not a conductor. I thought this rather extravagant, but upon his return he related his astonishment over the performance and vowed to return the next year for two performances by Abbado at the same festival. After that return, he sent me the DVD of the performance of Mahler's Third. It was everything he said it was, even as confined by a DVD. So, for the past two summers, my wife and I have made the long, expensive journey to Lucerne to hear Claudio Abbado conduct an orchestra that must be heard to be believed.

In some ways, the Lucerne Festival is a *Gesamtkunstwerk* of a mountaintop experience: the city is extraordinarily beautiful, nestled with its centuries-old buildings next to a large, pristine lake and in the shadow of seven-thousand-foot Mount Pilatus. The concert hall, designed by Jean Nouvel, has the finest acoustics I've ever heard, allowing for great clarity while still enhancing every sound in a warm reverberation. The Lucerne Festival Orchestra is handpicked by Abbado and includes soloists, chamber musicians, and orchestral musicians from all over Europe. They gather only once a year to perform with a conductor whose style is more facilitator than leader. Before they leave the stage following a performance, they embrace their stand partners and other friends in the orchestra as the audience pours forth its applause.

The music—again you just have to be there. When Abbado began Mahler's First Symphony last year, my mind had trouble computing that the sound was coming from musical instruments. It was more like the slow awakening of dawn, the sounds so soft that one was hardly aware of it. The next fifty minutes went by in what seemed like five—a performance both unified and heartfelt. I have never heard an orchestra play so sensitively. The next weekend, we heard Mahler's Fourth. This year, we heard *Fidelio* and Mahler's Ninth. Each performance extended my conception of the possible.

Mahler said, "To write a symphony is, for me, to construct a world." I always thought that statement hyperbole, until I experienced the musical summit in Lucerne.

12

Virtuosos a Dime a Dozen?

Winds of Change

NOVEMBER 2011

Last summer within a month, the *New York Times* arts pages trumpeted two eye-catching headlines:

VIRTUOSOS BECOMING A DIME A DOZEN

(August 12)

KING OF VIRTUOSOS IS WEARY OF HIS CROWN

(July 22)

Remembering that journalists seldom pen their own headlines, the two articles reward inspection. Is it time, two hundred years since the birth of Franz Liszt, for a reevaluation of that oft-used and abused term *virtuoso*?

Let's start with the dictionary definition: "a person having great technical skill in some fine art, especially in the performance of music."[1] Piero Weiss and Richard Taruskin refine the meaning further in their *Music in the Western World*: "A virtuoso was, originally, a highly accomplished musician, but by the nineteenth century the term had become restricted to performers, both vocal and instrumental, whose technical accomplishments were so pronounced as to dazzle the public."[2]

---

1. *Webster's New Collegiate Dictionary* (1973), s.v. "virtuoso."
2. Piero Weiss and Richard Taruskin, *Music in the Western World: A History in Documents* (New York: Schirmer Books, 1984), 430.

It was this thread that chief *Times* music critic Anthony Tommasini picked up in the "Dime a Dozen" piece. Tommasini noted the extraordinary number of young pianists before the public today who seemingly can play anything with absolute ease. The knuckle busters of yore, like *Gaspard de la Nuit* or *Petrushka*, are child's play for them. Looking for new challenges, they fall upon the Ligeti *Études* (considered all but unplayable when they appeared in 1986) or transcriptions by one-of-a-kind virtuosos of the past, like György Cziffra's "Flight of the Bumblebee"—in octaves. What once was extremely rare—jaw-dropping technical excellence—is now relatively (dare I say it?) common.

Tommasini cites a wonderful story in his article about this phenomenon, which merits full quotation.

> When the 1996 movie *Shine*, about the mentally ill pianist David Helfgott, raised curiosity about Rachmaninoff's Third Piano Concerto, [Juilliard faculty member Jerome] Lowenthal was asked by reporters whether this piece was as formidably difficult as the movie suggested. He said that he had two answers: "One was that this piece truly is terribly hard. Two was that all my 16-year-old students were playing it."[3]

With so many pianists playing so well, it becomes more and more difficult to dazzle. Superb technique has its limits—like the speed of light, one can only go so fast. When most pianists can reach that limit, what then?

There have always been musicians for whom virtuosity per se meant little. These are the artists who spend their years plumbing the depths of literature that, as Artur Schnabel said, is "better than it can be performed." As opposed to pianists who have the technique to play anything, these pianists have all the technique they need to play the music that matters to them, to paraphrase Tommasini. Indeed, Schnabel and his disciples (who include the majority of university-level piano professors) epitomize this ethos. But virtuosos were frowned upon

---

3. Anthony Tommasini, "Virtuosos Becoming a Dime a Dozen," *New York Times*, August 12, 2011.

as shallow showmen long before Schnabel's heyday: "Virtuosos are constantly tempted to indulge in an undue exhibition of their wonderful technic, and as many have succumbed to the temptation, the term *virtuoso* has come to be considered by many as slightly deprecatory, and the greatest artists usually object to having it coupled with their names" (W. L. Hubbard, *The American History and Encyclopedia of Music*, 1908!).

This helps explain the second headline. The "King of Virtuosos," Marc-André Hamelin, wants to move on. Blessed (or cursed) with the ability to play anything, Hamelin does exactly that, while also composing and transcribing in the grand tradition of the ur-virtuoso himself, Franz Liszt. Hamelin first came to prominence as the winner of a very specialized competition, the Rockefeller Foundation international competition for the performance of American music. His first recording featured William Bolcom's *Twelve New Études* and Stefan Wolpe's *Battle Piece*, not exactly standard virtuoso ear candy. His career since has been fascinating to follow, breaking new ground at every step. His repertoire ranges from Haydn to Alkan to Stockhausen, often in the same program.

After decades of concert artists traveling very prescribed paths, playing a limited, bankable repertoire, artists—mostly young—are beginning to explore other possibilities. And people are listening, thanks to venues like Le Poisson Rouge, a multimedia cabaret in Greenwich Village where classical and popular music coexist in an eclectic, dynamic environment. Its mission, stated on their website, is "to revive the symbiotic relationship between art and revelry." Shocking as this may seem to those of us who have done our best to separate the two in academia, doesn't this sound a lot like the hothouse salon culture of Paris in the 1830s as Liszt, Paganini, Chopin, and others launched the virtuoso age?

There is something fun about virtuosity that we've lost to too many cookie-cutter competition players and the all-flash, no-soul technical exhibitionists. Perhaps the somber reverence we pay to "music that is better than it can be performed" hinders us as well. We all know the stories of Liszt as consummate showman, but let's not forget he was also considered *the* Beethoven pianist of his age. Today, we don't encounter any "Beethoven pianist" wandering into virtuoso territory, or vice versa, except maybe Hamelin. These two tracks are seen as mutually exclusive.

But must that be so? Granted, it takes an enormous heart and an all-encompassing intellect to embrace both, but perhaps this is the true definition of *virtuoso*—someone whose lack of technical impediments allows for the realization of whatever musical ideal is at hand. Again, Liszt suggests it is possible; his *Études d'exécution transcendante* refer not to "transcendental études" as we usually hear the title translated, conjuring up Emersonian philosophy, but rather to études that transcend their execution. To play them successfully, one's technique is so complete that the experience of the music is the prime concern, not the playing of the notes.

Anyone who seeks to perform at the highest level pursues this transcendent experience in whatever repertoire is at hand. It is not a matter of always playing all the notes—think of the deeply rewarding recitals you have heard with some clinkers. We have also heard many a reliable, note-perfect pianist who disappoints. True virtuosity will never become matter-of-fact, as long as astonishment is possible for the human race.

Or, as Liszt himself wrote, "Virtuosity is not an outgrowth, but an indispensable element of music."[4]

---

4. Franz Liszt, *Gesammelte Schriften*, vol. IV: 1855–59 (Leipzig: Breitkopf & Hartel, 1910).

13

Interlude

In 1992 Richard Chronister, executive director of the National Conference on Piano Pedagogy, asked me to speak at its biennial conference. Attended by a mere eighty teachers when it was founded in 1980, the conference had grown quickly, and by 1992 nearly nine hundred teachers came to Schaumburg, Illinois, for a three-day event titled "The Pianist's Road to the Future."

Richard envisioned several keynote addresses to the entire assembly and asked me to talk on "that part of the pianist's career which produces income from performing." By this time in my career, I was as busy as I would ever be as a performer (not that I made much money from it), so I agreed.

Richard and I shared a contrarian streak, so when I submitted my title "Stuck in the Parking Lot of the Present: The Solo Performing Career, circa 1992," he agreed. While I certainly did not consider myself a successful performer, the bio printed in the conference proceedings told the audience the following:

> Robert Weirich has performed in musical centers throughout the country, including Alice Tully Hall at Lincoln Center in New York, the Kennedy Center in Washington, D.C., Chicago's Orchestra Hall, and at such summer festivals as Tanglewood, Ravinia, and Marlboro. He has returned to the Eastern Music Festival for the past eight years, most recently performing the Brahms Piano Concerto No. 2 and an all-Beethoven recital with the legendary violinist Josef Gingold. As music director of the Skaneateles Festival in New York's Finger Lakes District, he has received an *Adverturesome Programming Award* from ASCAP and Chamber Music America. He has taught at the Peabody Conservatory in Baltimore since 1985, having taught previously at Northwestern University and Tulane University. His column, *The View from the Second Floor*, is a regular feature in *Clavier* magazine.

14

The Solo Performing Career

A Keynote Address at the
National Conference on Piano Pedagogy

OCTOBER 21–24, 1992, SCHAUMBURG, ILLINOIS

By my calculations, this talk takes place at approximately the midpoint of the various keynotes here, a fact that may or may not have symbolic meaning. It could be a sign of great honor, suggesting that this conference devoted to the "road to the pianist's future" considers performing for remuneration central to one's life as a pianist. It could also be that the organizers hoped that a great black hole would open up at this mystic midpoint, sucking me and everything I say to would-be "concert pianists" out into the void. If the latter is going to occur, please let it be now.

For alas, I do not have much good news. In fact, I have three words of advice to anyone who wants to make a career of playing the piano in public for money: *seek professional help.*

I will return to those words after a while. In the meantime, since we are talking about the "road to the future," we must first talk about the "parking lot of the present." I think that is the correct metaphor: everyone in the music business is parked in a gigantic parking lot, and we are so busy at work that most of us can't remember where we left our car. If I were to call the present a traffic jam, it would suggest we are all madly trying to get to the same place, using the same avenue. Such is not the case, in my opinion, but that's another speech.

First some definitions. If we are trying to make a living as a performer, I am going to assume that we are looking for an average annual income of $50,000.[1] That's respectable, although hardly in the league of third-year attorneys or first-year plumbers. If you have $50,000

---

1. In 2023 this would be $105,772.

left as take-home pay—after deducting expenses for travel, hotel, and meals on the road, management fees, paying your press agent, absorbing the cost of a new photo session, keeping up your professional wardrobe, sending Christmas cards to all the presenters who engaged you during the last three years, and paying off your telephone bill[2] for calling home now and then—that means you probably have had an income from your performing fees of $80,000.[3] That's an overhead of 37.5 percent for the accountants among you. By the way, I assure you that somewhere along the line you will also pay a real accountant to handle the inevitable IRS audit. To make $80,000, you would need to play forty engagements at $2,000; or twenty-five engagements at $3,200; or sixteen engagements at $5,000; or if you are Itzhak Perlman, two engagements at $40,000. Obviously, if you are Itzhak Perlman, you will be asked to play a good many times more than twice in a year, and you can therefore make a good deal more money than the piddly sum of $50,000 that looked so respectable just one paragraph ago.

"Now, wait a minute," you say. "I'm not interested in making a living performing—I just want to get paid for an occasional concert." Fine. Here is an example of what you can expect: I was offered $200 to play a piano sonata by Hugo Weisgall on a good series in Baltimore this year. When I calculated the fact that it would take at least one hundred hours to learn the piece to my satisfaction, I realized I'd be making two dollars an hour. I also realized, upon looking at the piece, that each of those hours would be unpleasant and that I would probably never play the piece again. I said no thanks. It might have been different if those hours would have been enjoyable, but at two dollars an hour, I would be making substantially less than the guy who asks if you want ketchup with your fries. For that you need a DMA?

I think I will not be telling professional secrets if I admit to you that plenty has been the time that I have played full concerts or a concerto, spending far more than one hundred hours in preparation, for less than $2,000, the lowest fee mentioned above and also the lowest fee a former competition-winning student of mine will be paid this year. On the other

---

2. This preceded the day of cell phones.
3. $169,235 in 2023.

hand, it isn't that often that I play on the same series as André Watts or Murray Perahia. We must now, as we crane our necks looking for the parking lot's exit, consider the presenters and the organizations that actually pay you to play. For most of the concert artists whose names you recognize, those organizations are predominantly orchestras; if you are making much money these days as a performer, you are playing a lot of concertos. If you are being engaged by orchestras, it means at least two things: First, the management considers you a safe draw. They assume that no one in the paying public is about to come hear a nobody on stage with their expensive orchestra, so you'd better not be a nobody. Second, the conductor already knows you and respects your work, because there is no way he or she is going to risk his/her professional standing with an untried soloist. Recital series are practically gone—the college/university series has been either wiped out or cut back in these hard times, and the remaining community-concert-type series are much more likely to engage something called Voice of the Turtle than you, a classical pianist. Getting to know these presenters is itself a full-time job; there are many of them out there, but every other struggling performer is cold-calling them at the same time you or your manager is.

Oh yes, and have I mentioned you have to play *really* well? To reach the acceptable level of perfection, you have probably chosen to attend an institution of higher learning where the curriculum allows you one hour a week with your major teacher—and five hours a week in the required foreign language course. In addition, you have to work twenty hours a week in a part-time job to pay the five-figure annual expense of your higher education, and on your one night off, you will not be able to go hear a recital by a visiting artist because the college has cancelled the concert series to save money. Instead, you might go over to the new computer learning center the college has spent money on and do your theory homework.

Now that I've offended nearly everyone, there is one more observation to disclose about this parking lot we're in. It's actually on two levels, you see. On the ground floor are the schools, their faculty, and students. On the upper level are the presenters, the orchestra managements, the artist representatives, and the conductors. And there is one big problem: the ramp between the two is nowhere in sight. For the most part, the activities of one parking lot have very little to do with the other. Every now and then, students from the lower level will win a competition sponsored by the upper level and suddenly find themselves on the upper level without so much as directions to the comfort facilities. If the young musicians find their way to the upper-level exit and start a career, it is usually a matter of extraordinary luck or sheer talent, which is the same as extraordinary luck. Any other (please pardon the expression) intercourse between the two usually occurs when an extremely tenacious, rebellious individual tunnels through to the other level and learns the game from within.

In the meantime, there is the audience, whose money and approval fuel the whole endeavor, and who is sought after by performers and presenters alike. This audience is parked in a separate garage several miles away, since most of them shop at a different mall anyway: Walmart. Many of them have little idea what it's like to attend a live concert of "classical" music. Most of them assume it is elitist, expensive, and boring. In many cases, they are right. Look, if you will, at the typical college audience at, let's say, a faculty recital with free admission. Are all the piano students there? No. How many of the other faculty? Hmm, not so good there either. Faculty from other schools in the area? There's one! Local teachers? Yes, a few. Other nonpiano majors from the school? Very few. People from the community? A handful. Total attendance: fifty or sixty. Sound familiar? And that's *on campus*, where the ground should be most fertile.

There! Now I have offended everyone.

It doesn't take an MBA to realize that we are in a business with some structural problems. We can choose, like the tunnelers, to outmaneuver the problems, or we can try to change the way we do business. I'd like to talk about some ways to change the business.

Let's start in the music schools. It was Busoni who had the nerve to say in writing, when he was first teaching at the ripe old age of twenty-four in a conservatory in Helsinki, that a music school exists for its own perpetuation. A century later, we have become very good at teaching students to succeed at going to school. If they go on to teach, they continue the tradition with peerless authority. We are an industry unto ourselves, with some systems that are open to question. Many is the piano student who will play in more jury situations in music school than in recitals. Many are the schools where students end up in music education or pedagogy because the performing faculty, in their all-knowing kindness, suggests to the student that their chances of "making it" as a performer are slim.

What can we do? First of all, we can get rid of the woebegone assumption that "making it" means conquering Carnegie. We need to send our *best* students to lead programs in education, not those who can't make it as performers! We're condemning the next generation if we do otherwise. Second, we need to design our schools and departments in such a way that we are not all imitation Juilliards. Not every school should try to turn out performers. Each school could build on its strengths, turning out musicians of resilience and flexibility who would unite in what should be our common effort: to make music a more necessary part of our culture. Third, these schools committed to training performers should emphasize artistry rather than perfection. Take the focus off juries, with their "more-than-five-wrong-notes-is-a-B-minus" attitude. Encourage live performances of every size and shape. Get off campus; go to retirement homes, hospitals, churches, prisons, music stores, public schools. On campus, get out of the concert hall—go to a dining hall, or a student lounge, or the library atrium. Do something other than the usual seventy minutes of music with no words exchanged and even less personality revealed. Finally, stop producing specialists, whether they be performance specialists, ensemble specialists, or pedagogy specialists. We all need to know as much as we can about everything. It's all related: if you can accompany a Schubert song with sensitivity, you have a better chance playing the sonatas, and if you try to play a Schubert sonata without knowing the songs, you are going to miss the boat entirely. If you try to teach the Schubert sonata without either experience, you are committing a crime against the past, present, and future of music.

And what is the point of playing the Schubert sonata at all? Once we get past the personal edification rationale, we are left with the desire, perhaps even the duty, to play it for others who can't play it themselves. Performers need an audience, and I think we can do something about that part of the business.

Back at the garage, all the organizations parked on the upper level are just as stuck in the status quo as we in academe are, except they are closer to the bottom line. In short, they are willing to change faster if it means their survival. They are looking for audiences, and they are finding that their traditional audience is fast disappearing and that new audiences are staying away in droves from anything as old-fashioned as a straight piano recital. So how do we performers present ourselves in new ways without doing aesthetic damage to the art we love?

There are numerous ways. To cite a few examples: Yo-Yo Ma plays the cello as well as it can be played, but more than that he projects a persona that exudes enjoyment, love, even ecstasy. People love to be around him! He is constantly performing new works, including a piece for "hypercello" by Tod Machover. He has even ventured into improvisation, making a recording with jazz singer Bobby McFerrin. If you don't know that recording, proceed to the nearest record shop immediately.

Another example: the Kronos Quartet performs only works written in this century, most of them by composers of their own generation. They dare to dress in something other than the required formal dress. They bring a lighting engineer with them on tour. Their recordings have broken all the rules of classical-record production and, at the same time, have broken quite a few sales records. They are a string quartet that has spawned a cottage industry with a budget that exceeds $1 million; they have a staff of five full-time people and three part-time. In short their organization itself is larger than many artist managements. If someone had suggested ten years ago that a string quartet would make over a million dollars a year playing avant-garde music, they would have been committed to an asylum. But it happened!

Success as a performer involves a good deal more than how well you play the instrument. In several seminars tomorrow, you will hear about that "good deal more." After you've listened, if you still want to pursue a career as a paid performer, I ask you to remember two things.

First, you need to have an artistic vision and believe in it with an unswerving faith. That vision is the car that will get you out of the parking lot. One of the most difficult things about a career in art is that no one is waiting for you to make it. Only after you arrive does your audience realize they've needed you all along.

Second, I come back to my opening advice: *seek professional help*. You need to think of your career as a small business that, with some luck and a lot of hard work, will grow into a bigger business. You need what any small-business person needs: some working capital (i.e., money in the bank) and the help of people who are professionals. You'll have to pay them, but the whole point is to position yourself so that people will pay you for what you do. You need to hang out with people who are performers themselves, learning from them, seeing how they have managed so far. In this regard, unfortunately, we professors sometimes aren't much help.

And finally, may I say to my fellow professors that it's time for us to get out of the parking lot too. Instead of worrying about the dip in the demographic curve that paints a gloomy picture of fewer and fewer music students out there, let's start educating the millions of people who will never be professional musicians of any sort. Let's bring Schubert into the living room of our neighbor. Let's make music and invite some people into our *own* living room! Let's help our students learn how to develop an audience, bring that audience closer to things in the music anyone can hear, instead of obsessing over the Neapolitan relationship in the coda. Let's cancel a few committees and go to a concert ourselves.

This business of music needs to be as interlinked as our knowledge of music itself. To make a performance, one needs only three things: a composer, a performer, and a listener. As educators—yes, even as pedagogy teachers—our duty is to all three.

IV

■ On Becoming a Teacher

Let us first annihilate the cliché that those who can't do, teach. Good teachers have discovered entirely different skill sets from the ones used for playing. So-called artist-teachers can exist in both worlds, but it is likely they will be better in one than the other. It has to do with their priorities, of what comes first for them.

Another clarification to consider: there is no such thing as a piano teacher. The piano is a complex machine without a brain that learns nothing from your instruction. You'll note that it has no ears, so anything you tell it is preposterous. It can only respond to your touch.

One *might be* a music teacher. Music can be the subject of the sentence but cannot be the object of the verb *to teach*. Again, we can't teach music anything—it knows much more than we do. We can learn from music, but we can't teach it anything.

We teach our students. We teach them *about* music and the piano, but the object of the verb is other humans, equipped with the same senses we have—sight, hearing, taste, smell, and touch. We may focus mainly on sight, hearing, and touch, but who is to say an advanced student can't smell a chord or taste a tangy dissonance?

While the senses are our objective monitors (the ear determines louder or softer, the eyes discover the score's D-natural or D-sharp), both student and teacher have within them an expanding universe of subjectivity. Our lives exist on many levels at once. Little Johnny may be dealing with a bully on the school bus and finds it hard to think about anything else. Sharon just joined the debate team and wonders how to balance that work with her piano. Professor Jones just learned her salary was cut by 10 percent due to state budget shortfalls. Psychology 101 barely begins to cover all the sensitivities needed. Yet the teacher is the adult in the room. Their subtle empathy in this constantly changing playing field separates the good from the great.

When you first start to teach, you know none of this. I first taught piano students when I was a high school student myself, undergoing my own transitions. Luckily, I was also a fairly intuitive person who liked smart, eager kids, so it felt as natural to teach as it did to play in those days. I didn't become a teacher so much as I simply started teaching.

I think I truly became a teacher, though, during two tumultuous years on the faculty at a prep school in Vermont. It's a long story.

I came of age in the late 1960s, a period of rebellion and strife on every front. The night before my first day at a summer job after high school graduation, Robert Kennedy was shot. I had chosen to attend the Oberlin Conservatory of Music in the fall, and my four years there profoundly changed me. As I worked hard to become a performer, I grew away from my provincial Midwest background. As I approached graduation, the sensible next step would have been graduate school so that I could continue on my path to a performing career. However, I chose *not* to go on to graduate school because I wanted to be independent of my parents. I would always be beholden to them if they paid for my graduate education. So, after graduating in the top of my Oberlin class, I went home to a summer in which the only job I could get was selling ice cream from a truck. For ten hours a day, I listened to its electronic music box blast "Beautiful Dreamer" out of the rooftop speaker.

One day in early June, a letter arrived from the Oberlin placement office regarding a teaching position at a small preparatory high school in Vermont. The school was seeking its first full-time teacher of music who would also teach English. I had not studied piano for four years at a school like Oberlin to sell ice cream, so I applied via the requested letter. A few weeks later, I received an invitation to come for an interview (at my own expense, by the way).

Vermont Academy occupied a beautiful hilltop in the village of Saxtons River. There was one gas station, one diner, and a couple of white-steepled churches on the main street. Tenney's Lumber Mill was just south of the center of town. I never knew the population, but it couldn't have been more than four hundred. As I got to know the school, I learned it enrolled boys fourteen to nineteen who couldn't get into Andover or Deerfield or who were thrown out of Tilton or Tabor.

These were hard times for elite private schools. I was offered the job for $4,800 a year with room and board. "Room" meant that I lived in the student dorm serving in loco parentis. "Board" meant that I ate three meals a day in the dining hall with the students. I was only three or four years older than the students.

The culture of the school favored all things athletic. Unless you were a team coach in charge of a sport during "high-intensity-activity" period, you might be conscripted to handle towels at the gym. I escaped this by becoming involved in student drama productions. The senior members of the administration wanted me to start a glee club, but the boys at this time were into Jefferson Airplane and the Grateful Dead. In my first semester there, I offered a course in music appreciation, which drew an enrollment of five.

It was in this extremely uncomfortable situation that I became a teacher. Forming a glee club would have been as impossible as teaching a piano. I had to find a way to connect to my five music appreciation students. I had a lot of LPs of very modern electronic music, and I had taken a course in electronic music at Oberlin. So, in the classroom I played Morton Subotnick's *Silver Apples of the Moon* and Luciano Berio's *Visage* for them. These sounds were new and intriguing to them, and rather quickly they started discussing what bands like Pink Floyd were doing. I asked them to bring their recordings, and we talked about commonalities, like how to describe that sound or what is the form here. As we developed a vocabulary and an appreciation for innovation, I took them *backward* in music history and listened to things like *The Rite of Spring* or Bartók's Concerto for Orchestra. I talked about individual instruments and what it takes to play them. They in turn brought Eric Clapton records and gave me an introduction to the electric guitar. I was working on the Bartók Piano Sonata at that time, so I played it for them on the Yamaha console in the room. Over time we developed a very cordial relationship.

Then there were the two English classes I was assigned—one for freshmen and the second for sophomores. The senior English faculty basically shrugged their shoulders and wished me luck. I was a reader and liked the subject but had no idea what to assign and in what order. At some point, I asked the headmaster why he thought I could teach

English. He answered that I had written a good letter of application. Caveat auctor! (Let the author beware!)

The students needed remedial work. I tried to teach them to diagram sentences, but that went over as if I had asked them to memorize Shakespeare. We tried reading a Shakespeare comedy (*Much Ado About Nothing*), and that was also a bust. I finally tried Kurt Vonnegut, and that they liked. *Cat's Cradle* beat out *Slaughterhouse-Five*, but that gave me the idea to expand into science fiction with Robert Heinlein's *Stranger in a Strange Land*. This allowed us to talk about words like *grok*. I challenged them to make up words of their own. At least they were reading and found writing about what they read not so onerous.

I was hardly a successful teacher of English, but my goal was to foster in the students an appreciation of books and good writing. If that feeling somehow settled into their being, they could tap it again when needed.

The following three essays were written for *Clavier* in 1985, my first year of teaching at the Peabody Conservatory. During my interview there, the dean asked me why I loved to teach. I didn't have a ready answer, so I spent months thinking about it and came up with what is essentially one long essay, but because of column-size limits, I wrote it as three connected parts. Rereading it thirty years later, I am embarrassed by the attempts of a young writer to sound wiser than he was. I have tried to take some of the bluster away and leave what were pretty good ideas for someone still learning to teach.

The fourth essay was written ten years later, during my time in the woods. I had had a two-year vacation from university teaching and was looking forward to returning to the studio. I can feel the enthusiasm, the desire to engage again with new students full of potential.

The final essay looks back at the fervor of young pianists all chasing the dream of becoming the next great virtuoso as they sought conservatory training in nineteenth-century Europe. Based on quotations from Amy Fay's 1880 book *Music-Study in Germany*, we see that even 150 years ago, teachers had different approaches, not to mention different temperaments. Fay's book was enormously popular in its day, going through twenty printings before 1912. The New York *Musical Courier* estimated in 1891 that about two thousand Americans lived in Berlin, and almost all of them were music students!

15

Why I Love to Teach

The View from the Second Floor

SEPTEMBER 1985

My view from the window on the second floor has changed this new academic year. In August I said goodbye to friends and colleagues at Northwestern University, packed up my tents, and joined the nomadic tribes of American professionals who keep the post office in business handling their change of address cards. Early this month, I will settle into a position on the faculty of the Peabody Conservatory of Music in Baltimore. No more sweet shop across the street; instead, I will probably frequent Louie's, an ingenious enterprise that combines a bookstore in front with a restaurant in back. Since Louie serves oysters, something I sorely missed in the Midwest, he can be assured of my patronage. The change in working atmosphere will also affect my view: I eagerly anticipate the challenge of teaching in a major conservatory, even though I know I will miss the eclecticism of life on a university campus. To paraphrase some old sage: you pay your money, and you take your chances.

During my interview at Peabody, I was asked a simple, direct question that has haunted me ever since: Why do you love to teach? For some reason, I had never put all those words in one sentence and asked it. It is a question that deserves—and by this time has received—some serious thought on my part. Its exploration leads one down many paths, and my attempted answers will span three essays in a row. This month we will look at several definitions and techniques of teaching. Next comes an examination of the tasks and results of teaching, what makes a good teacher, the subtle and sometimes painful relationship of teacher and student, and at last, how we as teachers come to love our work.

As unimaginative as it may seem, I started my exploration with the dictionary, looking up the transitive verb *teach*. *Webster's* first definition is

---

"to cause to know a subject." This deceptively simple answer only opens up other questions. A volume could be written on how it is possible to cause this knowledge—are there teaching techniques everyone should employ? A second volume would have to consider that word *subject*. Do different subjects demand different methods of teaching?

Another dictionary definition is ripe with philosophical possibilities: "to cause to know *how*" (emphasis mine). As much as I like that definition, I leave it to the reader to go back to Plato and Aristotle for an adequate exposition on those five little words.

A few of the dictionary definitions were negative: "to make to know the disagreeable consequence of some action" was illustrated with the sentence "I'll teach you to come home late." I don't think that kind of teaching will ever usher students into a state of grace with late Beethoven. I was saddened by the definition "to seek to make known and accepted, as in 'experience teaches us our limitations.'" As wise as that statement is, we teachers know an even truer example: nothing teaches us our limitations better than teaching itself.

My favorite definition was "to guide the studies of." While it implies action on the part of the teacher, it also indicates that the student has to participate in order for the process to work. I also liked "to instruct by precept, example, or experience." This suggests that teachers do indeed "know how" and that this know-how serves as the motivating force of their daily actions.

This final interpretation appears often in a wonderful book called *Masters: Portraits of Great Teachers*, edited by Joseph Epstein and published by Basic Books (1981). It is a collection of critical appreciations of significant teachers, written by former students who have themselves achieved distinction in their fields. Since so few teachers have left records of their pedagogical methods, it is illuminating to read the reflections of prominent men and women as they discuss how a teacher caused them to know a subject.

To illustrate teaching techniques, Epstein begins with some Socratic teasing, answering every question with another question. He then turns his attention to those gifted with a sonorous lecture style who bedazzle their disciples with verbal fecundity. The pianistic equivalent might be the teacher who sweeps the student away on the power of his or her own playing during lessons. Epstein continues the roll call of techniques by denoting sympathetic discussion, passionate argument, witty exposition, and dramatic derring-do as applicable in the classroom. He's right—who among us hasn't at some time coaxed a crescendo out of a student using any or all of those methods?

Epstein also likes the last of *Webster's* definitions of teaching, prominently mentioning the power of personal example among his techniques of teaching. An anecdote from Pulitzer Prize–winning poet Anthony Hecht succinctly sums up the variety of ways his Kenyon College professor of English, John Crowe Ransom, influenced him:

> I find it very difficult in retrospect to say exactly what it was one learned from Mr. Ransom, to point to particular notions or propositions. For one learned from him not facts or positions, but a posture of mind and spirit, a humanity and courtesy, a considerateness that inhabited his work as it did his person.
>
> And one learned to pay attention to poetic detail.[1]

---

1. Joseph Epstein, *Masters: Portraits of Great Teachers* (New York: Basic Books, 1981), 187–88.

16

Why I Love to Teach II

The View from the Second Floor

OCTOBER 1985

At a certain point, it becomes difficult to separate teaching from the teacher. Teaching is a performing art that requires the teacher as intermediary between the subject and the student. In his book *Masters*, Joseph Epstein lists three characteristics that all successful teachers seem to share.

First, they love the subject they teach. Please make note of the verb—they don't merely like it, or respect it, or find it occasionally intriguing. They love it, are obsessed by it, think about it when they are not actively engaged with it, are lifted to ever higher planes of awareness by it. There is a darker side as well: the subject can anger them, frustrate them, depress them. It is a romance that is as volatile as the love between two people. One day can be heavenly; the next can seem hopeless. The one thing this ardor can promise is that you will never be unaffected by the subject at hand. It will always matter.

Second, teachers fond of their subjects take great satisfaction in arousing this same sentiment in their students. They want to pass on to their students the affection and devotion that has meant so much to them. They are trying to give the next generation something enduring, something that the previous generation of teachers passed on to them. They become aware of their place in a long and grand tradition, and this knowledge imparts real pleasure.

Finally, all successful teachers have the ability to convince their students that the subject matter is deadly serious. They are able to make them suspend their ingrained adolescent apathy and take notice of something that may never have seemed all that important. Given enough time, these teachers are able to instill in their students not only the belief that what they are being taught is important but that their very lives depend on it. It is this quality that ignites the fire to learn.

When I was eight years old growing up in the farm country of Ohio, my first teacher, Vera Getz, told me that more than anything she loved "classical" music. That was tantamount to receiving stone tablets from on high telling me it was all right to love it too. In our society, little boys especially need permission to love something, particularly when it does not fit the norm. Much later, in my last year of graduate study, I have a vivid memory of Claude Frank illustrating the simplest of Mozart melodies (the opening of the slow movement of K. 503), pausing to repeat it again for the sheer enjoyment of it. "Isn't that beautiful?" he asked as his person radiated warmth for the music itself. I wanted nothing more at that moment than to enter this world in which beauty could transform the commonplace.

Still later, as a teacher myself, I became aware of the desire within me to arouse this devotion in my students. One learns quickly that the success rate can be variable, because each student has a different capacity for love. When that capacity is great, though, there is nothing that compares to the joy of teaching. Who hasn't experienced one special lesson in an otherwise bleak afternoon? Even though you connect with just one student, it is enough. The rest of the day, you walk with a jauntier step; you find yourself humming whatever the student was working on, and you have the ineffable feeling that you have made a difference.

Making the subject seem deadly serious can be tough work, though, especially in music. Students already know that what you are teaching them won't make them millionaires. They sense that music doesn't hold a serious place in the minds of most people in our society, since it is more often thought of as an entertainment or a social occasion. The talented and ambitious students to whom these realities may not matter are likely to have their own ideas about what is important, and strong ones at that. Lessons become a battle of wills between your ideas and theirs: incipient concert pianists are not known for their tiny egos. Finally, there is the frustration and discouragement that come to all teachers: it is simply not possible to reach every student. Many will come to be taught, but few will exert the energy needed to learn, no matter what you do. It is comforting to realize that great teachers have poor students too.

Still, great teachers have fewer poor students. Why? Could it be that these teachers value the subject more than they value their relationships with their students? Could it be that they are willing to forgo being liked by the student in favor of upholding the integrity of the subject? It is possible that these teachers realize they cannot create a love of music by trying to make the student love them.

The subject must come first.

17

Why I Love to Teach III

The View from the Second Floor

November 1985

Perhaps this is the most obvious answer to why one can love to teach: the love of the subject comes before everything else and colors our interactions with students who are learning to love the subject too.

Our love of music can be internal. We can meditate upon it, listen to it inwardly, be moved by it in solitude. But teaching is different, more like performing—it is outwardly directed, always involves at least one other person, and depends to a large extent on the strength of the interconnections we feel. It's like a runner's high—all that activity brings on an increased sense of well-being.

It is ironic that teachers receive respect and honor in most societies, albeit meagerly remunerated. Perhaps that imbalance comes from the fact that our work, while crucial, is essentially ephemeral. We lead students to wisdom; we do not produce it. Working with the young at a major turning point in their lives, we pass on a tradition that began centuries ago and puts us in touch with musical giants such as Bach and Mozart. We light sparks in minds that have not yet known fire. Once that passion for learning is well stoked, we help to focus, refine, and sharpen the intellect, hoping to create the concentrated blue flame of technical and musical craft. What's not to love?

If we do our jobs completely, we help to foster the fusion of emotion and intellect described by the British literary critic John Middleton Murry:

Then came, out of that extreme and absolute division, a sudden unity. A new kind of consciousness was created. Mind and

Heart, which had been irreconcilable enemies, became united in the Soul, which loved what it knew. The inward division was healed.[1]

There is much to love about helping students with this journey. Again, though, there is seldom anything concrete to which we can point and say, "I did that." Teachers can lead students to a better instrumental technique, but the students have to produce it themselves. We can shape an interpretation of a work, but again, it's the student who brings the piece to life in a performance. I am distinctly uncomfortable when someone congratulates me after one of my student's performances. I have merely guided the student; the praise belongs to the one who realizes the music onstage.

It's simply not possible to measure the larger effect you have on students, on the fusion of emotion and intellect Murry describes. It may be years before students have an inkling of the profound yet subtle changes in consciousness you have helped create. Often we have to be quite farsighted to recognize the results of our teaching. It's too bad that we seldom get to see the end results.

I suspect the reason we love teaching has everything to do with potential. Within each student is a potency, a capacity for effect. We help to form and then to unleash their powers; we help them to define their intentions. We deal everyday with young people for whom the question "Who am I?" has not yet been answered, and we play a part in our students' inevitable wrestling match with that question. We should help them keep the question alive. Learning is not an accumulation of scraps of knowledge; it is, rather, a continual transformation, a growth that begins at a certain point in life but never ends. The question should never be completely closed for any of us. There will always be something to explore or examine, something to challenge our conceptions, something to give meaning to our existence.

---

1. John Middleton Murry was a British literary critic who married the writer Katherine Mansfield. Here is another Murry quote worth remembering: "There is nothing more dangerous to the formation of a prose style than the endeavour to make it poetic." *Semper caveat auctor*!

If teaching addresses questions on this level, it is impossible not to love it. Whether we are teaching five-finger positions to six-year-olds who haven't even dreamed of asking themselves who they are, or whether we're attuning the percussionist in class piano to the requirements of four-part voice leading, we are helping them realize music is a craft that is part of something bigger than themselves. They are addressing their own potential.

Teaching helps us keep questioning ourselves as well. Our students show us that we don't know all the answers, reminding us of the complex interactions involved in our work. They continually give us the opportunity to think in the future tense. Who knows where all that potential could lead? H. G. Wells, never one to think small, leads us to consider an infinity of possibilities:

> All this world is heavy with the promise of greater things, and a day will come, one day in the unending succession of days, when beings...shall stand upon this earth as one stands upon a footstool and shall laugh and reach out their hands amidst the stars.[2]

---

2. H. G. Wells, "The Discovery of the Future" in *Annual Report of the Board of Regents of the Smithsonian Institution, 1902* (Washington, DC: Government Printing Office, 1903), 392.

18

September

Out of the Woods

Whenever September rolls around, the teacher in me feels a stirring akin to that of New Year's Day. September marks the beginning of the school year, and a fresh start like this suggests endless potential. The die is not yet cast; everything is still possible.

Throughout America students return to school. They come in all shapes and sizes and from every conceivable background—some are guileless first graders, others off to college hundreds of miles from home. Yet they all have something in common: before them lies growth. In the days and months to come, they will learn new things, connect to more of the world around them, and they will change.

The fancy word for this is *ontogeny*. My dictionary defines it as "the development or course of development of an individual organism." All students walking into school this month are deep into their own ontogenies, whether they know it or not.

As they settle into the classroom, their attention comes to rest, in varying degrees, on another individual, the teacher. What incredible potential lies in that moment, this commingling of ontogenies. From this point forward, so much could happen, and therein resides the singular excitement of September.

I believe this thrill may be greatest for a studio teacher. I base such extravagant hyperbole on three irrefutable facts: (1) we work with individuals, not classes of thirty or four hundred; (2) we teach a subject that touches every part of our beings; and (3) the subject is considered by much of society to be essentially useless.

Despite economies of scale, teaching someone to make music by singing or playing an instrument is still a one-to-one enterprise. The student and teacher occupy a room together for the sole purpose of the student learning new things, connecting to more of the world, and changing. The medium of this growth is music; the teacher serves as a guide. It is a powerful relationship, existing in few educational arenas today, and for this reason music teachers are potentially extraordinary forces in their students' lives. Where else can students regularly receive the undivided, constructive attention of an adult dedicated to their success? Teachers have the potential to be among the strongest influences students will encounter.

With that dire pronouncement hanging in the air, let me digress to reinforce the fact that we teach people through music. The person comes first, then the music. There has been so much emphasis in our profession on the sanctity of the score, the unconditional reverence for the great composers, and the absolute rules of stylistic tradition that teachers forget the child sitting at the piano just wants to grow. We think that by indoctrinating our students in the rules as they are passed down, we are teaching. That's *not* teaching—it's brainwashing! Beethoven will survive without us; little Susie Smith may not.

Each face that comes through the studio door has a person behind it. We guide our students in their growth, using as a tool a subject that educates every facet of the human being. To make music is one of the highest human accomplishments—we exercise our physical abilities, intellectual powers, emotional responses, and at music's highest levels, our spirituality. To play an instrument well requires a remarkable degree of physical awareness and control that combines the joys of the athlete with the Zen of the yoga master. To absorb a piece of music—to know its structure and history, its grammar and syntax, to hold it all within the mind—stretches the intellect as fully as mathematics or a foreign language. The centuries of musical thought are as challenging as the entire written literature of a civilization, and there is sufficient diversity in the world of music to arouse the highest IQ.

Despite progress in science and medicine, we still cannot explain how or why music touches the emotions. Therein lies the third area for growth: to respond fully to music's emotional message. What other discipline allows the student to tap the gamut of intense feelings through art?

To listen to Tchaikovsky's Symphony No. 6 (the "Pathétique") with open ears is to encounter grief. Playing Chopin's D-flat nocturne, the pianist may sense feelings of love, affecting—perhaps even increasing—his own ability to express the emotion. Ultimately, music leads her students into the realm of the spirit. Words stop at the threshold, requiring one to complete the journey on faith, but all the forces of the physical, intellectual, and emotional are at hand.

At the center of it all is the music teacher. The potential for good—indeed, the responsibility—is nothing short of overwhelming. What other subject can do that? Name one other adult in a young person's life who has more potential influence.

The teacher's obligation is complicated by the fact that we live in a society that considers music a frill, a nice extra that parents or school districts add if there is time and money left over. No one expects much; parents, students, and teachers are happy if everyone is having fun. What a waste.

There is a hidden irony, however. Anyone who studies music beyond the fun stage must really value it. In the face of criticism from friends and little understanding from parents, some students keep studying. It is the potential for meeting these students that increases September's thrill. With them we form a secret society, a fellowship of musicians; echoing Schumann, we belong with these special students to a *Davidsbund*. We see the world differently, pursuing something the Philistines can't understand.

This is the toughest part to endure. It takes courage to follow a course of study that society deems useless. Then again, what purpose is there in a rainbow? The other evening, I was in the house absorbed in something when I looked outside to see the most perfect rainbow I'd ever seen. Its left foot began just across the lake in the sunshine, and from the water it rose to arch southward across a gradually blackening sky, spanning the lake en route. Its seven colors were crystal clear for perhaps a minute before the light changed and the rainbow gently faded.

I cannot tell you the rainbow's use to society. It is an accident of the laws of physics, yet seeing one has a universal impact on us. We usually assign it a symbolic meaning, that something better is coming.

I'll accept that. Let every musician aspire to the purpose of the rainbow. Welcome back, September.

19

A Look Back with Amy Fay

The View from the Second Floor

JULY–AUGUST 1990

In November 1869, Mississippi-born Amy Fay arrived in Berlin to pursue serious piano study. Already twenty-five years old, she had attained at best the level of talented amateur, but she was determined to do better. For the next five years, she sought out the most reputed teachers, practiced her fingers to the bone, absorbed the culture and art of Europe, and wrote letters home filled with candid observations on her activities, both musical and social. The collected letters appear in the book *Music-Study in Germany*, published in 1880. Reading it today, one is startled to recognize that patterns of piano study really haven't changed much.

Amy arrived hoping to gain admittance to the new conservatory recently opened by Karl Tausig, the first of Liszt's students to achieve a career comparable to his master's. News of this school must have created quite a stir; not only had Amy heard of it in far-off America, but a number of Europe's finest signed on as faculty or enrolled as students. Tausig, however, was often away on tour, and the work fell to his assistants. Amy landed in the class of Herr Ehlert, who by her account was a "splendid teacher, but very severe, and I am mortally afraid of him." Her earliest experiences in the conservatory were the sort that produce intense anxiety:

> *The girls in my class are three in number, and they all play so extraordinarily well that sometimes I think I can never catch up with them. I am the worst of all the scholars in Tausig's classes that I have heard, except one, who is a young man...Many of the girls played magnificently, and I was amazed at the technique that they had, and at the artistic manner in which even very young girls rendered the most difficult music, and all without notes. It gave me*

*a severe nervous headache just to hear them. But it was delightful to
see them go at it. None of them had the least fear, and they laughed
and chattered between the pieces, and when their turn came they
marched up to the piano, sat down as bold as lions, and banged away
so splendidly!*

It took a while for Amy to gain admittance to Tausig's studio,
but she attended his class lessons. What she saw could not have been too
promising: "His idea of teaching is to utter such cries of encouragement
as 'terrible, shocking, dreadful, oh God, oh God!' He would then push
the pupil aside violently, play the passage himself, and tell the pupil to
do it just so." One can predict the resultant tears. By August of 1870,
Amy at last played for the master, only to be undone by his cajoling.
It hardly mattered, though, for about this time Tausig announced that he
had had enough of students and was closing the conservatory in October.
This brilliant pianist, whose playing was described as the most perfectly
finished of the time, simply could not tolerate the weaknesses and
inadequacies of pianists less fortunate than himself. He died of typhoid
fever a year later, only twenty-nine years old.

Amy next went to Theodor Kullak for lessons, although she did
so with mixed feelings. No less an authority than John Knowles Paine
had recommended Kullak to her before she left America, and Tausig
had told her that Kullak taught as well as he himself did, for whatever
that was worth. Amy knew of one student driven to desperation by the
treatment he received at Kullak's conservatory, who "from being deeply
melancholy over it, actually committed suicide!" Amy, however, found
Kullak enchanting, patient, and gentle in comparison to Tausig. She was
also surprised to find that he played quite beautifully: "Why in the world
he has not continued playing in public I can't imagine, but I am told that
he was too nervous. He knows by heart everything that he teaches, and
he plays sometimes with me, sometimes before me, and shows me all
sorts of ways to playing passages. I am getting no end of ideas from him."

Amy studied with Kullak until December 1873, but the honeymoon
lasted less than a year. By the summer of 1871, Amy wrote home:

In one respect Kullak is a more discouraging teacher than Tausig, for Tausig only played occasionally before you, where it was absolutely necessary, and contented himself with scolding and blaming. Kullak, on the contrary, doesn't scold much, but as he plays continually before and with you, with him you see how the thing ought to be done, and the perception of your own deficiencies stands out before you mercilessly.

She plugged on nonetheless, and her letters reflect a growing musical sophistication. She met the aging Friedrich Wieck, heard all the great musicians of the day, and kept practicing, despite the lack of real help from Kullak.

In the summer of 1873, she had the experience of a lifetime: studying with Liszt at Weimar. At this point in his career, Liszt divided his time between Rome, Budapest, and Weimar, and whenever he came to that small German town, young pianists from all over Europe congregated around him. He made himself available to as many as he could and never took money for his time. Amy was awestruck, completely swept away by Liszt's humanity:

Nothing could exceed Liszt's amiability...and instead of frightening me, he inspired me. Never was there such a delightful teacher! And he is the first sympathetic one I've had. You feel so free with him, and he develops the very spirit of music in you. He doesn't keep nagging at you all the time, but leaves you your own conception. Now and then he will make a criticism, or play a passage, and with a few words give you enough to think of all the rest of your life. There is a delicate point to everything he says, as subtle as he is himself.

Her letters are full of telling details of Liszt's teaching; every lesson showed another side of his personality. Then there were the students, some already before the public. Amy probably met musicians of the stature of Klindworth, Nikisch, de Pachmann, Moszkowski, Scharwenka (these latter two studied also with Kullak), and Sophie Menter. In July she wrote home:

Liszt is such an immense, inspiring force that one has to try and stride forward with him at double rate, even if with double expenditure, too! Today I'm more dead than alive, as we had a lesson from him yesterday that lasted four hours. There were twenty artists present, all of whom were anxious to play, and as he was in high good-humor, he played ever so much himself in between. It was perfectly magnificent, but exhausting and exciting to the last degree.

She returned to Berlin in the fall, but lessons with Kullak were less than inspiring:

When you play for him, it is like looking at your skin through a magnifying glass. All your faults seem to start out and glare at you... He never overlooks a technical imperfection, and he ties you down to the technique so that you can never give free rein to your imagination. He sits at the other piano, and just as you are rushing off he will say, 'Don't hurry, Fräulein,' or something like that, and then you begin to think of holding back your fingers and playing every note even, etc.... When you play to Kullak, you feel as if your wings were suddenly clipped, and as if you were put in a harness!

Within a month, she bid Kullak adieu and began studying with yet another master.

* * *

Ludwig Deppe is one of the better-kept secrets in the history of piano teaching. To her good fortune, Amy met him at a musical party given by another American living in Berlin. Kapellmeister of the Royal Opera, Deppe conducted, composed, and played the violin well enough to join his piano students in sonatas. Although never a performing pianist himself, he became obsessed with the physical aspects of piano playing and developed a scientific approach to the instrument. From Amy's letters, it is clear that he made an immediate change in her playing. She writes in great detail of his approach to scale playing and how after careful practice of his methods she at last achieved the pearling scales she had longed for, but not attained, under Kullak. She willingly put aside her plans for a debut to go back to square one with Deppe: slow practice, hands separately.

Amy worked with Deppe for about eighteen months. He was at all times patient, industrious, and specific in his instruction:

> Deppe...shows me how to conquer the difficulty now. He takes a piece, and while he plays it with the most wonderful fineness of conception, he cold-bloodedly dissects the mechanical elements of it, separates them, and tells you how to use your hands so as to grasp them one after the other. In short, he makes the technique and the conception identical, as of course they ought to be, but I never had any other master who trained his pupils to attempt it.

One of her final letters home summarizes her experiences and shows a remarkable equanimity in dealing with so many influences:

> With regard to playing in concert, I find myself doubting whether on general principles it is best to get one's whole musical training under one master only, as Fannie Warburg [one of Deppe's prize students] has done; for my experience teaches me that though nearly all masters can give you something, none can give you everything. If, with my present light, I could begin my study all over, I should first stay three years with Deppe, in order to endow the spirit of music that I hope is within me, with the outward form and perfection of an artist. Next, I should stay a year with Kullak, to give my playing brilliant 'concert dress,' and finally I would spend two seasons with Liszt, in order to add the last ineffable graces—(for never, never should an artist complete a musical course without going to LISZT while he is on this earth!)—The trouble is, however, that one master always feels hurt if you leave him for another! No one can bear the imputation that he can't 'give you everything.'

More than a century after her immersion in all that Europe had to offer, Amy Fay's experience feels remarkably familiar.

V

■ My Teachers

> I have come to believe that a great teacher is a great artist and that there are as few as there are any other great artists. Teaching might even be the greatest of the arts since the medium is the human mind and spirit.
>
> —John Steinbeck[1]

When I was in the woods, I wrote several essays about the teachers I encountered during my student days. It was an opportunity to fondly recognize their influence, but I also wanted to reassemble the memories in a more up-to-date understanding or, put another way, to *re-member*. Meanings will have changed between the time I started lessons at age seven and how I felt forty years later when I wrote the essays. And now, with *this* writing, I again re-member, a couple of decades later still.

The section begins with three essays that concentrate, with one exception, on my teachers before the college years. They are full of stories, for these are the things we remember most easily. Stories loom large in our lives, so much so that they help us form our choices and values. We are in many ways the sum of our stories. Paulo Freire, author of *Pedagogy of Freedom*, said "I cannot be a teacher without exposing who I am."[2]

Looking back, I can say that my teachers were not afraid to be themselves. Of course, I perceived each of them at the time with the eyes and understanding of a child. You will soon meet Mrs. Getz, my

---

1. John Steinbeck, "Like Captured Butterflies" in *California Teacher Association Journal*, edited by J. Wilson McKenney (November 1955): 7.

2. Paulo Freire, *Pedagogy of Freedom* (Lanham, Maryland: Rowman & Littlefield Publishers, 2000), 87.

first teacher. At the time, I saw only the good—her warmth, patience, and love of music. I happily accepted this freely and gratefully. Did she have shortcomings as a teacher? Yes, I can now see that she should not have described the correct hand position as a "claw." It took me years to get rid of tension in my hands but were it not for the love of music she instilled in me, I would not have tried to become a better pianist.

You will also meet George Toot, whose job description as "band director" barely begins to hint at his sophisticated musical taste and understanding. He drafted me to play trombone in his band, a group that performed transcribed classics, modern original works, and only occasionally something popular. I remember once a professional soprano singing opera arias with the band. *Madama Butterfly* at Tuslaw High School? You must be kidding! In my freshman year, he programmed the Overture to *The Barber of Seville* and worked with an attention to detail that I later learned was rather extraordinary. He opened my eyes and ears to music that I would never have encountered if I had been only a pianist.

There are two ways of looking at his influence. Because of him, I surely became a more curious musician with a broader range of interests. On the downside, this excitement about music beyond the keyboard may also have diverted my attention, distracting me from the hard work on piano technique and repertoire building needed during those formative teen years. All in all, I consider Mr. Toot a godsend.

The teachers I describe here inspired me. They gave me good information for the most part, but their real contribution to my education was to light a fire that otherwise would never have found oxygen to burn. Plutarch said, "The mind is not a vessel to be filled, but a fire to be kindled."[3] These teachers had the necessary book of matches. Given my experience with them, I think it is probably true that "we teach as we were taught." I would like to think that this was my goal as a teacher.

It is clear from the essays that I was a rather impressionable youngster, given to superlatives. If Mrs. Getz liked "classical music," it must be the greatest music in the world! Thinking back on this, I don't

---

3. Plutarch, "On Listening to Lectures" in *Moralia*, vol. 1, Loeb Classical Library (Cambridge, Massachusetts: Harvard University Press, 1927).

believe I worshipped Mrs. Getz. It was more that she was giving me a choice—she liked this music, so perhaps I would find it worth liking as well. Until she entered my world, I didn't know this was an option. Mr. Toot broadened my horizons, not only to Wagner and Puccini but to modern American composers like Copland and Persichetti. Both teachers opened the doors to self-education, since as mentioned earlier this was the time of the televised Bernstein *Young People's Concerts* and the Columbia Record Club. I took advantage of these as often as I could; by the time I went to college, I had quite the record collection.

I call the reader's attention to one word near the end of the third essay: *messy*. A teacher's impact depends so much on the psychological pathways between the parties. If the defense mechanisms are well developed, it could be as ships passing in the night. I enrolled in Philosophy during my student days at Oberlin but dropped out within a week with no memory of the professor at all. It wasn't his fault—I simply had no interest then in the subject, and he didn't say anything to change that in the first few class sessions. If the channels are too open, the opposite can occur. The student can become dependent on the teacher's praise for the motivation to work. This also happens when the teacher bullies the student into producing—the student may do so to avoid punishment without developing intrinsic motivation. It *is* messy!

One thing we can agree on: it's never boring. When the human mind and spirit are involved, it will always be soul stirring.

20

Mrs. Getz

Out of the Woods

OCTOBER 1996

As another school year begins, I find myself thinking once again about teaching. This time I don't want to dwell on theory or noble ideals. I'm simply remembering my own teachers, men and women into whose hands I fell by happy accident.

When my mother and father decided that I, age seven, should take piano lessons, they took me to a teacher named Vera Getz. At the end of her driveway hung a neatly painted sign that said, PIANO INSTRUCTION. As far as I know, that sign is the main reason Mrs. Getz became my teacher. We passed that sign every time we drove the five miles into town. There were undoubtedly other piano teachers around, but Mrs. Getz happened to live on the road to town.

The little boy who walked into Mrs. Getz's living room that fall couldn't wait to get started. For years, whenever we visited my paternal grandparents next door, I always ended up messing around at the player piano. After my third cousin Stanley showed me how to play the beginning of "Silent Night," I simply had to figure out the rest. Trips to Grandma's now became pianistic hunting expeditions as I found the keys that would play "Hark! the Herald Angels Sing," "Auld Lang Syne," and a few others on my own. Before I knew it, the upright was relocated (with no little effort) to our house, and I found myself in Mrs. Getz's living room.

At my first lesson, she taught me to count quarters and halves, the location of middle C, the numbers for my fingers, how to figure out the lines and spaces in both the treble and bass clef. She gave me my first method book, assigned the first piece (all on middle C), and taught me a piece by rote she called "Peter, Peter, Pumpkin Eater," which involved an ascending and descending five-finger pattern in the right hand accompanied in the left by a blocked tonic chord and one incomplete dominant seventh. I'm not sure, but I think this was her standard first lesson for all students. I was well into my thirties before it occurred to me that this might be a bit much.

We raced through the first method books, and for Christmas she gave me two pieces of sheet music. I fell in love with "The Skaters' Waltz." My simple joy fueled hers, and she showered me with warm attention. Next came *John Thompson's Second Grade Book*. She supplemented the Thompson series with exercise books, sheet music, and a "pop" book that gave the melody and chord symbols. Sometime in that first year of lessons, she assigned the Thompson arrangement of Schubert's Serenade and began to play it for me. I still remember the glow of her face as she told me that this was her favorite kind of music. When I asked what she meant, she explained that this was "classical music." Until that time, I had no idea one kind of music might be different from another, but I knew if Mrs. Getz thought that classical music was special, then it must be the greatest music in the world.

As I outgrew John Thompson, Mrs. Getz would sometimes go to her hall closet and bring out the pieces she had played. Her background was always a bit fuzzy—as far as I know, she didn't finish college and sometimes mentioned that her own teacher was a student of a student of Liszt. When she played, though, I felt a power that went beyond training. To my youthful ears, the music coming from her fingers was a force of nature. Her "In the Hall of the Mountain King" thundered mightily; when she played "Rustles of Spring," I could feel the spray of the splashing water on my face. She passed on her feeling for music less by instruction than by osmosis; she shared something that came from the center of her being, something that transcended words. I reveled in every moment of it.

I studied with her until I was fourteen. If either I, my parents, or Mrs. Getz had been more sophisticated about music study, I probably should have moved on sooner, but as it was, I was almost to college age before my family conceded I might have what it takes to "make it" as a musician. She was the first to admit that I needed a teacher who knew more than she did, but it took a while for us to find one. In the meantime, I learned lots of pieces that I played with great sweep and approximate finesse. I liked music that was loud and fast and sight-read the rest, sometimes even at lessons. We went through the old Schirmer classical sonata volume, and I still remember a few lessons during a Mozart slow movement when I had to stop to wipe the tears from my eyes. I apologized to Mrs. Getz, who thought her sixth-grade student was overcome with the beauty of the music. Actually, I was nearsighted, and my eyes were straining to read the notes for the first or second time. Once glasses were prescribed, my feeling for Mozart disappeared entirely.

Given the coincidence of Grandma's upright and cousin Stanley, it was perhaps inevitable that I would take piano lessons. It was Vera Getz, though, who struck the spark, blissfully unaware of theory or noble ideals.

21

Mrs. Leach and Mr. Toot

Out of the Woods

DECEMBER 1996

After the last column about my first piano teacher, I share with the writer Flannery O'Connor "a certain embarrassment about being a storyteller in these times when stories are considered not quite as satisfying as statements and statements not quite as satisfying as statistics." The memories, however, are still flowing, and I want to pay tribute to a few more of my teachers, working without the safety net of either statements or statistics.

I nearly quit lessons when I was fourteen. Mrs. Getz, my beloved first teacher, told me she didn't have anything else that she could teach me. One day my mother came to the piano while I was practicing and asked if I would like to take lessons with a professor at Malone College, the nearest institution of higher learning to Massillon, Ohio. I said, "No, I don't think so." I was learning the first movement of the Grieg Concerto at the time and was perfectly happy to go it alone.

Wiser heads prevailed, and that fall I started studying with Kay Leach, whose tall and serious demeanor immediately intimidated me. It could also have been the Bach partita that replaced the Grieg in my assigned pieces or the twin Steinway grands in her studio, a long way from Mrs. Getz's living room Acrosonic.

Mrs. Leach acquainted me with many of the big issues of artistic playing, and I learned a great deal from her in the three years I studied with her. However, it took me the better part of two years to get over the fact that I was really nervous in lessons. I never admitted it to anyone, especially my mother, who would pick me up after school, drive across two towns to get to Malone, and then wait for an hour in the car while I had my lesson. Mrs. Leach was not unkind, but she meant business, and suddenly lessons weren't fun anymore. I had to fill out a practice card each week: ten hours minimum was expected, and there were more than a few weeks that I didn't make it. She assigned Bach, Mozart, and Schumann instead of Grieg, Rachmaninoff, and Zez Confrey. Luckily, she knew more about playing the piano than either Mrs. Getz or I did. She had another high school student, a boy a year or two older named Stanley Varn. Soon after I began studying with her, she made a point of inviting me to a Malone recital on which Stanley played. To my utter dismay, Stanley played better than I did. All the things she kept telling me regarding tone, clarity, and style, he already did. So, I got to work.

After my second year of study with her, Mrs. Leach presented Stanley and me in a joint recital. When I think back on it, I'm amazed I ever performed again. There was the inevitable comparison with Stanley, whose confidence was as certain as it was galling. Then there was my mother's nervous breakdown over the whole *affaire du concert*: what to wear, the guest list, the arrangements for the reception, and her own competition with Stanley's mother. Finally, two days before the recital, I broke my glasses in gym class. My nearsightedness even then was severe enough to make my father wonder if I would find the piano when I walked out on stage.

I survived because of another remarkable teacher, our public-school system's most appropriately named band director, Mr. Toot. While I didn't start a band instrument in the fourth grade, Mr. Toot noticed me at the piano making up accompaniments to the little tunes the other kids were playing on their flutes, clarinets, and trumpets. He drafted me soon thereafter to accompany the older students, promoting several of us in a fairly extensive concert tour of the local PTA meetings. When I was in the eighth grade, a year before I started studying with Mrs. Leach, Mr. Toot decided he had to have me in his band and hatched a plan that neither my parents nor I could refuse. He offered me the choice of any instrument, with free lessons and instrument rental as long as I played in the band. I chose the trombone.

In comparison to the Grieg Concerto, the trombone was fairly easy, so I didn't have to work too hard. However, I got much more from Mr. Toot than trombone lessons. The band was a social laboratory, the exact opposite of my lonely trips to Malone with my mother. During marching season, it even provided physical exercise, and there was so much to explore inside the band room. Mr. Toot let me take his full scores home to play on the piano; it never occurred to me that this might be difficult. When Mrs. Leach assigned the Mendelssohn Concerto in G Minor, Mr. Toot told me I could play it with the band if I arranged it. He even bought me the orchestral score. There was no curriculum or instruction—just do it. "By the way, the French horns sound a fifth lower than written—good luck." He had a serious stereo system at his house, and when I went there for a trombone lesson, he'd crank it up and blast us both against the wall with the Philadelphia Orchestra playing Wagner overtures. *That* was fun!

He taught me passion for music. I'd probably be a better pianist today if I had practiced more for Mrs. Leach during those years, but thanks to Mr. Toot, I'm a musician today.

22

Professors Winter and Howland

Out of the Woods

FEBRUARY 1997

This column finds me still absorbed with memories of my teachers. Beyond the fond reminiscences, I am trying to discern the nature of a teacher's influence. I know that every day I influence my students in some way, yet I cannot discern the exact nature of that influence. I would like to control what students take from me, and my hope is that honest reflection about my experiences as a student will help me to understand this delicate relationship.

In my senior year of high school, I studied with Daniel Winter at the College of Wooster. Despite a relatively short time in his studio, I now recognize that his influence extended far beyond just playing the piano. Mr. Winter was an Eastman graduate who studied with Cecile Genhart. He worshipped Beethoven, in particular the Op. 111 Sonata, and spoke eloquently of the glories of Bach, Mozart, Schubert, and Brahms. He performed both *Die schöne Müllerin* and the B-flat Sonata of Schubert during that year and would often depart from whatever we were doing in a lesson to demonstrate a fantastic moment of beauty from either work. One day I arrived for my lesson and noticed Copland's *Piano Fantasy* on his piano. I owned recordings of several Copland works and asked him about this piece. He spent fifteen minutes showing me the abstract work, then sent the score home with me for further investigation, trusting that I would relish digging into it.

Mr. Winter tended to speak in the tone of someone reading from stone tablets carved on high; as an impressionable seventeen-year-old, I believed every word. He was utterly convinced that technical work outside of the repertoire was useless, yea verily, antimusical. He detested most French music and had nothing but disdain for showpieces of any ilk. In short, he was passionate about both his likes and dislikes.

Music was absolutely central to his being; the fervor of his convictions bowled me over.

Nearly thirty years have gone by since I studied with him; this is the first time I tried to sort out his influence. It can be no coincidence that I played the Op. 111 Sonata on my senior recital four years later or that my final graduate recital at Yale included the Copland *Piano Fantasy*. It is also no accident that I was nearly thirty before I tried to figure out piano technique and didn't play the Tchaikovsky Concerto until age forty.

That his influence was so strong says something about both of us. He clearly lived by his convictions, and I wanted a strong role model. I was on the verge of deciding which way to go with music. My parents, in particular my father, had doubts about music as a field of gainful employment. They had no clue why their otherwise sensible son was so engrossed in music by dead Europeans. Mr. Winter understood me, and I thrived on it.

If the balance in our personalities had been slightly different, his influence would have diminished. Had Mr. Winter been less passionate or less vocal about his beliefs, I might have looked elsewhere for inspiration. Had I been more certain of myself, or my parents been more encouraging, I might have found him opinionated or overbearing. Learning could have taken place in either instance, but I doubt that the connection between student and teacher would have been as significant.

* * *

Inda Howland is another teacher whose influence I recognize every day I make music. She was a short, leathery woman in her sixties who taught eurhythmics at Oberlin. She had burning, shamanistic eyes and walked with the grace of a leopard. Because I was too shy to risk other people laughing at me moving about in her eurhythmics class, I snuck in the back door by enrolling in her advanced ear-training course. The first class was a revelation; she came into the room, sat down at the piano, and played a harmonic progression of five or six chords, then asked us to play it back to her. We were a class of mostly pianists with perfect pitch, so we were ready in three tries, but try as we might, she kept telling us it wasn't right. After fifteen minutes, she played just the first chord and told us to play it exactly as she did. We were completely puzzled because we knew we were playing the right notes. What she wanted was the right sound; in the words she eventually shared with us, "the right trajectory of the sound," going the precise distance at a particular speed. It was unlike anything we had heard before, and most of the first term was spent learning to listen all over again. It was indeed advanced ear training; no piano teacher before or since made me listen with such intensity. Her teaching method was almost completely experiential: she never told us how to do it—in fact, she refused if we asked. Instead, by painful trial and error, we had to experiment until we got it. She was a stern taskmaster, spurring us on until either she gave up in disgust or, by some miracle, we got it, whereupon we were rewarded with a smile that put the sun to shame.

Perhaps her influence on me was the magical quality she brought to the classroom. While my other classes were rooted in fact and rationalism, Inda dared to suggest that it couldn't all be put down on paper. We had to listen with a ferocity that started a chemical reaction between our spirit and the music, and the result was never the same. The challenge was to learn through experience how to control the process.

While modern pedagogy strives to teach how to do things right, it occurs to me that the study of teaching will never boil it all down to one to-do list. It *is* mysterious; there is no way to know which teacher will have the greatest impact or which student will look back thirty years later and remember such detail. It is also messy; with the good comes the not so good. No one has it all right.

23

Interlude

The *Clavier* editors gave me carte blanche regarding subject matter, so I tended to write about whatever was on my mind. As a result, topics could vary widely from month to month. In collecting the *Clavier* essays in book form, though, I realized there had to be an organizing principle centered on the thematic material.

This section centers on memories of my later teachers. You've already read three columns about my earliest instructors; the essays that follow summarize my three principal postsecondary teachers. Two of the essays were never published in *Clavier* and relate memories of my Oberlin teacher Emil Danenberg and my Yale mentor Donald Currier. The first appeared as a program note to a Schubert series I organized at Northwestern University, two years after Danenberg's untimely death in 1982. The second was requested to honor Mr. Currier's retirement and was published in the Yale School of Music alumni magazine in 1989. The remainder of the essays return to these two important figures as well as touch on the remarkable Claude Frank, a beloved teacher and musician whose death in 2014 is still mourned by his many students. These are strong memories, stories vital to who I am. We never outgrow memories of our teachers.

These stories begin in the distant past (as a child of seven, for example, or a graduate student of twenty-four), then become the subject of essays by a middle-aged college piano professor. Now, decades later still, he is writing again, remembering, one more time. I am reminded of a Beethoven coda—the recap is over, but we seem to be starting a second development. A better metaphor may be *pentimento*: in painting, the presence or emergence of earlier images, forms, or strokes that have been changed and painted over. These essays scratch the surface of earlier essays, which in turn were the first sketches or attempts at creating a canvas.

Throughout this journey, the stories are personal enough that I debated including some of them. While I'd like to claim that my admitted insecurities are behind me, I find I still need to expunge some of these demons, even in retirement. Revisiting these essays, I am shocked by how much pleasing my teachers meant to me, both emotionally and motivationally. I also note the "father figure" issues. Are these inevitable? We all have fathers and families—we might as well admit to them. Our students probably look at us this way too—better to be aware of it than hiding one's head in the sand.

I come upon a phrase we have already seen in these essays: life is messy. I first used it in 1997, and you will again come across it in the 2010 piece on Mr. Currier. There is power in accepting one's foibles. Even today my mentors help me reconfigure my neuroses. And here's a tidbit not mentioned in the essay about Claude Frank: he once told me I wasn't neurotic *enough*!

24

Program Note for
an All-Schubert Recital

Northwestern University

JANUARY 1984

All pianists have teachers. Natural facility and immense talent will take you only so far. There is simply no way to master the requirements of first-rate musicianship and pianism without a little help along the way.

I was fortunate to have a lot of help, the kind that nurtured and challenged at the same time. As a student, I had no idea why I enjoyed the piano as much as I did, but looking back now with the assurance of hindsight and experience, I can say that all my teachers must have known what they were doing.

Emil Danenberg was one of those teachers. Ushered into his presence with a group of quivering freshmen at Oberlin, I admit to some terror (a back injury that left him physically impaired gave him a slightly gnomic appearance), but he also impressed me as a person of significance. His ubiquitous gray suit and the countenance of Schoenberg (one of *his* teachers) glowering down from the studio wall contributed to this impression. Mr. Danenberg let you know in no uncertain terms that he took his job seriously—at the first lesson, you were assigned reams of études and serious pieces: Beethoven sonatas, Bach suites, and yes, Schoenberg as well as other twentieth-century revolutionaries were typical fare. I remember him assigning a Chopin scherzo in my sophomore year and referring to it as a "party piece." He took music seriously, and so did his students.

He expected you to work hard, but I don't remember him telling anyone to do so. Consequently, everyone worked hard. Those who didn't went into other fields. He also never talked about beauty, but you could tell from the furrowed brow and the intense concentration he exhibited when demonstrating in a lesson that beauty was indeed uppermost in his mind. He hated conceit of any kind, especially musical. When once a student explained a ritard made in a Chopin étude as a technical facilitation, he exploded with epithets that made clear that the easy way out was not an option for *his* students. When I once suggested a redistribution in the Ravel Toccata, his answer was, "Sure, if you want to sound like…" naming a pianist known more for flashing fingers than musical insight.

Every year, the Danenbergs invited the students to their home on Prospect Street for a holiday party. Mr. Danenberg always announced these events to us with "Come over Saturday night. I'm going to cook." And then he would threaten us with some inedible-sounding delicacy he had as a boy in Hong Kong. Inevitably, though, it was Mrs. Danenberg who did the cooking, and the two of them introduced us to the joys of living well. Veal Marengo was accompanied by a history lesson on the dish itself and a learned discussion of its preparation in various parts of France. If he was feeling particularly magnanimous, Emil would command Mary Ann to "Get out the slides," and he would treat us to a vivid account of their most recent gastronomic tour of Europe, complete with details missed by the *Michelin Guide* and always centered on the precise meal eaten at a certain restaurant at an exact time of day.

He had that kind of memory. An avid collector of facts, he could tell you the program played by a visiting artist at Oberlin twenty years previously. He scanned the *New York Times* for humorous or ironic bits of interest, posting the "squibs," as he called them, on his bulletin board. He was an opera buff and a sports fan at the same time—his idea of a great Saturday afternoon was watching a football game on television with the sound off while listening to the Met broadcast on the radio.

By the time I left Oberlin, Emil had become dean of the conservatory and was very shortly to become president of the college. He was amazingly effective as the school's leader, but it came as no surprise to those who had witnessed firsthand his dedication to music and his powers of concentration. He simply applied those energies to something else.

Two years ago, on January 16, Emil Danenberg died at the age of sixty-four. His passing left those who knew him deeply saddened that he had been taken at such a vital, productive time in his life. While immersed in teaching a lesson, I sometimes catch myself saying something to a student, only to hear it re-echo in my mind in Emil's voice. This weekend's programs celebrate Schubert, one of Emil's favorite composers. I studied only one piece by Schubert with him, yet I find myself drawn to this music increasingly as time goes on. At a memorial concert given by a group of his students two years ago in Oberlin, Frank Weinstock and I played the slow movement of Schubert's *Grand Duo* for four hands. Afterward, the group quite naturally began to converse about food, exchanging stories of *nouvelle cuisine* expeditions in our respective cities. The conversation grew increasingly animated until someone suddenly asked, "Do you realize what we're doing?"

I felt Emil's presence in all of us at that moment and knew for the first time the true magnitude of a powerful teacher's influence.

25

Thirty-Seven Years of Giving: A Thanksgiving to Donald Currier

Yale School of Music Alumni Magazine
MAY 1989

Fifteen years ago this spring, I trekked up the Stoeckel Hall stairs for the first time to room 46. It was a Saturday morning, and auditions were in progress. The door at the end of the fourth-floor gloom opened to reveal a darkly intense gentleman of rumpled build in a tweed jacket whose seriousness of visage was heightened by the way he peered over his glasses. He ushered me in with what I took to be Ivy League politeness, and as I sat down to the piano, he stood immediately to the right of the keyboard and fixed me with a powerful stare, again over those tortoiseshell glasses. My fragile ego hunkered down to weather what portended to be a chilly audition.

Then he smiled. The clouds dispersed, and without uttering a word, he seemed to say, "All is not as it seems, my nervous young man." With that unspoken message, Donald Currier began teaching me.

There is much to learn from a man who doesn't believe in answers. Lessons with Mr. Currier seldom involved directions of the "take-time-at-this-cadence" variety. Usually his first response after allowing a complete performance of a movement began with a question. "How does this phrase work?" "What do you think the composer is doing at this cadence?" "Did you like what happened going into the second theme? Do you remember what happened? Where *is* the second theme? Well, let's work on this!" Thus began the quest for a shared discovery about music, which was itself the answer.

Similarly, there is much to appreciate in a teacher who lets you in on his humanity. That grin on audition day suggested a delightful and varied personality behind the dour exterior. As Mr. Currier gradually became Don, he invited students out to his home on Mulberry Point for dinners of bluefish. He counseled patience with the problems of reaching adulthood, endured hours of our career doubts, and managed to become a friend while never losing the objectivity of a teacher. It was quite a balancing act, and I wish he would break down and tell me how he did it.

This May, Donald Currier retires from thirty-seven Yale years, and those close to him know that he must be dreading all the nice things people will say about him. That Yankee sense of self-deprecation will have him squirming through this and other testimonials, but the facts of his life and career remain. It is time to honor those facts.

For example, it is a fact that I have never encountered a more astute, insightful pair of ears than his. He has a way of listening to you play a piece and then saying the one thing that brings the problem you felt, but were unable to define, into focus. It is seldom a bromide for success ("practice this slowly twenty times and call me in the morning"). Rather, he somehow gets into your thought processes and removes the blockage, allowing you to solve the problem yourself. Those of us who teach know how difficult that is. Donald did it all the time.

Yet each lesson was different, and seeing him in action during the weekly master class was an education in itself. One student would receive a lesson in stylistic awareness; the next would experience an immersion in the Currier School of Limitless Coloristic Potential at the Piano. He worked with effectiveness on literature ranging from pre-Bach to Yale student composers. One day, to my everlasting amazement, I brought in a dense, complex piece, the ink barely dry, written by my friend and student colleague Martin Brody. On first hearing, Don had accurate, helpful suggestions about the structure and dramatic possibilities. When I reported the ideas to Marty, he was even more surprised than I, since Don had intuitively understood what turned out to be a recondite game of pitch relationships Marty had embedded in the piece.

When left on his own at the piano, Donald gravitates unabashedly to music of a lyrical persuasion. While he would confess great admiration for the three Bs (Bach, Beethoven, and Brahms), his soul belongs to Mozart, Schubert, and Chopin, his eyes glowing at the mere mention of their names. He has a deep sympathy for the French Impressionists, and his chamber playing is *sans pareil*. But if one were to seek the composer with whom Donald Currier identifies most closely, it would be Schumann. The quicksilver temperament, the extreme joys and corresponding depressions, the literary bent—all bespeak a character that finds its mirror in our friend Donald, and those who have heard his performances know that Florestan and Eusebius were not figments of a fevered, nineteenth-century imagination.

If Don prefers his piano playing *legato cantabile*, he wants his martinis dry and his beef rare. No Eusebius when it comes to living the good life, over the years Donald has shared his enjoyment of the finer things with his students and colleagues. During my Yale days, there was always at least one general studio party per year and several smaller dinners or nights out with various groups. Until the advent of Charlotte (an event seen by all who know him as his greatest triumph), he handled the chef chores on his own. He is an excellent cook (although Charlotte is better), and I have never seen him happier than after a dazzling repast of his own making, leaning back at the table to breathe a sigh of pure contentment, knowing that at this particular moment, there were no questions to ask, no answers to seek. At one such occasion, as his young guests engaged in making meaningful utterances, he popped our philosophical balloons with the comment "Oh, youth today are such prudes!" Since this was during the height of the sexual revolution, astonishment reigned. But soon, his postprandial glow returned, and now that I am fifteen years older, I see his point.

Cyril Connolly said it a bit differently, with perhaps less dramatic impact: "Youth is a period of missed opportunities." For the past thirty-seven years at Yale, Donald Currier has worked with students to show them where the opportunities were hiding. His style has been to let the students think they've discovered them on their own. It has required a selflessness that cannot have been easy for this man whose inner life is so complex and rich. He has never been one who lives vicariously through his students, and so his teaching has been a kind of giving that is not based on getting something back.

So Donald, now it's your turn! Think of sitting back from Yale's table with thirty-seven years' worth of students around the groaning board. Imagine the look in all those eyes as they contemplate you heaving a sigh of relief over having pulled off a meal like that! Consider how many ears you have introduced to gourmet music making. Try to envision all those apprentice chefs cooking up a storm, improving their skills over the years, experimenting with new dishes, deepening their appreciation of old favorites. We wish you long happiness now with time to pursue your own muse, and we send you a one-liner, borrowed from J. B. Priestley, to trot out at any appropriate moment: "One of the delights known to age, and beyond the grasp of youth, is that of Not Going."

And Donald, thanks for dinner...

26

Reflections on Oberlin and Yale

Out of the Woods

APRIL 1997

Between 1968, when I entered Oberlin as a freshman, and 1977, when I left Yale with the Master of Musical Arts degree, I studied piano with three remarkable men. It is not difficult to recognize how they influenced me musically. However, it has taken me all twenty of the intervening years to understand the deeper role they played in my life. Because I now do what they made their careers doing—work with young people who have chosen to devote their careers to music. I've spent a lot of time thinking about who they were, how they interacted with their students, and how they interacted with me in particular. It has sometimes been confusing to think about this, since the feelings of the past so easily blur into the recollections of the present.

Of one thing I am certain: what I needed then as a postadolescent, not-quite-formed adult is not all that different from what my present students need. I remember my carefully concealed anxieties: Was I good enough? Would I be able to make it? Would I find any friends? Would I be as good as my teacher's other students? It was daunting, but I was too good an actor to show my real feelings.

I knew nothing about the teacher to whom I was assigned at Oberlin, Emil Danenberg. I had never met anyone like him and soon learned he was one of the most respected teachers at a competitive school. I could also sense that I was behind the curve when compared to my fellow students, so between wanting to please him and to catch up, I worked like a madman. "If I could only satisfy him," I thought, "be not only good enough but the best, perhaps I could win him over." I turned him into an Old Testament god; I have no idea how he felt about this or if he even realized it. I came to love him, but the fear never entirely went away. He was incredibly generous, giving me free lessons for an entire summer a year after I graduated. Before the summer of my junior year, he took great care to prepare me for a first visit to Europe, giving me the location, menu, and fee structure of half the restaurants in Vienna. His accuracy and good taste substantially broadened this country boy's culinary experience.

I entered Yale in 1974, following marriage and two years teaching at a Vermont prep school. I was dying to get back to serious study. My new teacher, Donald Currier, must have thought I was a wild horse; so eager was I to catch up on what I had been missing. Mr. Currier could be moody, but his demeanor more often tended toward the kindly Ivy League professor. He had the highest standards but gave no sermons. He encouraged but let the students set their own goals. This worked exceedingly well with me, since I had enough ambition for two or three. He gently guided me musically and quickly became a close friend. Again, he was generous to a fault, giving me extra lessons, hiring me for odd jobs around his house, inviting us to dinner, and nearly always picking up the tab.

I'm struck by the way these two men were opposite aspects of a father figure: the first a Zeus—stern, demanding, giving only conditional approval; the second was more like Robert Young in *Father Knows Best*—warm, supportive, approval more assured. I'm also struck by how I needed them as fathers, quite simply because I was not yet ready to go it alone.

And then there was Claude Frank, who represented everything I wanted to be: a superb musician, an inspiring teacher, a performer with a real playing career. "If only I could please him," I thought, "I will have arrived and consequently be worthy of making my way in this noble profession." Mr. Frank taught master classes at Yale in those days and occasionally took on a lucky student full time. He chose me to study with him privately for six weeks in my first year, a great honor indeed. In my final year, Mr. Currier was on sabbatical, so Mr. Frank was my only teacher. I tried mightily to please him and felt I failed. I'm not sure he would agree with this—we never talked about it. The point is I convinced myself that I did not meet his expectations, and that has bothered me for twenty years.

Like his own teacher, Schnabel, he wanted a different piece at every lesson, memorized and ready for performance. When one week it's Beethoven's Op. 101 and the next it's the Brahms "Handel" Variations, and they are both new, that's very demanding. Because I could not do this to my own standards, let alone his, I felt I failed. Additionally, everything I played needed to be "more beautiful," an invocation I heard at every lesson. Was my playing so lacking in beauty? He wanted me to feel more and to project that feeling with more openness of character. Was I really not feeling or projecting the music? It seemed to me, in my vulnerable state of trying so hard yet missing the mark, that he wanted me to be a different person, one who was more confident to express his feeling, one who could *be* Schumann instead of one who attempted to play him.

That, at least, is how it seemed to me at the time. It was terribly unsettling. In the wisdom of middle age, I can see that he had only the best intentions and that his high expectations spurred me on to a greater effort than I might have exerted under less pressure. He could not have known the effect he had on this seemingly confident overachiever—remember, I was a pretty good actor. The toll I paid during much of the next twenty years, though, was the feeling that I would never learn fast enough, never played beautifully enough, never satisfy the internalized father. I'm writing now to expunge the demons. It wasn't his fault.

The point is that we as teachers are only half the equation—we never know what is going on inside the heads and hearts of our students. We exert enormous influence, perhaps more than we realize. We forget how vulnerable students can be; these bright, eager young people are more complex than we think, especially the quiet ones. A tossed-off remark at the end of a long day can live for years in the heart of a sensitive student. It is an awesome and frightening responsibility.

27

Mr. Currier's Passing

Winds of Change

July 2010

On January 7, 2010, Donald Currier, my teacher during the three years I was in residence for graduate study at Yale University, died at the age of ninety-one. While this article may be part eulogy, it's not intended as such. Instead, I want to think about what it means to "study with someone."

The phrase itself is not used in every discipline. It arises most in one-on-one teaching; we use it all the time as musicians, perhaps even taking it for granted. In any field in which the master-apprentice model is the norm, one might hear this simple statement, spoken with both respect and pride: "I study with..." In higher education today, the preferred terminology centers on *student learning*, even to the point of avoiding the word *teaching*. However, "to study with" might be the highest of all objectives. The phrase connotes simultaneous learning, bringing the learned and the learner together to study, and eventually a mastering of the subject, again accomplished together.

Donald Currier taught at Yale from 1951 to 1989. He had been there for twenty-three years before I first met him on the top floor of Yale's Stoeckel Hall. Lessons occurred there for the next three years, and recitals were played in the recital hall across the street. And then I graduated. It seems like such a short time in the long unfolding of both our careers.

But Don wasn't just my teacher—I studied with him. This difference could have been in the way our lessons proceeded. He wasn't a man to rely on codified solutions. His instructional method, if he would admit to anything that formal, usually involved asking questions, and our combined efforts to find answers led to a shared exploration of the music at hand. One literally studied *with* him, at the same time as he studied.

Given the fondness that many of his students felt for him over the years, it's safe to say that studying with him worked for a lot of us.

In any close student-teacher relationship, the learning seldom stops when the studio door closes or the semester ends. This is where it gets tricky, or so I realize thirty-four years into my own teaching career. The boundaries can't help but blur somewhat. Don gave me extra lessons without asking for a fee; hired me to do odd jobs around his house during summers; helped me pick out the first piano I ever bought; cosigned for the loan I took out to buy the piano. On the day I flew off to my first college teaching position, he drove me to the LaGuardia shuttle service. In short, he became more than a teacher—he was a friend.

This wasn't confusing at the time—I needed someone like him, without knowing why. I was in my midtwenties with a couple years of teaching experience at a boys' prep school under my belt. I'd had a fairly sheltered childhood but was determined to make it on my own. I worked really hard as a student and was proud that all my teachers thought well of me. Once I left Yale, I never sought out someone else to "study with." I wanted to be on my own—and was. Don did not try to hold on to me in any way as a student, and our friendship was a strong one well into the 1990s. When he retired from Yale in 1989, he invited a group of us who had truly "studied with him" to a long weekend at the Yale-at-Norfolk estate in the Litchfield Hills of Connecticut, where we tried to have serious discussions about the "meaning of it all" but had much more success toasting his career and devising the Currier motto for music making: "No fuss, no muss!"

It was only later that I began to question where "studied with" ended and friendship began. I had blurred the two so much that it was all a continuum for me. There came a point where I needed to disentangle the threads and in the process had to withdraw somewhat. This hurt Don, but I couldn't explain to him what I was going through. We remained friends, but the old closeness was gone. When he died, we hadn't spoken in over a year.

I write so intimately about this because I think when we study with someone, whether we are the student or the teacher, we enter into one of life's most dynamic yet precarious associations. It's the next closest thing to being part of a family. And what family is without a scar or two? Don's extending his friendship into our relationship was always good-intentioned, but there was no way he could have known I was needier than I appeared. I became dependent on him for some things that a teacher shouldn't have to provide. And who knows—maybe he needed to feel needed? Life is messy. So is studying with someone.

A disquieting irony in all this is that I am now older than Don was when he taught me at Yale. In fact, I turned sixty the month after Don's passing. Such a concurrence has a way of making one think about life's cycles. I reflect on the students who have studied with me. I have probably left a scar or two myself—perhaps unrecognized, perhaps not. I know that I am much more careful about how close I allow myself to get to a student now than I was earlier in my career. Every day I have to rediscover the appropriate boundaries with every student as we work together. The lines are constantly in flux, for all of us.

Yet how fortunate we are to study with another person who loves music as much as we do. From one side, we witness someone who understands and embodies the artist's life, who by working with us at a crucial time in our development grants us entry into that most select throng, the musician's guild. From the other, we re-experience the excitement of everything being new, of youth's limitless energy to press on, of knowing that the best is yet to come. It is a relationship few are accorded, and it is with us until our last days. Thank you, Don, for all that and more.

28

Mr. Danenberg Reemerges

Out of the Woods

MAY–JUNE 2001

One of my winter reads this year was a book called *Evenings On and Off the Roof*, Dorothy Lamb Campbell's fascinating account of the groundbreaking Los Angeles concert series founded by Peter Yates and his wife, the pianist Frances Mullen. Frustrated in the 1930s by the absence of serious chamber music, the couple built a rooftop studio on their small West Hollywood house for intimate concerts. They invited local musicians to perform the most challenging repertoire for a small but eager audience of similarly starved music lovers. The series, dubbed Evenings on the Roof, soon outgrew the Yates' studio but continued its pioneering ways for many years thereafter.

It makes for a good story, especially when on page 42 a name leapt out at me that brought the story much closer to home.

One of the local performers was a UCLA undergraduate named Emil Danenberg. Campbell relates the story of how Danenberg performed in one of the first Evenings on the Roof, an all-Schoenberg program attended by the composer in late January 1940. He then underwent a drastic operation for crippling arthritis leaving him in a plaster cast for two months. He emerged to perform Roy Harris's Piano Sonata and Little Suite while still in a neck brace in June of the same year. He was scheduled to open an ambitious Beethoven series in October but suffered a heart attack. Yates chronicled what happened next in a letter to his closest friend:

> *[The day he was scheduled to play,] Emil discharged himself from the hospital more or less by walking out…and called to say he would play. Which he did, scarcely able to stand up, played better than he has ever played for us. I had to hoist him up the stairs for his last bow.*

Two years later, Danenberg apparently ended the series as well; Campbell writes of his performance of Op. 111 in June 1942, at which Otto Klemperer turned pages for him.

All this has particular significance to me because I studied with Emil Danenberg at Oberlin. His students all knew that Schoenberg was an important figure in his life: a somber photograph of the master held a place of honor on the studio wall. The rest was personal. In my senior year, I learned Op. 111 and played it on my recital, yet he never told me this story.

The power of Emil's story kept nagging me, not so much the facts themselves as that he never told me. Did he think I wouldn't care? That I'd care too much? Was it no longer a part of his active memory, having occurred more than thirty years before? Was it simply too personal?

I might have chalked it up to Emil's reticence and not thought more about it until one of my own students said something that struck a spark. In a lesson, I referred to an idea as having occurred to me "in a previous life," and he said, "Oh, you must have some great stories—you've done so many things."

At that moment, my only concern was to get him back to his Beethoven sonata and out of my house of memories. My past seemed insignificant; I had never had one of the century's greatest conductors sit at my elbow during late Beethoven. However, my student simply wanted to know me, just as I had wanted to know Emil. Where does one draw the line?

About the same time as memories of Emil toppled over one another, I was reunited with my first real student whom I will call CVG. As an undergraduate philosophy major at Yale, CVG studied with me when I was a graduate assistant. Twenty-six years later, I invited him to give a lecture and master class at my school. His life has had as many chapters as mine. He began his lecture with two stories about me as a young teacher. They weren't that flattering, but CVG remembered the incidents fondly and as important to his development. I let myself wander through my own memories of our times together: working on sound in the Rachmaninoff Prelude in B Minor, on effect in Chopin's C-sharp Minor Scherzo, on form in Beethoven's Op. 90. I was surprised by how much detail I remembered. Later, he would visit me in New Orleans where I held my first college teaching job; we would exchange long, thoughtful letters during the year he spent abroad. For several years, we both lived in Baltimore but were each involved in different lives there, too preoccupied with personal needs to spend much time together. When he came to Kansas City for his class, I had not spent serious time with him in eight years. It was a bit of a risk for both of us.

The years melted away quickly, though. At one point in his lecture, I caught sight of the dazzlingly quick, guileless teenager I knew in New Haven. He reminded me of one of my former selves, the passionate, music-above-all twentysomething who taught from his gut and loved every second of it, before the scar tissue built up to cover the pockets of sorrow, before a lesson meant telling how as efficiently as possible.

He and I shared many stories at dinner that night and realized our ongoing story has a way to go before its denouement. Thinking about it afterward, it occurred to me that our various selves are always there, even when we don't admit them to present awareness.

We teach from our stories, whether we tell them or not. Emil's being communicated strength, determination, and courage—he didn't have to tell me the story of his hospitalization or of surviving a first performance of Op. 111 with Klemperer hovering over him. Nevertheless, his personality was undoubtedly formed by such experiences.

I tell my CVG story to bring part of my past into the present and perhaps to animate the reader's memories of their pasts—it matters. In the words of the poet Rainer Maria Rilke,

> Think...of the world you carry inside you, and call this thinking whatever you want to...only be attentive to what is arising within you, and place that above everything you perceive around you. What is happening in your innermost self is worthy of your entire love; somehow you must find a way to work at it...
>
> —Letters to a Young Poet

29

Phyllis Curtin

Winds of Change

NOVEMBER 2016

While I try to focus here on change as it transforms our profession and sometimes flusters its practitioners, I want to think today about something that doesn't change: the effect of artistry and its long-lasting impact.

These thoughts come to mind as I reminisce about the unexpected effect Phyllis Curtin had on my life. Phyllis was an admired American soprano who taught voice at Yale back in the '70s, who directed the vocal program at Tanglewood for fifty-one years, and who passed away this June at the age of ninety-four. She sang often at the New York City Opera in the '50s and '60s, created the title role in Carlisle Floyd's opera *Susannah,* and performed at the White House during the Ford administration. She was dean of the Boston University School of Fine Arts from 1983 to 1991 and every summer until 2014 gave Tanglewood her all. Among her best-known students: Dawn Upshaw, Cheryl Studer, Simon Estes, Sanford Sylvan, and Stephanie Blythe.

My connection to her began as accompanist to a few of her students at Yale. I greatly enjoyed learning the song literature and thinking about how her concept of vocal sound production could be transferred to the piano. Near the end of that first year in her studio, she asked if I would substitute for her regular accompanist in a recital in Vermont. Flattered beyond words, of course I said yes. That led to several more recitals, including the one at the White House. I was all of twenty-six, still a student. Photographs of that event hang in my teaching studio today.

The last recital I played for her was at Yale in 1980. We stayed in touch over the years, but I deeply regret that I didn't do more to extend the relationship. I last spoke with her in 2006, a brief moment in passing, again at Tanglewood. These memories go back forty years, yet they resonate as if they were yesterday.

We are lucky in our student days if a true artist appears to open windows to things we have not previously known. Phyllis did this in ways I did not recognize at the time but appreciate more fully now that I have lived into maturity.

If I am able to walk onstage for a performance with anything like the appearance of joy, it is due to Phyllis. She commanded the stage from the first footstep. Shy and uncomfortable in the limelight, I simply imitated her. I recognized this even then.

There was the time we were rehearsing in the theater at Tanglewood for a recital the next day. Between groups, she strolled around to relax and loosen up, stopped slightly stage right, and said something to the effect that she was standing on this spot singing in *Peter Grimes* in her student days when she realized that she had no idea how to sing. At the time, I thought she was just being modest, but I've come to realize she meant it. We can go a long way trying to accomplish our goals, and sometimes we get there without the basic fundamentals we need. This realization can take place throughout a career: Busoni said that he completely reworked his piano technique five different times in his career.[1] Most of us would probably consider his first technique pretty good. Artists are willing to work on themselves ceaselessly.

Phyllis herself told the *Boston Globe*: "A conductor hears a Stradivarius voice, and he wants to use it. It may not matter whether the singer has any taste, whether he knows the difference between Mozart and Puccini…His youthful, natural talent will probably carry him along for a few years, but then he'll probably disappear. And that's tragic."[2]

Another time we were rehearsing Aaron Copland's *Twelve Poems of Emily Dickinson*. It was my first real exposure to Dickinson's texts, but Phyllis told me how difficult it was for her to remember the words in Copland's settings because she had recently studied a new edition of Dickinson's complete poems that were a kind of urtext. Copland had only nineteenth-century editions to work from, and those texts were not always what Emily wrote. At the time, I wondered why she would

1. Pedro de Alcantara, *Indirect Procedures* (Oxford: Oxford University Press, 2013), 95.

2. Jeremy Eichler, "Phyllis Curtin, Opera Soprano and Former BU Dean; at 94," *Boston Globe*, June 7, 2016, https://www.bostonglobe.com/metro/2016/06/07/phyllis-curtin-opera-soprano-and-former-college-fine-arts-dean-dies/Smy0fr48ivCy5kscPQ11mJ/story.html.

want to confuse herself with more information than necessary. Now I recognize her dedication to digging into the submerged meaning in whatever she sang, spending the time required to find the essential.

Phyllis suffered increasingly in her life from a painful rheumatoid arthritis. It was apparent in the years I worked with her and became worse as she grew older. Still she persevered and brought so much joy to everyone who knew her. Dawn Upshaw shared a Mary Oliver poem called "Messenger" at Phyllis's Tanglewood memorial. I thought these lines particularly captured her spirit for which I am forever grateful:

> *Are my boots old? Is my coat torn?*
> *Am I no longer young, and still not half-perfect? Let me*
> *   keep my mind on what matters,*
>
> *   which is my work,*
> *which is mostly standing still and learning to be*
> *   astonished.*

VI

■ Pedagogical Confessions

As I was getting started in my playing/teaching career, the field of piano pedagogy was coming into its own, establishing itself as an academic pursuit deserving its own pedigree. The concept was that if one is going to teach piano, one should know *how to teach*. Some of the precepts included a devotion to lesson plans, that slow practice with one hand at a time was very important, and that a thorough knowledge of method books could make a big difference. John Thompson's *Modern Course for the Piano* was out; various other methods came and went. College degrees in piano pedagogy were instituted. Supervised teaching, in which senior pedagogy faculty members observe the apprentice teachers as they teach their students, became required. The pedagogy faculty members themselves may or may not have had experience teaching actual college majors to play the piano; their experience was in pedagogy, not performing. Finally, many of the curricula lightened the performance expectations; instead of a full recital, a half recital might suffice. In short, the graduates were not judged by how well they could play the piano; what mattered was that they knew how to teach.

In my youthful idealism, I had a lot of trouble with this. As a beginner, I did not always practice with one hand at a time. I liked the John Thompson books. Mrs. Getz never had a pedagogy course, and I survived pretty well. As a student at Oberlin in the wild and crazy '60s and '70s, I even lobbied the piano chairman to make the required pedagogy class an elective in the senior year. Turbulent as those times were, he went along with it. So, my first confession: I never took a pedagogy class.

When I joined the Northwestern University faculty, only seven years after *not* taking that pedagogy course, I had a lot to learn. A pedagogy degree program was in full bloom there, overseen by Frances Larimer, a nationally recognized authority. The School of Music had given a lot of thought to the structure of the degree: it could only be pursued by graduate students, and the name of the degree was Master of Music in Performance *and* Pedagogy. In other words, there was no lightening of the performance expectations; in a sense, it was a double degree.

I moved on to the Peabody Conservatory in 1985 and joined a faculty proud of its strong performance reputation. You don't doubt you are around *real performers* when you bump into Leon Fleisher in the elevator. I can't even remember if there was a pedagogy course when I arrived. However, there was a very active community preparatory department with an enrollment of two thousand students. A piano faculty of nearly forty served these youngsters, and the dean of the prep division, Fran Zarubick, sought me out to teach a very promising new student from China. Fran had previously been an administrator at the Community School of Performing Arts in Los Angeles, soon to become the Colburn School. There she came to know Richard Chronister, an imaginative teacher who founded the National Conference on Piano Pedagogy in 1978.

Fran decided she would attend the conference in 1988 and encouraged me to submit a paper for inclusion on the program. I was still steaming about a "teaching demonstration" I'd seen at the 1987 Music Teachers National Association conference. For me, the pedagogy bandwagon was in danger of spinning out of control. So, I wrote a paper called "Some Thoughts on Teaching, Once Removed" that expressed my concerns.

That MTNA teaching demonstration was staged as a reenactment of a supervised teaching experience in a typical college pedagogy program. In my paper, I outlined my concerns:

> Let's begin at the beginning. When a new piece is assigned, a student must learn the notes. Part of the teacher's job, of course, is to make sure they have learned the right notes. This seems so obvious; I shouldn't have to mention it. Yet, at the MTNA convention last March, when three young pedagogy students did teaching demonstrations with critiques from professionals, one student let the wrong notes go by in a passage that was repeated several times. To make matters worse,

this oversight was not mentioned in the critique. Perhaps they were both too embarrassed. I found myself wondering, though, "Could it be that the pedagogy student didn't know the notes were wrong? Could it be that she felt other things were more important to communicate to the student? But what can be more basic than the right notes?"

At this same teaching demonstration, another student, working with a rather average student on a Bach Invention, followed a lesson plan that was full of good ideas but which did not address the young human being at the keyboard in any way other than as executant of the lesson plan. The poor boy played Bach as if it were written in Swahili, and never once did the young teacher attempt to make it more alive for him. In fact, to my mind, she sterilized it even further by suggesting practice patterns that served to focus attention away from the musical meaning of the piece. They were good suggestions; they just weren't relevant to this student, who needed a remedial lesson in enjoyment. If anything is more important than the right notes, it's a sense that they mean something to the player, whether he be ten years old playing a Bach Invention or seventy years old playing Beethoven's Op. 111. Nevertheless, our young teacher chose to follow her lesson plan, and in my opinion, neither music nor pedagogy was served that day.

To my horror, the paper was accepted, and what's worse, my reading was scheduled as the last event of a three-day conference. If I read what I submitted, I was almost sure to be on the hit list of every one of the 716 registered attendees.

I was all ears during the conference and luckily learned a lot. Much of the program focused on how teachers observe—how useful observations can be made to their students that enable them to make predictions, draw conclusions, and take action. Indeed, how do we make pure observations, since we tend to give meaning to everything we see through our personal lenses? All the conferences planned by Richard Chronister involved the participation of thinkers from outside piano pedagogy. At this meeting, we were treated to the knowledge of Keith Golay (psychologist, educational consultant, and author), Robert Duke (music education professor), and Frances Scott (philosophy professor). Golay spoke of learning temperament and the four primary personality types, each of which possesses a unique pattern of learning, thinking, wanting, acting, and feeling. These are seen in the Myers-Briggs psychological profiles, where the terminology for the four types is *sensory-judgmental, sensory-perceptive, intuitive-thinking*, and *intuitive-feeling*. He made these easy to remember by giving each type an animal name and characteristic: bears, apes, owls, and dolphins. This became the take-home motif of the conference. Suddenly, I realized pedagogy's value.

I still had to deliver that paper, though, so I did what any other enterprising student would do—I rewrote it in the hotel room. The speech that follows is the first publication of what I actually said that day. There is a colloquial quality to it—by this late hour, everyone at the conference had let down their guard and behaved like longtime friends. Remember, too, that I am a performer by nature—I had to give a speech that people would want to listen to and maybe even laugh at the good lines. Feeling that the speech was too loose for the published *Proceedings*, I rewrote it again for the official conference record. I much prefer the tone of the speech, so that's what I chose to include here. Even though it is much less confrontative than the original paper submitted, it still asserts the dangers of teaching, once removed.

The essays that follow the speech delve into my aha moments as I tried to reconcile the performing and teaching worlds. In order to live with myself, I had to find the connections between them, since my duties at Peabody expanded from teaching studio piano to include chairing the Preparatory Piano Department and, yes, teaching the Conservatory Piano Pedagogy course. Blame it on that speech! As the reader might expect, my class was not a by-the-book unfolding of subject matter that might be approved by the National Conference on Keyboard Pedagogy. Like much else in my career, I did a lot of outside reading and followed Rilke's advice quoted in the previous chapter. I analyzed the "world I carried inside" and placed it at the center of the class experience.

30

Speech Given at the
National Conference on Piano Pedagogy
Drury Lane Theater, Lombard, Illinois
OCTOBER 22, 1988

This is my first attendance at a National Conference on Piano Pedagogy, and it has been fascinating to watch the conference progress. I think you will agree that Richard Chronister and Jim Lyke are master orchestrators. My problem giving a paper at this point in the conference is that I feel like the young student who is playing the last piece on the recital—it had better be good following all those others! The thing is: I've only been taking lessons for a few days! With only one hour to go of this National Conference on Piano Pedagogy, I find myself in what might be thought of as the enviable position of summarizer, and I hope to say what many of you might want to say if you were in my shoes. At the same time, I am in the decidedly unenviable position of having rewritten my paper twice since the sessions ended yesterday, partly because Richard suggested that I may want to incorporate my sense of the conference, and partly because everyone seems to be stealing what I have to say.

Six months ago, when I started this paper, I was attempting to reconcile two parts of myself: the performer and the teacher. I would like to begin by sharing that process of mutual self-understanding, if there is such a thing, and hope that you will recognize a familiar dichotomy.

I know that I am a performer, and that implies two modes of operation. Since there has been a lot of talk about the faculty of Drury Lane University being performers, I'm going to talk about what *we* do as performers. We have to learn 100 percent of the right notes and then play a ferociously high percentage of those notes in public when the time comes. We must not only follow the composer's indications but also that "ritard" doesn't always mean the same thing to Schumann as it does to Chopin. We must listen like crazy to every sound we make, evaluate it, decide what we like and don't like, proceeding by trial and error at great expense to our family's hearing and patience as they try to live with us. We have to discover interpretive possibilities, accept interpretive limitations, and somehow avoid schizophrenia. And thanks to Clara Schumann and Liszt, we have to memorize the whole damned thing!

So much for preparation. At the performance, we are of course highly spontaneous, imaginative, risking all. We walk on stage, daring an eye to ignore us, romantic heroes and heroines conquering all. We aim for peak experiences, even if we haven't read Abraham Maslow—the unforgettable, the ineffable magic of a moment that changes everything for the listener.

Those of you who have adopted the "menagerie school of personality traits" will immediately see that the performer in preparation is a bear (storing up knowledge, skills, and drills, trying to do the right thing) but that the performer onstage is exhibiting strong apelike tendencies (creative, immediate, in the moment, doing it *my* way). Did someone mention schizophrenia?

Which brings us back to the beginning—I know that I am also a teacher, as are all of you. Like Nelita True, I teach mostly advanced pianists. In teaching, and again let's use the first-person plural, we try to deal with all the things we do as performers in preparation: right notes, composer's indications, etc. But it goes a little further. We also must give the students ways to practice all the above—taking care that they have a technical approach that works, and an ear that hears with a sensitivity and even a yearning for the beautiful, and an ever-growing awareness of that next-to-impossible-to-define word: *musicality*.

Speaking for myself, I enjoy doing this with all my students, whatever the level or background, but so far none of them has ever had the good manners to approach the music just like I do—there is always a gap to bridge. To jump that gap, we must care about them as people, get inside their heads, sometimes be a friend, sometimes be a mentor, always be an example.

Again, two beasties rear their heads, and if I've been paying attention correctly, they are the owl (objective reasoner, systematic, conceptual) and the dolphin (good communicator, relationship oriented, people person).

Although the book says that only one personality type is imprinted on my genes, I am fairly certain that every day of my life as a performer and teacher, I am dealing with the whole blasted barnyard! And so are you.

The personal side of this ends with the admission that while I may have a few quirks about me, I am not schizophrenic. The reason is that these four apparently disparate temperaments all come together when they address something much larger than any of us—the music.

Music is an end in itself—we can enjoy it without knowing anything about it. Somehow or other, music goes right to some nonverbal part of the brain and elicits feelings and states of being that we really can't control. But if we are going to make music, we have to know a lot about it, and getting to that point is, as we all know, a rather involved road. It is a process—the process of learning notes, the process of making interpretive decisions, the process of finding a sound that gives us goosebumps, the process of falling in love with music. It may be possible to be a good performer and not be aware of these processes (intuitive apes!). But I am certain that a good teacher *must* be in touch with them.

The only way to be in touch with the processes is by doing. You can't learn to play a scale by reading about it—you learn by doing. This has been said. You can't learn to teach a scale by reading about it—you have to do it. This too has been said. Linking the two is an *awareness of the process*, and I don't think that has been said. The only way I know of coming to that awareness is by experiencing it as you yourself make music.

Beyond the awareness is something even more important—the strength of the music's image in the mind and heart of the performer. I'm sure you have all read critics' reviews that say, in essence, "Performer X played with mechanical perfection but had absolutely nothing to say." It could be that this performer was *too* interested in the process, had in fact gotten stuck in the "doing." It could also be that the initial musical idea was not strong enough or wasn't there at all. Fran Scott spoke of going from analysis to synthesis. I would suggest thinking of going from the initial musical idea—through the process—back to the musical idea, which now becomes a statement.

It's quite possible to write that review of teachers too: "Teacher Y taught with great skill but was so obsessed with the style that the substance was lost."

I've listened to a lot of ideas about the myriad things that need to go into a pedagogy course. I get nervous when a pedagogy curriculum focuses on teaching as an end in itself, losing sight of the basics of music making. My dictionary defines pedagogy first as the *art* of teaching, and only secondly as the science or profession of teaching. Art involves intuition. Science involves experimentation, and unless we know the chemistry of making music, we will have nothing of lasting importance to pass on to our students. Teaching cannot be taught once removed.

Teachers need to start with just as strong a musical image as performers, and additionally they need an awareness of what they are doing to communicate the image. At that point, the skills of teaching can take over, and of course they should be taught, but first the musical idea and the awareness of the process has to be there. My hope is that pedagogy classes will devote more time to these issues. Performance teachers need to do so as well—no one can be *too* musical! But rules of teaching divorced from one's own actual musical experience will not make good teachers. Supervised teaching internships will only improve a student's teaching if the pedagogy teacher and the student have the common bond of knowing firsthand what it is to make music. I think we will advance the effectiveness of piano pedagogy courses when the focus becomes an understanding of what is going on in one's own musical development, rather than memorizing a list of qualities that supposedly make a good teacher. It is not unlike the training of psychiatrists: before they are licensed, they undergo their own analysis!

For that kind of understanding to be achieved, performance teachers and pedagogy teachers must work closely together. This, too, has been said before. Maybe we should change our titles. How about *music* teacher specializing in pedagogy? *Music* teacher specializing in performance? It has been suggested that performance teachers should observe and work with teaching interns. I would love to! If I may suggest a reciprocal arrangement, I would also like to see all our star pedagogy students go home and sit down with their pedagogy teachers and work on something like the Schubert F Minor Fantasy for four hands!

No one has all the answers. We need to share ideas, brainstorm, and argue. I have gained a tremendous amount by being here: in my heart of hearts, I have stood and cheered for a couple of presentations. A couple of other times, I was ready to commit murder! I have learned from both extremes. I hope you have too.

Thank you.

31

Performance Power

The View from the Second Floor

OCTOBER 1986

In recent years, a spate of books has explored the psychological side of complex, often competitive activities. The *Inner Game* series by W. Timothy Gallwey is perhaps the most famous, and no one, certainly not I, would deny that such books can be helpful in changing physical habits as well as denting the mental tortures we tend to erect for ourselves. The one drawback is that these books are simplistic; they are mass market remedies for fixing everything from your golf game to your Wall Street acumen. Applying these correctives to the art of music making can sometimes illuminate a problem, but the solutions offered are ultimately limited.

Last spring, I came across a book that you won't find in the self-help section of the local bookstore, but it may well contain more useful advice than all the *Inner Game* theories combined. *Performing Power*, by H. Wesley Balk (University of Minnesota Press, 1985, 375 pages, paperback), is subtitled *A New Approach for the Singer-Actor*. Although written primarily for our friends in the theater, its main points offer many parallels to our work as pianists giving public performances. I recommend wholeheartedly this perceptive, lucid, and exhaustive treatment of the craft of performance.

Chapter one alone is worth the price of the book. Writing from the perspective of a musical theater director, Balk knows the performer's problems firsthand. These problems involve knowing too much, he says. We know we are tense, but the very act of trying not to be tense increases the tension. We know too much about what we want to become (actors, directors, critics, composers, et al.), yet well-meaning loved ones are happy to tell us just what we should "do with our lives." We analyze our art in such a judgmental way (this is good, this is not good) that we end up without any knowledge of what we are actually doing.

"Judgments," Balk writes, "are generalizations—another name for bad descriptions—and generalizations are the enemy of good performance." In something as complex as art (and life, for that matter), judgments rob our work of the power inherent in that complexity.

What can the artist do? Embrace the complexity, says Balk, but find ways to work with it that are communicative and descriptive without being judgmental. Much of the book is devoted to exactly that.

To do so, Balk explores what he calls "the modes of perception." We perceive the whole of existence through our five senses, and three of them, Balk says, are involved in the theatrical experience: sight, hearing, and touch, the last of which Balk expands into our perception of physical movement. These three modes become the facial/emotional (eyes), hearing/vocal (ears), and the kinesthetic (the body's motion). All of us tend to be attuned to one of these modes more than the others, whether we know it or not. Viewed in this way, it comes as no surprise to realize that audiences for concerts, theater, and dance are usually very different crowds; each audience tends to be dominated by a different perceptual mode. A concert audience will favor the ear, a theater audience the eyes, and a dance audience the kinesthetic.

Similarly, we learn basic skills with the help of one mode more than (but not excluding) the others. For example, in learning to spell, some of us may remember the sound of the letters (hearing/vocal dominant), others what the word looks like (sight), or what it feels like to write the word (kinesthetic).

The plot thickens when we realize that some musicians may not favor the hearing/vocal mode and yet must work with it to produce their art. How many students have you had who couldn't sit still through a lesson? They were probably kinesthetic dominants. Similarly, think of the students in whom the music seemed to play in the expression on their faces but had little meaning in the sound itself.

In reality, all three modes are important in the artistic message of performance, and Balk insightfully explores each of them. The actor, and to some extent the performing musician, must come to terms with all three modes, which are not only perceived but projected to the audience. When open to perceiving visually and kinesthetically as well as aurally, a concert audience will come away from a performance with more to remember and think about than if only one mode is addressed. You need think only as far as your enjoyment of *Masterpiece Theatre* on PBS for an excellent example. British actors come from a society that is largely hearing/vocal dominant, and one immediately hears the musicality of the language as spoken by these actors. The facial/emotional mode is exploited with subtlety and care (never approaching the mugging seen in American sitcoms), and the kinesthetic sense is likewise trained to carry whatever message fits the requirements of the part (remember Derek Jacobi in *I, Claudius*?). The implications for musicians are staggering, challenging, and in my opinion liberating. I am not suggesting we should act out the music, but it is important that we consider what messages our face and body project as we labor so diligently over the sound.

The plot thickens further as Balk explores mode interference, an extremely useful concept to teachers. Essentially, he says that any of the modes can interfere with another mode's ability to project the message intended. Physical tension at the piano may be a result of kinesthetic interference with the hearing/vocal mode's job. Balk gives several exercises that could be adapted for use by musicians that separate the modes for a clearer understanding of how they work. And finally comes the concept of mode combinations, which considers the ways the modes can be used together to reinforce the artistic message.

The writing is always exhilarating in its attention to detail; it embraces complexity without exhausting the reader. Interspersed throughout are wonderfully entertaining anecdotes, leaving one with the sense that Balk would be a delightful man to know. I am certain he is an incredible teacher. This reader (and student) will ponder Balk's pages for a long time to come.

32

Real Creation

The View from the Second Floor
FEBRUARY 1992

There are days when I want to rail against tradition. Why are performing musicians of the late twentieth century so concerned with doing everything right?

Few professions are as obsessed with the ways of past masters. We deify the "great performances," bowing and scraping before Schnabel's Schubert or Perahia's Mozart, erecting a short list of the musically correct. We spend years immersing ourselves in stylistic awareness, hoping to be faithful to an imagined ideal of the musical conventions of two hundred years ago. We strive for perfection but find the present inhospitable to our rarefied art. So, we retreat to the past, where we think such ignoble urges as spontaneity and risk-taking don't exist. Safe in the sanctified haven we create for ourselves and a few other initiates, we assure ourselves that our way is right!

I exaggerate for effect. Don't misunderstand; I like Perahia's Mozart as much as the next guy. I also like Curzon's and Gieseking's, Uchida's and Serkin's (both R. and P.), Lupu's and Bilson's. One is no more right than the other, even if Bilson might think he is. I also like the way a student of mine named Annie Chang played the F major sonata K. 332 last year. She was worried about doing it right, but it didn't stop her from making the piece her own, especially when she performed it. She played it one night in a master class for Leon Fleisher, who brought his considerable sense of tradition to bear on her performance. Annie's relationship to the piece changed a great deal in a short time; still, the performance worked as an artistic expression in the here and now. She didn't merely follow Fleisher's directions—she substantiated them.

All too often a student receives a competition criticism like "Inappropriate style" and wonders what they missed. They know they've heard about such things as beginning the trill on the auxiliary for years. Sadly, it's easier for judges, critics, and even teachers to wave the banner of Classicism or some other vague conceit than to deal with the whys and hows of real music making. I once heard a teacher say to a student, "It doesn't sound like Serkin." Thank you, Herr Professor, that's because it sounds like me, but clearly that's not good enough. It must not be right.

No wonder professional pianists quake and tremble when approaching the instrument. We have the accumulated wisdom of the ages bearing down on our shoulders: every article written about performance practice, every piece of the teacher's well-meaning advice, every recording ever made to which we compare ourselves. We can sense the Olympians aloofly listening over our now sagging shoulders. Perhaps we are the victims of our own success: the scholarship and exactitude we have achieved enchains us, leaving us with the pallor of the monk or the prisoner.

We've brought it on ourselves. It's not the tradition that confines us—it's our worship of it. Last summer I gave my first performance of the Brahms Second Concerto. I shook in my boots from the time I signed the contract. Ah, Weirich, it's the Everest of concertos; how fortunate you are to get to do it. In between bouts of euphoria, stories of disasters inflicted by this piece on several more-experienced pianists than I danced through my head. I listened to all the greatest recordings. I read a biography of Brahms; played through lieder, chamber music, solo pieces; practiced the concerto many hours a day. All that's fine, except I did very little to convince myself that I just might be worthy of playing it. Instead, I worried about whether it would be good enough, whether it would be right. The resultant performance hovered for me between miserable and barely acceptable but put things in immediate perspective. It's not whether it's right—it's whether it lives.

Another experience from last summer brought this home even more. I was scheduled to play contemporary composer George Rochberg's Violin Sonata with my friend Andrés Cárdenes in a chamber music festival. Rochberg was to attend rehearsals and the performance, so again I did everything I could to be a good, correct recreator. I analyzed the score, adhered to all the metronome markings, and listened to the composer-sanctioned recording. Before playing it for the composer,

Andrés and I made sure everything was in place and all markings strictly observed. It didn't take long with Mr. Rochberg, though, to realize he wasn't interested in how well we followed his notes. "Why are you playing that phrase so straight?" he'd ask of a boringly accurate presentation of his notation.

At one spot in the second movement, marked *fortissimo* with heavy accents, he asked me for more sound. Three attempts later, I gave it a good belt, and even after his congratulatory "That's more like it," I had to ask, "It isn't too harsh, is it?"

He shot back, "Noooo! It's a cry, a piercing cry from deep within! It's supposed to be harsh!"

In the third movement, he stopped us to say it was too slow. With each injunction toward movement, we felt increasing pangs of guilt as we moved further and further from the printed metronome marking. Finally, he said, "Look, don't worry about the page. This music is fevered, passionate, ardent. It's not on the page, it's out here where it can be felt."

I finally got the point. Music is too elemental to be confined to rules or notation. We are too well schooled. When Andrés and I performed the sonata, we both allowed ourselves to play louder and softer than usual. We played both faster and slower; we didn't worry about balance. It was a performance that had nothing to do with tradition, yet it was the composer who pulled it out of us. Here was a real creator, daring us to share in the creation, not just re-create according to the book.

If George Rochberg welcomed such participation, could Brahms and the rest be so different?

33

Watching Miss R.'s Class

The View from the Second Floor

APRIL 1992

Once upon a time, music excited us.

On a recent Friday afternoon, I visited a Piano Focus class at Peabody's preparatory division. Two girls and two boys, first and second graders all, spent a grand and noisy hour with their teacher Miss R. I sat in the back and tried to act like the furniture so as not to bother them. I needn't have worried.

Earlier the same Friday, I spent several hours listening to graduate auditions at the conservatory. There is a theory of learning called associationism that suggests mental elements are connected by relating contiguous experiences, or in plain English, we are more likely to learn something when whatever we experience happens on the same day. Here's what I learned…

At 4:00 p.m. sharp, the kids in Miss R.'s class burst into the room, wearing smiles and trailing music books and school packs. They exchange warm hellos, and Natalie breathlessly announces that today their new piano arrived. A high-pitched discussion of the pianos in their various living rooms follows, Zachary beaming with pride in his family's grand. When Miss R. asks who will be the first to play a piece, four hands shoot toward the ceiling. Natalie tells the class that she has called her piece "Scare," and I realize with a start that these are pieces they wrote themselves. Natalie's piece had a right-hand line with an F-sharp in it that clashed quite nicely with the left hand's F-natural. Everyone applauds when Natalie finishes, and Brandon mentions how much he liked the way the fifths and sixths worked in the bass. "Oh my," I think. Each piece gets its premiere performance, with Marie bringing up the rear with "Wild." It was that and more, ending with a big glissando from bottom to top that really brought down the house.

For the next hour, the kids worked for Miss R. with an excitement bordering on frenzy. They played their book pieces; they clapped rhythms from the board. They had a running duel going with Miss R. who offered them points if they could complete a task without mistakes, but should they mess up, *she'd* get the points. I never did find out the significance of the points, but the kids really went after them. Final score: Kids 14, Miss R. 1.

Toward the end of the lesson, they worked on constructing scales. First, they recited the whole-step–half-step sequence of the major scale, which they seemed to know as well as their ABCs. Then Miss R. showed them how they could make several different scales. They arranged eight pennies on a drawing of a keyboard, counting off "whole-whole-half," delighting in the measured exactness of it all. When they each had it right, they'd go to the piano and play the scale. Then they'd come back to their desks and put the pennies on a staff and place the cutout sharps and flats next to the correct notes. They got so stimulated by this activity that they would race to the piano as soon as their pennies were in place and then race back to their desks to complete the next step, happily colliding in the space between desks and pianos with each other or Miss R. They figured out scales in G, D, E ("Oh my gosh, *four* sharps!"), and E-flat ("Whoa, *flats!*") in ten minutes.

I was utterly charmed. Every now and then, one of them would look over a shoulder to see what the stranger in back thought of all this. Usually, they caught me with an idiot grin on my face, awestruck by their eager energy.

The rest of the day at the conservatory was another story. We had set aside the time to hear our own students audition for advanced degrees. We knew them, and they knew us—maybe someone should have reminded both sides. The students, pale and self-conscious, came nervously into the studio where teachers sat with clipboards and file folders, pens poised in judgment. The half-smiling hellos fooled no one. They played; we listened. They left the room; we discussed standards. It wasn't fun for anybody, and perhaps it simply can't be, even under the best of circumstances, but it makes me wonder. Isn't there a way to structure a musical education so that both faculty and students would celebrate something like a graduate audition as an honored moment in a student's life?

What happens between the ages of six and twenty-two that turns music making into agony? Even by the age of fourteen or fifteen, there is usually a lot of anxiety attached. Left to their own devices, I don't think the kids would take the play out of piano playing. Somehow, unintentionally, we teachers do it for them. Maybe we stop giving points too soon. Maybe the kids don't see the fun in our student recitals, where they must put on uncomfortable clothes and play one stupid piece just so (and by *memory!*) that they've worked on for months for a bunch of relatives and other adults who are also dressed up in uncomfortable clothes and sitting in uncomfortable chairs in a room where no one is supposed to talk. Yes, and look over there at how nervous the teacher is acting...

My Friday of epiphanies ended at home where I found my two-month-old son blissfully asleep. I want him to know music's joy, but I hereby vow that I will not put him through what I have been through, nor will I allow him to endure what most of today's students endure, sometimes at my own hand. There must be a better way.

34

The Spiral Curriculum

The View from the Second Floor

MAY–JUNE 1992

I'm looking for a unified theory of piano teaching, something that will explain it all. If physicists can search for one grand formula that symbolically represents the workings of the universe, surely we can find the key to a teaching approach that successfully guides, inspires, and empowers our students through each step of their musical journey. While Miss R.'s approach with Natalie and her six-year-old cohorts may be different from how I deal with an artist diploma student, the key should be the same. We share the same goals: unlocking the joys of music for our students, tapping their creativity, and giving them the tools for artistic expression.

No one will argue with the goals, but somewhere along the line, something usually goes awry. To find the key, we first should question several assumptions:

- Why do we reserve the honorific "master teacher" for those who work only with the most gifted and advanced? The Miss R.s of the world are at least as masterful as the big names.

- Why do we accept the weekly lesson as the norm at every level of study? Most university piano majors spend more time per week with their music theory professors than in their piano teachers' studios.

- For that matter, why do we accept a compartmentalized curriculum as either natural or efficient? In my experience, students seldom take what they learn in theory class about a German sixth chord and apply it to what they do in their piano lessons.

- Why do we turn piano playing into a test? We seem unable to think of any other goal for our students than entering them in a contest or putting them in a recital.

- Why do we insist that solo performance determines a student's advancement in music study? Surely we lose a lot of music lovers when the only choice we offer them is jumping through the hoops of performing in front of people.

The six-year-olds I wrote about last month learned theory and technique, played pieces in progress, started learning new pieces, and composed as a natural part of music study, all in the space of an hour. The key I am looking for would keep things just as integrated as they continue their study, even as the approach or method changes. The unfortunate likelihood is that, at some point, they will have a teacher who neglects the creativity inherent in composition and concentrates on polishing a few pieces to win a competition. Technique study will become separated from the music, and the students will start to practice scales as ends in themselves—fingers flying, bodies tightening, ears a million miles away. They will get into the rut of learning a piece, memorizing it, performing it, then starting the cycle again, with nothing to look forward to but the lessons in which they are told what they didn't learn correctly. We wonder why students can't sight-read when all we do is require them to memorize. We wonder why they have trouble memorizing when we let someone else train their ears. We wonder why they are so unimaginative when we never show them how to improvise.

I think it is no exaggeration to say that the future of the piano teaching profession depends on our finding this key. In *The Process of Education*, Jerome Bruner writes of the "spiral curriculum," his concept that the study of any subject involves revisiting the basic ideas repeatedly as one achieves greater mastery. Miss R.'s students are learning about theory, technique, and creativity in terms they can handle. Three years from now, the subject will not have changed, but the sophistication with which they address the piano and music will have increased. To keep our teaching focused and integrated to the students' growing awareness, we should keep our sights fixed on the long-term goals at each curve of the spiral, remaining flexible in our approaches and wary of assumptions.

Teaching at the conservatory level, I see a cross section of perhaps less than 1 percent of the students who begin lessons, and they are supposedly the success stories. For the majority, the words *joy* and *music* would not occupy the same thought. Their creativity is limited to playing the printed notes in a studied, stylistically approved manner. Very few have ever composed. If I ask them to improvise, they look at me as if I had asked them to speak Swahili. Their innate talent has gotten them this far; they have somehow survived our weekly ministrations and are now desirous, miraculously enough, of joining our profession. They are no longer children, and, God forbid, they want to be like us.

To whatever extent possible, I think we should declare war on the status quo. With my own students, I've already abolished the private weekly lesson: everyone still has an assigned time, but the door is open, and anyone who is free comes to observe and participate. We simply need more time together than the schedule allows. We're improvising, hoping to tap the spontaneity that will bring music to life. No one will enter a competition until they can view it as just another artistic outlet. There's more to do, but it's a start.

The profession's biggest battle is with the ignorance brought on by our isolation. We have accepted for too long that a conservatory teacher is different from a teacher of beginners, who in turn is different from someone teaching intermediate students. Beyond agreeing on goals, we ought to know a lot more about what goes on at each level. It's time for all of us to learn the spiral curriculum. It's the only way we will find the key.

VII

■ The Question of Sustainability

The essays ending the previous section suggest all is not well in the world of advanced piano performance. When I compared the youthful energy and excitement of Peabody Prep's beginners to the sour faces of the conservatory's applicants, I can't help but wonder what happened. Even this book's path has slipped toward discouragement. I related memories of my early lessons through rose-colored lenses, and while joining the ranks of performers may not have been easy, there was a general optimism about it. The teaching positions that followed seemed inevitable. Is this possible today? I don't know.

From my earliest writings, I have questioned some of the accepted aspects of the profession. A particular sore point is how isolated classical music is from the rest of American culture. Musicians surround themselves with others as immersed in the art as they are, so it becomes easy to ignore the insularity of the vocation. I have always believed that serious music was something everyone could—in fact, should— love, and I tried to proselytize in my humble way. Among the first to require conversion were my parents. While they were always supportive of their son, I never felt they truly understood my love for music. They appreciated the prizes and outer recognition, but I was "different" (i.e., not one of them). They are gone now, and I am haunted by the missed opportunity to connect on this level.

The essays that follow continue to question the status quo. Even though they span almost forty years, the attentive reader will notice recurring themes. Some of these essays also represent my attempt at rationalizing advanced piano study as a worthwhile end in itself, not as a means to a music career. In playing a senior recital, larger lessons are learned than the pieces on the program. Those lessons only become obvious if teachers adjust their attitudes and expectations. It should not be about upholding the highest, perfectionistic playing standard, adjudicated by an inner circle of "master teachers." As stated earlier, it should be about unlocking the joy of music, tapping students' creativity, and giving them the tools of artistic expression.

Finding joy in music can be a lifelong reward, always at the beck and call of the inner ear. True creativity expands into so many areas of life. If you can write a short original melody, chances are you can write a limerick for fun, or a poem to your sweetheart, or a letter to the editor. Among other things, the tools of artistic expression release a student's individuality. Their uniqueness can be heard in the tone they produce, in their projection of rhythm (infinitesimal spacing differences between notes), in the honesty they imbue in the melodies and the dimensionality they bring to the harmony. If lessons have such focus, goals other than preparing recitals or competitions become possible. What can be more satisfying than an inner communion with music—just you and the piano?

Music can also be shared with others in ways that avoid "performance," when one player is under pressure to deliver and others are required to listen and applaud. Why not join an ensemble? Choral singing has become more popular lately,[1] and amateur chamber music organizations exist in many metropolitan areas.[2] Groups of music lovers are likely to connect simply because they have this common sensibility. It wasn't that long ago that compulsory music class in the public-school system created many more potential members of the extended family of music.

In the NCPP speech, I urged teachers of pedagogy and performance to work closely together. Share ideas, brainstorm, argue! In the essay about the young Peabody Prep students, I urged more communication between teachers of beginning, intermediate, and advanced students. Somehow, we end up in strata; where there are territorial concerns, there is protectionism.

Ultimately, the big question is: Why are so few children taking music lessons in the United States? Before lessons begin, parents must

---

1. Grunwald Associates LLC and Chorus America, *The Chorus Impact Study: Singing for a Lifetime* (Washington, DC: Chorus America, 2019), https://www.arts.gov/sites/default/files/Research-Art-Works-ChorusAmerica.pdf.

2. Stephanie Griffin, "Playing for Pleasure," Associated Chamber Music Players (website), https://acmp.net/about-us.

overcome significant impediments. Lessons require the investment of time. Parents already overschedule their children if one is to believe the *New York Times*.[3] There is also the investment of money. While some parents will spend $1,000 a month for sports equipment and training, similar expenditures for music are rare. Is there a piano in the house? Is that piano in good shape? I personally do not think an electronic keyboard is a good substitute. In the long run, it's the organic materials like wood, felt, and ivory that make a deep connection as well as the natural, unsynthesized sound. The heyday of piano lessons was the nineteenth century—the instrument then was at the forefront of human technology. Today its place is usurped by the iPhone, by Facebook and Instagram, by YouTube and TikTok. All these things become competition for the time one might spend with the piano. Perhaps the most daunting factor of all is that the parents themselves have probably not taken music lessons. It has been decades since public-school music has contributed to the intellectual and spiritual mores of at least a generation of Americans. Parents don't know that their children are lacking something, since they themselves never had musical experiences. The whole family simply doesn't know what it is missing. It's an uphill battle. Is it surmountable?

Only if music study somehow becomes irresistible again. That word *irresistible* may seem an odd adjective, but what came initially to mind was *cool*, and in looking up that word in the thesaurus, one finds only other out-of-date words (*great, swell, dandy, groovy, out of sight*). This suggests how difficult it will be to make music study a necessary part of life.

Otherwise, it becomes a niche hobby, which it already is. How sustainable can this be?

3. Bruce Feiler, "Overscheduled Children: How Big a Problem?" *New York Times*, October 11, 2013; Dani Blum, "The Outrageous Costs of Overscheduling Your Child," *New York Times*, February 17, 2020; Shalini Shankar, "A Packed Schedule Doesn't Really 'Enrich' Your Child," *New York Times*, July 9, 2021.

35

A Call to Action

The View from the Second Floor

MARCH 1986

During the Christmas holidays, I received a card from a friend who had come upon some of my earlier columns, read them with enjoyment, but found them "a little sticky: too much love, love, love." This month changes that tune: there are several facts contained herein that suggest pianists are living in perilous times.

Pick up any paper in any metropolitan area and you will find at least one article on the decaying infrastructure. Roads are wearing out, bridges are dangerously unsound, and mass transit is grinding expensively to a standstill. The same is happening to the infrastructure of the "music business." Witness the state of our art:

■ The domestic piano industry in recent years has experienced greater financial difficulty than at any time since the Great Depression. Sales have not kept pace with rising costs, and foreign competition has caused both Steinway and Baldwin[1] the same sea of troubles that General Motors and Ford know so well. The government loaned substantial sums to Chrysler in its time of need, but last year Aeolian had to close its doors, despite vital management and a fine product. In the 1920s, there were over one thousand piano builders in the United States; today there are fewer than ten.[2]

---

1. Once one of the most recognizable brands in the US, Baldwin became part of the Gibson Guitar Company (now Gibson Brands) in 2001. It now manufactures pianos in China at the Baldwin Zhongshan factory.

2. According to https://www.pianobuyer.com, in 2022 there are three.

■ A piano technician friend recently told me that he was flown halfway across the country to work on a piano because there were no technicians in the area who had the skills necessary for maintaining the instrument at the owner's standard. It is sad that technicians are caught in the middle: fewer people are buying pianos, and even fewer take care of the ones they have. Therefore, no one wants to enter the field, resulting in the dearth of qualified technicians we now face.

■ Go into almost any of the major schools of music in the country and you will find a collection of instruments that are worn beyond the point of common decency. They should have been put out of their misery long ago. I speak not only of practice instruments: studio and concert pianos as well are literally on their last legs. Most administrators shrug their shoulders and say it's too big a problem to do anything about. What they mean is it would be too expensive.

■ Because, you see, college enrollments are dropping. In part this is a result of demographics: there are simply fewer college-age students out there. The curve will start up again in 1995, but that's a long dry decade ahead. In the meantime, there is the effect of our present socioeconomic ethos in the country. These days the MBA is king. Students pursue a career that promises "*m*any *b*ig *a*chievements," coupled with a bottom line that reads "*m*ore *b*ucks *a*head." We have all been barraged with back-to-the-basics reports implying that Susie and Johnny should learn to read before they learn to play the piano. Given this attitude and the fact that many public schools face declining tax bases, administrators curtail such supposed luxury programs as music.

■ It should come as no surprise, then, that the number of solo piano recitals by touring artists has dwindled. Promoters prefer dance companies and balalaika orchestras to solo pianists. It would seem that the public no longer fancies the gladiators of the keyboard. Explanations abound: one camp claims that today's soloists are nothing but robots, while another cites a public, raised on color television, who craves the visual stimulation of exoticism and constant movement. Either way, the result is the same: pianists are passé.

My alarm is neither fear of change nor crying for the good old days. I am looking at a profession whose edges are frayed, yet mending them would not be enough. In our case, patchwork remedies would be the equivalent of pinning wings to a caterpillar. What we need is a complete metamorphosis. How do we encourage the emergence of a butterfly?

The examples cited are trends, which are difficult to stop once they gain momentum. Ironically, many of the woes discussed are inherent in our free enterprise system. It does cost less to build a piano in Asia than in the United States. More people prefer to buy the less expensive piano, regardless of the quality. The frayed edge is that if American piano companies suffer, indirectly we pianists suffer too. Perhaps the answer to some of these dilemmas lies in recognizing the difference between expense and value.

As a nation of consumers, we all know about comparison shopping. It is relatively simple to find the lowest price. It is not as simple to find what we value, for that takes rigorous qualitative thinking. You have the right to find the least expensive piano. But will it give you the sound and touch necessary for a rewarding kind of music making? Schools can claim insufficient budgets and let their instruments disintegrate. But will their students ever learn what can be done at a good piano? How can a school with poor instruments ever hope to attract serious students? Even more sobering, how can it claim to educate such a student?

If we find it difficult to hold to our values as musicians, is it any wonder that the public at large has little regard for us? Of course it is necessary for our children to learn to read. It is also necessary that they learn to make a life, not just a living. I am fearful that our economically inclined young, loaded with basic skills, will never learn to imagine, question, ponder, argue, innovate, or dream. There was once pride in creativity. Artists were creators; what they said mattered. They placed the highest premium on quality, and the public respected them for it. Today artists are often commodities, bought and sold in the marketplace. It doesn't have to be that way: we need to live for our values and hold them up for all to see. We need to integrate our profession: one sector's problems are everyone's problems. We need to take action now.

36

If 8,118 Pianists Graduate Each Year

Out of the Woods

MARCH 1994

Several years ago, I began an article by making an educated guess about how many people studied piano in American schools of higher learning. The figures were astonishing and still are—I'd like to update that arithmetic with you.

The most recent *Directory of Music Faculties* published by the College Music Society lists 4,059 teachers of piano, give or take a few, in schools across the country. A full-time professor of piano at a conservatory or university school of music is likely to teach twelve to twenty students, ranging from freshmen to doctoral students. Other full-time faculty in college music departments may teach piano in addition to music theory or history and thus have as few as two private students or as many as ten or twelve, usually undergraduates. Some have part-time appointments, but they may have as many students as a full-time professor.

If we assign an average of eight students to each of the 4,059 teachers, we arrive at an estimate of 32,472 piano students enrolled each year in the American university system. If eight students on average seems too high or too low, please substitute some other figure to reach a total. Whatever the case, the number is not without heft.

If a quarter of these students graduate annually, we find 8,118 pianists stumbling into the "real world," which as we all know is a euphemism for "severely limited job market." Most of the graduating DMAs seek a place among the select 4,059, but according to a recent article in *Clavier*, there are only about twenty-five to thirty piano faculty openings in a given year. Many undergraduates enroll in graduate programs in music, since according to accepted wisdom, the devalued bachelor's degree won't get them very far.

Nevertheless, I do not want to spread gloom or stir the pot of depression. There is an extremely simple way out of all this, requiring only two steps. First, reject accepted wisdom. Second, take another look at the real world.

The accepted wisdom of a bachelor's degree in music (BM) is that it's not enough, but look at what it does represent. The recipient of a BM has several eminently marketable skills: concentration, discipline, the ability to follow closely an abstract schematic of something entirely conceptual (i.e., a score), more than a little physical coordination, the ability to work with a team (ensemble playing) and motivate oneself, and the ability to put the components of a task in sequence and carry them out (i.e., practice). This is just a start. Add to these the fact that a musician can learn new skills quickly and handle pressure, not to mention criticism. A musician's problem-solving ability alone should have employers standing in line waving offers in the faces of BM holders everywhere.

Musicians are, in fact, as employable as anyone else graduating from college today, as long as they do not search for work in their own field. This is where taking another look at the real world comes in.

In the accepted wisdom, there are only a limited number of openings in the real world for a pianist to make a living in music. We are told that a "concert career" is next to impossible and that competition for the few teaching positions is just as fierce. Given the numbers at the beginning of this column, most dedicated gamblers would prefer the lottery, where the odds are better.

Look, though, at the bigger picture. The real world needs us. In the public schools of the real American world, an average of fifteen cents is spent per student per year on arts education. That's all the arts, not just music. Remember when phone calls cost a dime? Tens of millions of students across the country are getting less than two phone calls a year concerning some of humankind's highest endeavors. In California, about 75 percent of the public schools have no music programs at all. These figures are not my approximations; they come from an American Council on the Arts study.

In the real world, in the town of Pittsburgh, there's a man named William Strickland who built a school (the Manchester Craftsmen's Guild) dedicated to giving poor, disadvantaged kids a chance to make art. He is a gifted and determined fundraiser, and for ninety-five dollars a square foot, he built a state-of-the-art facility that included a pottery studio and kiln, photographic equipment, and a concert hall. He points out that ninety-five dollars a square foot is a bargain, because his school has helped a great number of kids get off the street and find some meaning in life. The alternative, he says, is spending $198 a square foot to build a prison, which seems to be what society prefers.

Bill Strickland knows that the arts improve life. It's why I say the real world needs musicians. The arts provide more than enhancement; they provide a measurable betterment to life—in some cases they can even mean survival. Unfortunately, we get sidetracked by little things like the lack of jobs. Of course, it would be nice to have a greater need for piano teachers, but that won't happen until musicians change society's attitude about what we do.

If 8,118 pianists enter the real world each year, what a force for good that is. If they could organize themselves—along with the 4,059 piano professors, the 24,354 remaining college-level piano students, and the 20,000 *Clavier* readers—to educate society to what the arts can do for them, a lot could happen very quickly.

Where there's a need, there is usually a job. It's just that you might have to invent it.

37

Emotional Quotient

Out of the Woods

As I sit down to write this, the cover of *Time* magazine asks the question, "What's your EQ?" It's not your IQ, quoth the newsweekly; it's not even a number. The eight-page story is about emotional intelligence and suggests that this element of our psyche "may be the best predictor of success in life, redefining what it means to be smart."

The basic premise is that one's IQ isn't the only thing that determines success. It may not even be the main thing. This will come as no surprise to piano teachers.

EQ as predictor of future behavior is the result of experiments psychologists have done with children. In one example, the doctor offers a four-year-old a marshmallow and tells the child that he needs to run an errand, but if the child can wait and not eat the marshmallow until he returns, the nice doctor will give him a second marshmallow when he gets back. Once the doctor leaves, some kids eat the first marshmallow right away. Others toy with it and eat it after a few minutes. Some work hard not to eat it; they play games, sing songs, even try to sleep. Those who succeed get the second marshmallow. According to experts, these same kids are more likely to get more goodies when they grow up. The experiment has been going on for twenty years; proof exists that those who learn to accept delayed gratification are the likely winners in the game of life.

On numerous occasions in these essays, I have extolled the virtues of musical training for children, and now it appears there is yet another reason for all good parents to take their children to the nearest piano teacher. I can think of few better examples of delayed gratification than piano study. (Those few that come to mind involve stringed instruments in the alto clef and double reeds.) Once after a recital, a piano teacher came up to me and said that what I was doing amounted to false advertising: if I were to be completely honest, I should only perform with a large sign behind me with a caption stating, IT'S NOT AS EASY AS IT LOOKS.

Alas, we who teach know that. Our student enrollments have been going down because most people, especially those of a tender age, do not want to study for years before they sound good. There are too many other pursuits that provide instant gratification, like television, computer games, the internet, and social media.

The fact remains, however, that those who know (or learn) how to wait are the ones most rewarded. As teachers, we see it all the time with the students who persevere, who somehow believe that the best is yet to come. Reasoning—"if I do my homework tonight, I'll do better in school tomorrow"—can prevail over our baser impulses. "If I eat the marshmallow, it's gone."

The *Time* researchers go even further and suggest that giving more attention to EQ may be the way out of the present societal malaise. Daniel Goleman, a Harvard psychology PhD and the author of the new book *Emotional Intelligence* that inspired the *Time* article, sees practical applications everywhere:

> When street gangs substitute for families and schoolyard insults end in stabbings…when the majority of the children murdered in this country are killed by parents and stepparents, many of whom say they were trying to discipline the child for behavior like blocking the TV or crying too much, it suggests a demand for remedial emotional education.

Goleman goes on to say, however, that there is only one "neurological window of opportunity." By midadolescence the brain's prefrontal circuitry has matured; the neural patterns determining our actions and feelings have been set. Translation: out-of-control teenagers are not likely to become successful adults.

For a long time, I have thought that studying music is a kind of emotional education. It cannot teach one to have feelings; rather, it teaches one about one's own feelings. Some of this comes from the music itself; quite a bit comes from the situations inherent in the study of music.

For example, children preparing for a recital learn all about delayed gratification. If I practice today and every day for the next few weeks, I'll play my piece really well on the recital. Furthermore, the reward is intrinsic: the children know when a performance is good, and they feel good about themselves. Each new piece represents a task with new problems to solve; each successful solution increases the child's confidence, not just in music making but in problem-solving.

Even when our experiences in music are less than positive, the study itself is a worthy proving ground. All musicians know about performance anxiety. Even playing for a lesson can bring it on. This is a common problem throughout life, one we should learn to overcome. Every human being experiences anxiety at some time in life; how we deal with it determines our success. Those who have learned to live with some anxiety in music study have had rehearsals for the butterflies that come with a job interview or a speech to the PTA.

There is another word that comes to mind that summarizes this balance of mind and emotion: *harmony*. How fitting that it is a musical term. While the notion of EQ may come right off the pages of today's press, the idea, if I read it correctly, has been around a long time. Plato wrote in the *Timaeus*:

> All audible musical sound is given us for the sake of harmony, which has motions akin to the orbits in our soul, and which, as anyone who makes intelligent use of the arts knows, is not to be used, as is commonly thought, to give irrational pleasure, but as a heaven-sent ally in reducing to order and harmony any disharmony in the revolutions within us. Rhythm, again, was given us from the same heavenly source to help us in the same way; for most of us lack measure and grace.

It seems so obvious. Then why are so few children taking music lessons in this country?

Perhaps it has something to do with the prefrontal circuitry of the parents who themselves sit before the television, or the school boards that cut music from the curriculum to save money, or the politicians who scrap the National Endowment for the Arts. It's too late to expect those people to come to us. We must figure out a way to get through to them.

38

No One Is Just an Artist

Out of the Woods

NOVEMBER 2002

To escape the clamor of the headlines, I sometimes allow myself a fantasy: what if all the world's leaders were artists or musicians? Imagine international disputes solved by heads of state during chamber music sessions together. Picture concert halls, built with money previously used for armaments, filled with audiences eager to hear music of the past and present, thanks to public arts education supported by tax dollars.

Dream on, you say, but don't wake me just yet—there's a point to be made eventually, and it's apolitical. I'm not thinking of amateurs like Richard Nixon tickling the ivories, or Bill Clinton and his occasional bouts with the saxophone. A more likely role model might be the pianist Ignacy Paderewski, who served as prime minister and minister of foreign affairs in Poland, helping to bring that beleaguered country back, however briefly, from the devastation of World War I,[1] or author and playwright Václav Havel, president of the Czech Republic since 1992,[2] who was a leader before holding office in the Czech struggle against Communism.

Artists have proven they can be world leaders, so my fantasy has some basis in fact. Unfortunately, people in the arts seldom imagine themselves leading the PTA, let alone a nation's government. We are too immersed in the intense demands of our work, the monastic pursuit of excellence, or a nonexistent perfection. It's a pity, since a musical education can be a first-rate preparation for a multitude of careers, up to and including leader of the free world.

---

1. Paderewski signed the Treaty of Versailles for Poland in 1919.

2. Havel was president of Czechoslovakia from 1989 to 1992, then president of the Czech Republic from 1993 until 2003. He died in 2011.

A previous essay enumerated the skills and abilities well-trained musicians have built into their beings. I'm surprised that music school admissions offices don't proclaim these indirect benefits of music study. Can you think of an active musician who is not self-motivated? These are people who don't quit until the job is done, and if it isn't complete yet, they come back the next day eager to finish it. They are excellent problem solvers, able to sequence solutions into bite-size, doable steps. Their ensemble experience has taught them to work as part of a team, and when called upon, they can function as the leader of the group. Did I mention they can work under pressure? They've even done it all in front of an audience.

If I were the personnel officer of a *Fortune* 500 company, I'd bend over backward to have employees with such a range of talents. Yet every May, our graduates slink out the university gate, heads hung with discouragement as they seek employment. Many accept day jobs in fast food while waiting for their big break.

Why not put these skills to full and lucrative use? What is truly amazing is the fact that most music students aren't even aware they are so employable. The fault lies within the culture of the music school, where performing and teaching are the only careers deemed successful.

Alas, I think we faculty are to blame for this. By dint of hard work and determination, we have managed to eke out careers in what we love. We perform concerts, accept appointments to teaching jobs, and succeed in a field that is challenging, competitive, and all consuming. Our days are filled with practicing, teaching, and service to the profession and the academy. Our students see us as busy, engaged in the art, productive— and they want this for themselves. They do not see their teachers wondering if other avenues of employment might better cover the monthly bills. "Art above all!" is the conservatory rallying cry. I know of institutions that will only award tenure to piano professors if they have had students win major competitions. "Publish or perish" is alive and well in universities everywhere; good teachers are sent packing because their résumés do not include that esoteric monograph no one will read. Immersed in such a culture, it is no wonder that faculty have little imagination about what lies beyond a music career: we are too busy surviving our own.

This is a call to reexamine our premises. A life in music can be glorious, but it's not the only career available. In the studio and the practice room, we focus so much time on specialization (depth) that there is little time to consider the wider aspects of our work (breadth). John Dewey wrote that "No one is just an artist and nothing else, and in so far as one approximates that condition, he is so much the less developed human being."

Musicians can contribute richly to society; our skills, abilities, and, most of all, values have never been more needed. We should encourage our students to think more imaginatively about their career possibilities. By doing so, we might just change the world.

39

The Boston Marathon and the Edge Effect

Winds of Change

JULY–AUGUST 2013

The deadline for this column arrived as the Boston Marathon attack unfolded.[1] For five days, we watched madness spread across a city, paralyzing the Athens of America, usurping thought and rationality as horror reigned supreme.

At the same time, I happened to be attending the finals of a high-level piano competition. Five gifted, exceedingly well-trained young pianists, all desirous of a prize worth more than $100,000, played their best, jumping through the hoops erected to display their talents. They were the same age as the Tsarnaev brothers.

Such a gulf is hard to fathom, yet this is the world we live in. In one case, two young men brought a city to a standstill and gripped the nation's attention through acts of incomprehensible violence. They acted alone [or so it seems as I write], killing, maiming for who knows what inner purpose. In the other, five young people played the piano in a marathon of another sort. They, too, acted alone, but behind them stood years of support from parents and teachers, untold hours of dedication to a craft, and the attention of audiences small and large who cared enough to come hear the results of this quest for personal excellence. Alas, very few Americans knew anything of these five musicians as we collectively trembled over the insanity in Boston.

Perhaps during that week, some of our fellow citizens turned to music for solace. The arts help us define ourselves, help us understand who we are and how we feel. Those of us around music everyday know that it makes us better people. It would be the perfect time

---

1. Even though this happened less than ten years ago, some readers may not remember the details. For further information, see https://en.wikipedia.org/wiki/Boston_Marathon_bombing.

to mount a campaign for the return of arts education to the schools, although another sector of the populace would protest, just as the NRA claims that banning assault rifles would not save lives. There is insanity everywhere.

At times like this, we feel helpless as activists for a better world. We practice, teach, and immerse ourselves in the daily demands of our art-centered existence. We feel blessed to live such lives. Generally, we stay among our own kind. We feel our influence is slight.

I am convinced this does not have to be the case. Musicians have many skills the world needs. We just need to be willing to come out from our comfort zones.

We are trained to see the big picture, holding the scope of an entire composition in mind while simultaneously tending to the smallest detail. Despite this, we don't often think globally. We are content to stay in our safe communities of fellow musicians, whether that is the local teachers' group, a college faculty, or a garage band. Our music doesn't seem very important to the world around us, so we hide in our affinity groups, satisfied by occasional successes like a student winning a competition, or getting a better-paying job, or selling a few CDs. In the scheme of things, these ends are insignificant. Perhaps we should redefine "success."

I urge you to listen to Yo-Yo Ma's talk "Art for Life's Sake," this year's Nancy Hanks Lecture on Arts and Public Policy at the Kennedy Center.[2] Ma offers a decidedly global approach to what musicians can do for society, encouraged as he was by Senator Edward Kennedy to pursue public service as a musician. He also cites Pablo Casals as an inspiration, who once told him, "I am a human being first, a musician second, and a cellist third."

Unafraid of big ideas, Ma seldom stays in his comfort zone. An idea I found particularly compelling concerns the "edge effect."

---

2. Yo-Yo Ma, "Nancy Hanks Lecture 2013: Yo-Yo Ma," streamed live April 8, 2013, https://www.youtube.com/watch?v=TWsdrjUhol4&t=1432s.

In ecology, where two ecosystems meet, such as the forest and the savannah, the point of intersection is the site of "edge effect." In that transition zone, because of the influence the two ecological communities have on each other, you find the greatest diversity of life, as well as the greatest number of new life forms.[3]

What does this say about our safe little affinity groups? Is it any wonder we feel impotent within them? But get out to the edge and mingle with another set of bioforms and look out! Creativity will happen.

"The edge effect," Ma said, "is where those of varied backgrounds come together in a zone of transition—a region of less structure, more diversity, and more possibility. The edge is a time and place of transformation and movement."[4]

Here's a formula for change in our profession if there ever was one. Imagine: MTNA groups with members of *different* backgrounds; college curricula with *less* structure (thereby spawning graduates with different backgrounds). More possibility. But it only happens at the edge, not in the safe center where things stay the same.

Imagine something even more challenging: musicians who go out to the edge where things are less predictable, even dangerous. An edge where poverty is the norm, say. And the musicians don't just play for the children and run back to their comfort zones—they engage them in music making at their level. This is El Sistema, the revolutionary music education program begun in Venezuela by José Antonio Abreu thirty-three years ago with only eleven students in a parking garage in Caracas. Today over three hundred thousand students are learning to play orchestral instruments and perform together in ensembles of every level throughout the country. Many of these students come from very poor backgrounds; the success of El Sistema has transformed whole communities.[5]

---

3. Ma, "Nancy Hanks Lecture."

4. Ma, "Nancy Hanks Lecture."

5. This is a continuing story. Abreu died in 2018 and Venezuela has undergone crippling economic problems. The current leader of the program, Eduardo Méndez, said, "We will have to multiply into thousands of Abreus."

Abreu has said, "The huge spiritual world that music produces in itself ends up overcoming material poverty. From the minute a child is taught to play an instrument, he is no longer poor. He becomes a child in progress, heading for a professional level, who'll later become a citizen."[6]

Yo-Yo Ma referred often in his speech to the "citizen-musician." Note the order of the words.

Might things have been different if the Tsarnaev brothers played music instead of wrestled and boxed? What if they had been drawn into a musical ensemble that gave them the sense of family and acceptance they so sorely missed? We will never reach potential students like these unless we get out of our boxes of safety and conformity. We don't have to do it alone. Real change occurs not so much by one person's efforts as by an intermingling of many. Ma's Silk Road Project is the edge effect in action, artistically in the cross-cultural influences of many musical styles, as well as in the kinds of programs the Project sponsors. Many are educational, grassroots events that meet the young students where they live.

In videos of the Silk Road, you'll see the founder of the Project, Yo-Yo Ma himself, blending into the fabric of the whole. He is one of many, the citizen-musician connecting at the edge.

---

6. See http://elsistema.org.

VIII

■ The Institution

Behold the Institution, humankind's invention to give order to the widest range of activities. The word's many meanings include the idea of beginning something (to institute) but can also connote something firm and dependable, something decisively established. It can also be an organization or simply a workplace. Consider the massive institution of higher learning, within which dwells the smaller institution of advanced musical education, and within that are abundant practices or traditions that could also be thought of as institutions (e.g., the institution of tenure). These modes of operation advance our goals and smooth the rough patches encountered along the way.

I credit the institutions in which I landed for great assistance in acquiring a foothold in the profession. After two years teaching in a Vermont prep school, I attended the Yale University School of Music for graduate study. At that time, Yale's doctor of musical arts degree was unlike any in the country. The traditional master's degree took two years, but in the middle of the second year, one could apply for the master of musical arts degree, in essence a conditional DMA. Upon acceptance to the program, a third year in residence was required for courses, another recital, and written and oral exams. If all went well, one emerged in three years with an MMA degree and the promise of a DMA. The final decision was based mostly on your success in the real world, defined as making a significant mark in whatever you chose to do. The final recital and exam were almost beside the point.

I chose to teach and perform. Therefore, getting a job was high on my to-do list if I wanted to get the DMA. In my last year in residence at Yale, I applied to two university teaching positions. Tulane University responded with an invitation to visit. I was about to undergo another of those institutional rites of passage: the interview.

The bare bones comprise a live performance, a teaching demonstration, meetings with various constituencies, and a social interaction or two (usually involving a meal). While it's true that they are interviewing you, you can also find out a lot about them and their hopes for the department. Interviews in those days were great fun. Today, the interview has lost its glow as budget overseers often require selection committee members to pay for their own drinks and dessert.

Tulane's music offerings were organized into a department, a designation in university terminology suggesting both its size and management. It is usually overseen by a chair who answers to a dean higher up in the bureaucracy. My first chair, Francis Monachino, was a singer and opera director who had produced a cash cow for the department in the form of the Summer Lyric Theatre. Frank was extremely supportive of my efforts, and I remember him with great fondness. The former chair, Peter Hansen, a harpsichordist/musicologist, was also very active in the musical life of New Orleans. He had written a book, *An Introduction to Twentieth Century Music*, that was *the* text in its day. We had many meals together, and I often performed with his wife, Doris, an excellent violinist. I give such personal background to illustrate that it was the institution itself that led to these close friendships and opportunities for musical growth.

It was also the institution that permitted me the opportunity to stretch my wings. Tulane wanted a place on the musical map in New Orleans, so I was allowed, even encouraged, to perform often—I gave three solo recitals in the first five months of being there. I also started a weekly chamber music series called "Music at Midday," held in a modern chapel on campus every Wednesday at noon. Advanced students, other faculty, and musicians from the New Orleans Symphony performed chamber music, often with me, thus allowing me to learn important masterworks like Schubert's *Die schöne Müllerin* and various sonatas and trios by Brahms. Since the programs were presented on campus in the middle of the day, an audience materialized regularly. Forty years later, the series is still in existence!

Sometime during that first year at Tulane, the Rockefeller Foundation (another institution), announced a competition to be held in 1978 for the performance of American piano music. With a mission to "improve lives and the planet, and unleash human potential through innovation," they did not find it outside their mission to encourage performers (with no age limit) to engage with both traditional and contemporary piano music by American composers. This was right up my alley—I had always been attracted to this music and already played works of Copland and Elliott Carter and more modern works by Yale composers. I set about learning two pieces I considered masterworks by truly contemporary composers: George Crumb's *Makrokosmos, Volume I* (written only seven years earlier), and C. Curtis-Smith's *Rhapsodies*, which required the performer to bow the piano strings among other avant-garde techniques. The finals were held at the Kennedy Center, and I placed third.

After only two years in New Orleans, I was invited by the Northwestern University School of Music to audition for a position in Evanston, Illinois. While the competition win helped, I owe a lot to the recommendation of Philip Nelson, my dean at Yale, that I was considered. Another institution—the old-boy network! Northwestern's dean, Thomas Miller, was then president of the National Association of Schools of Music, and people at this level share information. I was treated to a very nice interview and still remember the fine dinner at Café Provencal with the piano chair, Arthur Tollefson.

Only three years later, Art left Northwestern and I became piano chair at the ripe old age of thirty-two. Two years after that, I was interviewed for the deanship at the College-Conservatory of Music at the University of Cincinnati. The search committee must have immediately seen that their candidate looked good on paper but was too young for such a job.

I tell the story to give the reader a sense of how a career can develop and how institutions play a role. The essays that follow are my past attempts at recognizing the various kinds of institutions created to advance musical education in America. Those holding positions in the field are so accustomed to the systematic practices and assumptions that institutional influence on our thoughts and habits is seldom recognized. The essays look at practices such as auditions, commencement, and the ideal (in my opinion) piano department. I touch on summer festivals and adjudications, which I have enjoyed on the West Coast. The final essay relates my experiences over three remarkable days at a liberal arts university when everything had consequence, something that can happen only in an institution where substantial programs are maintained and valued. I just happened to be the lucky participant in all three. I hope the reader will relate to both the joys and frustrations one encounters when working within something larger than oneself. Were it not for institutions, we would face the world alone, unable to wield the power for good that can stem from the unity of purpose fostered by an institution.

40

On Auditions

The View from the Second Floor

MARCH 1990

During the last full week of February, the Peabody piano faculty hears roughly 150 auditions for openings in next year's class. In May we'll hear another hundred or so. This goes on all over the country from midwinter through spring, and every year I tell myself to write something about auditions; surely I've learned something listening to all those aspiring pianists. So this is it, teachers! The column to share with your students—Weirich tells all, the inside scoop!

Dear students, I'm going to tell you the most inconceivable fact first: the faculty listening to auditions really wants you to do well. We are not audition ogres, monsters with enlarged ears that hear the minutest mistake. In truth, we are usually on our best behavior and actually enjoy listening with our colleagues to all this fresh talent. Each new student coming in the door presents us with the potential for a rewarding musical and personal relationship. With that in mind, you should realize that we are positively inclined to hear good things and that we want you to be comfortable, because then you are most likely to do your best.

Needless to say, we will want to hear you play the piano, but there's more to an audition than that. A faculty member looking at you as a prospective student wants to know what you are like as a person. After all, if we accept you, we're looking at several years of contact with you, and being human, we want that contact to be enjoyable. This is where clean clothes, neat appearance, eye contact, and not complaining about the onstage piano will win you points. This is also where we read your application material; you'd be surprised at how interesting we find those five-hundred-word essays.

As for the playing part of the audition, there's no big news here. We're listening for the same things you work for every time you perform. How far along are you in achieving these things? The farther along you are, the more we want you, because in case you haven't noticed, music is a never-ending study, and you are more likely to succeed when you have the basics out of the way by the time you enter college. On the other hand, we don't expect perfection; if you could do it all right now, you wouldn't need us or the school.

We also look for what many an optimistic parent calls "promise," as in "my child may not hit all the notes, but he's got promise." Unfortunately, that's not an easy one to call. "Promise" to one person may be "laziness" to another. The rule of thumb here is: the older you are, the less you should count on promise.

More than anything, we look for individuality, that quality that makes you unlike anyone else we've heard. Over one hundred years ago, Anton Rubinstein said ruefully, "Everyone plays the piano well these days." It's even truer today: not only are we likely to hear a lot of standard issue playing, but quite often we hear a lot of the same piece. *Mirabile dictu*, it doesn't take all that much to stand out; all you have to do is play a non-warhorse with some personal conviction. Couple this with an occasional smile when spoken to, and you'll be surprised at how much we seem to like you. Remember, we want you to do well.

An audition should work both ways: not only do we find out about you, but you should find out as much as you can about us and the school. A lot of that should be done long before the day of your audition. Think of it as homework; you should know why you are applying to a particular school. If you want to study with a particular teacher, contact him or her well in advance of the audition. This lets you know if the teacher can take you and gains you an especially interested pair of ears at the audition. If you don't have a particular teacher in mind, you should. You are about to spend $17,000 a year if you go to a private school, and for that kind of money you should know what you're getting.[1]

If possible, play the audition in person. You are much less an individual on a recording, and even more to the point, you will have missed seeing the campus, meeting with your prospective teacher, and pumping the local students for the inside dirt. You may like the

---

1. That was the figure in 1990. Today it is more like $60,000. That figure, too, will soon be exceeded as costs rise.

teacher but hate the campus, or vice versa. You'll never know unless you show up in the flesh. Use the visit to take a sample lesson with the teacher; it's a good way for both parties to get a sense of how well they might work together. By all means, hang out with some of the natives; no one knows more about what's going on at a school than its students. They may appear aloof and unapproachable, but only a few years before, they were in your shoes. They might tell you more than you want to know.

All that travel will be expensive, so be realistic about which schools you apply to and how many. If you do your homework, you should plan to apply to no more than three or four.[2] After the audition, you'll be able to make an informed choice based on your experience, which is much better than relying on rumors of University X's reputation or College Y's social scene. You had the good sense not to be born during the baby boom, so you'll find it's a buyer's market out there. Enjoy it while it lasts—it's probably the last one you'll ever know as a musician.

---

2. Students I know today think nothing of applying to many more schools than this. Perhaps I am missing something. One can still apply for the "reach" school, a couple of good schools approaching reach status, and one safe school without breaking the bank with application fees.

41

Mestiere at Commencement

The View from the Second Floor

MAY 1985

They say it's a sign of age when an entire year goes by and you don't feel any older. It's particularly true here on the second floor, surrounded by graduating seniors who have been intensively involved in what the Italian diarist Cesare Pavese called *Il mestiere di vivere* (the business of living). The Italian phrase implies craft as well as occupation, whatever is necessary to one's profession or art. In the past year, I have probably changed little, but these students have gone through senior recitals, suffered the anxiety of measuring up in exams, and tasted the fear of rejection in graduate school auditions. They have been learning who they are and what they will do, finding their *mestiere*. Now they are about to graduate, leaving me here by the window, wondering how it all happened so fast.

While there is sometimes pain in watching them leave, there is also a sense of renewal that comes to teachers as we observe the ebb and flow of students. For me, it is one of the most rewarding aspects of teaching. Students come to you, ready to learn, a blank page waiting to be filled. Eventually they leave you, to some degree changed by their contact with you, taking with them the fruits of your interaction. I try to give them knowledge in the hope that they will transform it into understanding, passing it on to others directly through teaching or symbolically through music.

Every spring the flowers tentatively expand into the warming air around them, eventually bursting forth in uninhibited color and beauty. Likewise, every spring our graduating students look for space to grow, seeking to root themselves in a crowded and frantic world that is unaware of how desperately it needs more flowers. The difficulties that arise are often staggering. Nevertheless, the flowers persevere, and our graduating seniors should be just as dauntless.

The music world is crowded, but it is open to those who try something new, or do things in a different way, or manage to do things better than they've been done before. That world is not awaiting them; new musicians must be prepared to knock loudly at several doors and be ready to get the foot in fast and firmly. My advice to them is to find or create a niche that is theirs and theirs alone. I tell them: don't try to be another Ashkenazy—we already have one who's very good at it. Don't expect a competition to be the catapult to a musical career. Don't apply for teaching positions when your résumé looks the same as those of the 150 other applicants. I ask myself, "What advice can I give that doesn't begin with 'don't'?"

One of the chief components of artistry is uniqueness, the strength and individuality of the message in one's art. That singularity develops only if we strive to exceed the standard of "fitting in." Competition juries are looking for someone special. Job applications are screened by committees looking for qualities in the applicants that will contribute something new to the university community. Perhaps the most positive advice I can give the graduates is "Dare to be unique." How is that done? Very simple—just dare to be yourself.

In his book *Poetry and Experience*, Archibald MacLeish quotes a Chinese poet whose timeless words beautifully address the issue of making a life as a musician. "We poets struggle with Non-being to force it to yield Being. We knock upon silence for an answering music."

A musician's business of living involves creativity. May you create a life that will allow you to immerse yourselves in your art. Godspeed, graduates.

42

The Ideal Piano Department

Out of the Woods

JANUARY 2003

Another New Year dawns—a time of hope or a time of melancholy, depending on your outlook. Here we go again, for better or worse. Always the eternal optimist, I prefer to think that things really can improve, given determination and a bit of luck. In this season of resolutions, let's think positively, even imagining the unattainable. Perhaps we'll accomplish more than we expect.

What if we envisioned an ideal piano department in higher education? If there were no limitations on personnel or finances, what would we want in our wildest dreams?

I would start with faculty collegiality beyond the pleasantries of daily coexistence. Hellos in the hall are nice, and commiseration at juries considerate, but I'd like more. Teaching individual students behind closed doors is a lonely endeavor. There is no feedback except an occasional comment from the student. The last time a colleague saw me teach was at my interview; I have never seen them teach. I dream of a department in which colleagues spend time observing one another in the studio and then discussing it over lunch. This has nothing to do with formal evaluations—it's simply an admission that we are in this together and could help each other improve.

Such a discussion would also make pedagogy a topic of concern for the whole department, not just the province of the pedagogy specialist. If our students attempt to make a living in music, it is almost certain that teaching will be part of their livelihood. Yet schools continue to offer separate degrees in performance and pedagogy, as if their graduates will do one or the other. This is not healthy. Similarly, we maintain a separate major for collaborative pianists, with teachers dedicated only to the chamber music and song literature. In my ideal department, everyone would do everything, both students and faculty.

With so much interaction, the notion that the doors between studios could be more porous is not so far-fetched. On at least a daily basis, I am reminded that I cannot be all things to all my students, so nothing would please me more than their taking an occasional lesson with a colleague, and I in turn might teach one of their students when asked. I wrack my brain trying to understand why such an idea would not have been considered in the past. Is purity of pianistic bloodline so important? I fear that our personal insecurities are mostly to blame, but surely it need not be so.

In my ideal department, students and teachers would spend more time together. Seeing a student for one hour a week barely enables name recognition, let alone musical training. I have always been astounded that upon the completion of 120 hours of contact with the major professor (fifteen hours per semester times eight semesters), a bachelor of music in performance is awarded with the blessings of the National Association of Schools of Music. High school students work longer at McDonald's to earn pocket money.

I know many college-level piano teachers try to spend more than an hour each week with their students, but it's tough to accomplish, given one's own teaching load and the students' full schedules. Studio classes contribute extra contact time, but seldom does the individual faculty member receive load credit for this effort. Group lessons are another approach: typically, three students meet with the professor for a period of two hours. Within this time, the professor might spend forty minutes with each student while the others listen. The advantages are several: the students learn three times as much repertoire and get a double dose of the professor's musical concepts each week. The disadvantages are in the areas of scheduling (making a compatible class of students with similar needs or achievement levels) and a perception on the students' parts (erroneous, in my opinion) that they are not getting as much personal time with the professor. It should be noted that in nineteenth-century German conservatories, the usual method of teaching involved students grouped in classes which received two one-hour lessons a week, and the director determined the number of students per class, which was often more than three. Perhaps things today are not as bad as I think.

I would also like to suggest another possibility for my ideal department, also taken from the nineteenth century: most of the major teachers of the time had several assistants, usually handpicked and trained by the master. Today we employ graduate assistants (GAs) to teach secondaries or class piano, but the major professor seldom contributes to their training as teachers and never lets the GA loose on his/her piano majors. What better way to instruct future teachers than to instill in them the values we find most important and then observe them working with our own younger advanced students? The major professor might be able to take on more students with the aid of assistants, sharing instruction time with the well-trained intern. With the additional tuition income from more students, the school could afford more assistantships to attract the best graduate talent.

My space is nearly gone, and I have not even begun a financial wish list. Could it be that asking for more money for good practice pianos and a larger scholarship budget is the easy part? Of course we need these— everyone can agree. It's much harder to change the way people think about the subjective issues—did you really say you want to watch me teach, and then talk about it? Surely you jest!

Yet all it takes is an open mind. We don't have to do things the way they've always been done. Few professionals have as much control over their workplace as college teachers. Just go find another open mind and start talking. You have nothing to lose but your sense of helpless isolation.

43

Summer Music Festivals

The View from the Second Floor
APRIL 1985 AND FEBRUARY 1986

I write of the joys of participating for the first time in a summer music festival. It was such a good experience that I return to the topic a year later, finding that the second time was just as good as the first.

One of the loveliest perks of the teaching profession is that many of us have lighter schedules in the summer. With students off on family vacations, independent teachers have the luxury of moments to themselves. With limited university class offerings, the professoriate may find they have three months to practice or write that book that's been sitting in the corner of the den for ten years. Almost all of us have the chance to do something a little different from the rest of the year.

Last summer I engaged in a busman's holiday as an artist-teacher at a six-week music festival. Plenty of people do this, but I never had. I went back to the festival the next summer and had a completely different, perhaps even more valuable, time. It seems that each summer is unique since the mix of people in attendance changes from year to year.

Perhaps it was getting away from the usual pressures of the job. Perhaps it was the stimulus of new people, all of whom were talented and interesting. Perhaps it was the challenge of reaching new students in a short time, knowing that if you were to have an effect on them, you only had six weeks to do it. Perhaps it was the chance to set a schedule that was entirely your own; if you wanted to get up and practice at six in the morning, you could. It was all these and more.

The festival tends to be your entire world while you are there. That can have its drawbacks, but often the advantages are far more enticing. Living on campus, it is possible to drop in on orchestral rehearsals, something I never have time for in my life outside the summer. To hear the Verdi Requiem or a Sibelius symphony taken apart and reassembled by a skilled conductor is a tremendous experience, which need not end with your student days. Then there are the concerts themselves: I usually heard five per week, and there were more than that available. Informal chamber music and four-hand readings find their way into the spare hour between dinner and the evening concert. Finally, there are the performances in which you take part, receiving the stimulation of new chamber partners, adapting to an intense rehearsal schedule, and reaching a new audience. It's the kind of thing that fosters the peak experience, a result of complete immersion in the work at hand. I think it is more likely to happen in the summer because every moment of the day is packed with intensity. Everyone knows that they will be going home in only six weeks. The attitude becomes "Let's live every minute to its fullest potential."

It can be a similar experience for the students. They are eager to try their musical wings away from home, and since they usually come from far and wide, they meet other students with very different backgrounds from their own. Some have played concerti with orchestra; others have never even heard an orchestra. Each learns from the other: the stars learn humility and that, at a certain level, there is no one "best" artist; the less experienced learn that they have something unique to say as well, which is easier to discover around like-minded people.

The students from that second summer provided me with a wealth of good memories. There was the seventeen-year-old from Boston who played "La campanella" as if it were one of the simplest pieces in the repertory. She played it in a master class with Misha Dichter, whose only comment was "How do you do that?" Then there was the workshop at the beginning of the summer that I led attempting to gain an understanding of why we do what we do. I asked one question to get them thinking, a rather vague and existential inquiry into the nature of our art. A fourteen-year-old girl from Connecticut promptly answered the question as well as I could myself, complete with philosophical implications. As I stammered for something to say, the hour looming large before me, I knew this was no ordinary group of students. And lest you think that this summer festival was entirely serious, I should mention a picnic at which a bucket of water balloons suddenly appeared. (Rumor has it a faculty member brought it.) It had been a long time since I'd felt that sharp slap and then the cold, shocking ooze dripping down my back. Thanks for the memories, kids.

My only sadness is that I didn't think of going on some kind of summer musical vacation sooner. All the usual excuses would occur to me: "I can't get away…It's too expensive…Who will water the plants?" You *can* get away if you plan ahead. If you only have a week, there is probably something available that won't cost you your Christmas fund, and in the bargain, you will come back feeling refreshed and excited about what you do. If you have a longer time, the choices become enticing indeed, with numerous possibilities in some of the more splendidly scenic parts of the country. If you are looking for something for your students, a great number of the camps and festivals offer some financial aid. Every other aspect of the student's life is taken care of—resident health professionals, counselors in the dormitories, and the chance to hear more music in one place than they've ever heard before. There is literally something for everyone in the summer's musical offerings. Do yourself a favor—you'll love every minute of it.

44

Peak Experiences Redux

Out of the Woods

JULY 1997

Every now and then, a peak experience comes along, surprising us out of our doldrums. When that happens, it always makes me wonder why I let myself sit around in a funk for so long.

In May I was in Spokane, Washington, to serve as an adjudicator at that city's Young Artists' Festival. In the course of a week, 1,700 young musicians, dancers, and visual artists present themselves to an "expert" for written comments, a grade, and some one-on-one work together. There were six adjudicators in the piano area alone. The students, ranging in age from six to twentysomething, enter various events, such as "fifth-grade sonatina" or "eighth-grade Romantic." If there are twenty-four students in the "seventh-grade contemporary division," an adjudicator will hear them in four classes of six students, with each class lasting seventy-five minutes. In that time period, the students play their pieces, and the adjudicator writes comments as they play, then in whatever time remains works with each student. If you pay attention to the clock, it's possible to get five minutes with each student, sometimes more. It sounds like drive-by teaching, but with some quick planning, you can turn this into a thirty-minute session that involves all the students for the whole period.

So, for six straight days, in the week that followed finals week at my university, that's what I did from 9:00 a.m. to 5:00 p.m. It should have been exhausting; instead, it was exhilarating. Listening to twenty-five sonatina movements in a row should have driven me crazy; instead, I left the building humming Clementi. The entire week was like that; I enjoyed every minute of my time there. I'd forgotten a simple truth: when everything "goes right," work is play.

We have all had these glorious experiences, and this time I want to make mine last. More precisely, I want to have more control over the frequency of the experience; it should be possible to create—or at least to encourage—peak experiences instead of simply waiting for them to happen. Is there a trick to making everything "go right"?

If there is, I believe it begins by understanding just what was so good about the experience. Please forgive the self-centeredness of this essay, but it's the story I know best just now.

From the teaching standpoint, I felt I had an immediate rapport with almost every student. The work was swift and by necessity focused on one issue, two at most. I could help the student improve immediately and then move on to the next student. Given the shortness of time, I sometimes became wildly inventive; other times I trotted out my tried-and-true lines and realized how effective they were all over again, since these students had never heard me say them before.

No wonder my thirsty ego was so gratified; in a situation such as this, it's easy to view oneself as a miracle worker. Before I let myself quibble away the good feelings, though, what else happened?

The weather was beautiful, seven straight days of sun and warmth. Spokane is a lovely city with pine-covered hills lapping at its outskirts; through the center of town runs a river, which tumbles over a series of cascades made all the more dramatic by the sudden spring melt off. In the 1970s, the city fathers built a spectacular park around the falls; there are bridges, overlooks, jogging trails, ponds, and lots of greenery, making it one of the most people-friendly cities I've ever visited.

After the first day of judging, I joined three of the other piano adjudicators for dinner. We set off on foot from the hotel knowing only that somewhere along the river was a restaurant with a terrace for alfresco dining. We wisecracked about getting lost, which didn't happen although we had no idea where we were going. We laughed our way through dinner as each of us told various life stories to new and appreciative ears. Three hours went by in a flash as four strangers with very similar interests became fast friends. Dinner together became a ritual we observed each night; by the third night, our number had grown to ten, and even our serving person took a couple of turns in the joke telling.

It didn't hurt that the food was terrific. I had salmon, which I adore, three times in three nights. The gift shop in the hotel had an espresso bar for morning caffe latte fixes, which I also adore. The hotel restaurant served a splendid breakfast of fresh fruit and yogurt, which helped me feel less guilty about all the salmon I was eating at night.

In the mornings before breakfast, I threw on my running shoes and headed for the park. In the evenings after dinner, I read or wrote letters in my room. Each day had a completeness and a certainty that every minute would count.

I've described a lovely working vacation, one might say, a peak experience that was a function of its time and place. The trick is to reproduce these elements every day.

Lovely surroundings, friends, good food, and some time to oneself for both exercise and rest are under your control, but I don't know many musicians who indulge themselves often in such luxuries. We are too busy working at our work, and in the process, we never play.

We are also too self-critical. As I analyzed my teaching after the fact, I doubted my success, wondered if it were as good as I thought. In Spokane all I had to do was work on one or two issues. Of course, the students improved: I was the one defining the improvement. I am quick to find shortcomings with myself, nipping the peak experience in the bud. As musicians, we are trained to find the wrong note; we learn by finding what's wrong, paying much less attention to what's right. The negative rears its ugly head. In the flow of the peak experience, however, I saw myself doing great things and kept it up all week because I let myself go with the feeling. The immediate rapport I felt could not have happened without my feeling good about what I was doing. I viewed myself as successful in establishing rapport; therefore, I was successful. The rest followed.

Peak experiences are just waiting to happen to you. All you have to do is suspend disbelief—in yourself.

45

Three Remarkable Days

Out of the Woods

DECEMBER 1997

There are some obvious advantages to teaching in a university: bright students, a regular salary and benefits, and a studio to go to outside one's home come immediately to mind. A recent three-day period at Syracuse University, however, substantially exceeded these basics, reminding me just how rich the experience of an American university can be.

On Wednesday nights, I teach a section of Freshman Honors Seminar that is designed to take fifteen bright but inexperienced former high school seniors and help them become sophisticated, curious scholars eager to lap up everything the university has to offer. My job is to provide a sampling of activities that will whet their intellectual appetites.

Some meetings are more successful than others, such as the Wednesday when I took them to a drama department production of Cole Porter's *Anything Goes*. Hardly intellectual, you say. Remember, please, that this generation grew up watching *Mean Streets* on the late-night movie instead of *Monkey Business*. Remember, too, the subtle finesse of Porter's lyrics:

> *You're the nimble tread of the feet of Fred Astaire,*
> *You're an O'Neill drama,*
> *You're Whistler's mama,*
> *You're Camembert!*

Throw in the screwball plot, the period splendor of a transatlantic liner, and some of the most energetic tap dancing I've seen on any stage, and you have the ingredients for a grand night at the theater.

At one point, I looked down the row and saw the students' faces reflecting the bright stage lighting—each one focused intently on the action, completely engaged, smiles in various degrees adorning their features. They were hooked, and I was delighted. This would have been reward enough, but I must admit I was having at least as much fun. I confess that I am an absolute sucker for musicals, and this one was no exception. I blinked back tears of joy at finding so much talent onstage, so much energy so effortlessly released, right here at my university. Oh, to be that young again. After an eighteen-hour day, I left the theater completely rejuvenated.

The next morning, I was at the airport for a different sort of university assignment. A few weeks earlier, the dean had told me that the school of music would receive a substantial bequest from an alumni couple who were then in their eighties. The university wanted to plan a special event to thank them and had hit upon the idea of taking the music school, or more precisely a representative of the music school, to them. I was asked to join the chancellor and members of the development office in Massachusetts for the occasion.

This time, my exhilaration came in meeting a couple who were about to give their entire estate to a university music school. They knew the money would be used by talented young people who would eventually contribute to humankind through their creativity. They were quite comfortable talking in such terms: they believed that music is one of the blessings of humanity, that the greatest good of all is beauty, and that they could leave no more important legacy than an endowment for music scholarships. As they talked about their reasons for giving the money, they let their emotions show. There were tears of happiness that their money would nurture talent, as well as tears of relief that the decision had been made and that when the end came, a part of them would live on in many lives for many lifetimes, engaged in making beautiful music.

Less than twelve hours earlier, I had been immersed in the energy of youth, and here I came face to face with a couple in the winter of life, who nevertheless exuded a glowing warmth of spirit. I believe all of us in attendance felt how lucky we were that a university brought us together.

The final event in this three-day stretch came on Friday when I gave a speech for the faculty at the Remembrance Scholars Convocation. A bit of history is in order. Only days before Christmas in 1988, terrorists bombed Pan Am Flight 103 as it flew over Lockerbie, Scotland, en route to the United States. There were thirty-five students from Syracuse University on that flight, returning home for the holidays from a semester of study abroad. Within a year, the university established thirty-five scholarships to be awarded annually to rising seniors in memory of those who were lost. Each fall, a week of remembrance activities leads up to the convocation, a solemn ceremony attended by parents of the victims, the new scholars and their parents, and a goodly representation of the campus community.

Giving that speech was a real challenge. What I said doesn't matter here. What is so noteworthy is that the members of this university family have chosen to address the tragedy head-on. This happened to *our* students: these parents lost *their* children in an unspeakably useless act of violence. The grieving continues, as does the healing. The Remembrance Scholarships celebrate the best and the brightest among our students and remind us that values such as idealism and courage are to be cherished and nurtured. It is good to assemble once a year and say these things. It is good to admit that, yes, we are a family, albeit a large and incredibly diverse one.

The ceremony ended with the alma mater, and for the first time I understood why we refer to the university as "mater."

IX

■ On Composers

In his book *Sound in Motion*, David McGill begins a chapter titled "Selflessness" with the statement "Art falls into two main categories: binary and ternary."

By this, he means that certain arts, like painting and sculpture, require only the creator and the viewer, but music requires three: composer, *performer*, and listener. In times past, the composer was much more likely to be a performer as well, but for at least the past century, most composers have needed performers to bring their music to life. Exceptions to the rule, like Rachmaninoff or Rzewski, are rare. Even these two composer/pianists had many other performer advocates during their lifetimes, from Horowitz and Moiseiwitsch to Hamelin and Igor Levit.

Since the entire pantheon of composers from the common practice period is no longer with us, the task falls on performers to keep their music alive. McGill raised an important point: performers cannot be "selfless" if they are to do more than play the right notes at the right time at the prescribed dynamic level. Re-creators are essential to music's transmission.

Over the years I wrote for *Clavier*, I occasionally offered odes to various composers—thankful for their existence, in awe of their accomplishment, and sometimes marking their anniversaries. The entirety of Western music is beholden to J. S. Bach—how could one let the three hundredth anniversary of his birth go by without a love letter?

Other times, I wrote about my studio's deeper dives into milestones of the repertoire. It's hard not to celebrate getting closer to the twenty-four preludes and fugues of the *Well-Tempered Clavier, Book I*, or the twenty-four études by Frédéric Chopin.

The two essays on Aaron Copland reflect both my own affection for his music as well as his ninetieth birthday, a date he barely outlived. We have now passed his 122nd birthday! It will be interesting to see if his music attracts performers in the future. Another essay, written early in my teaching career, bemoans the routinization of the repertoire. Even then, I'd heard certain pieces so often that I created a list of "Nobody's Old Favorites" to encourage varietal spice in programming. A more recent essay looks at how "modern music" can bring the great music of the past into the present.

Central to all we do are the composers, the creators who have devoted their souls' metaphorical blood as well as literal sweat and tears to a composition's fruition. Brahms gave nearly twenty years to his First Symphony before he felt it worthy of performance. To do the composer justice, performers need to understand the role of every note. The original conceiver has brought these compositions to existence from absolute silence. A tall order? Yes. But playing the right notes at the right time at the prescribed dynamic level barely begins the journey.

46

J. S. Bach at Three Hundred

The View from the Second Floor

MARCH 1985

On March 21, 1685, a son was born in Eisenach to Johann Ambrosius Bach and his wife, Elisabeth, née Lämmerhirt. He was the eighth and last child of their union, and like the children of the Bach family for generations, he was to become a musician. No one in the family could possibly have imagined the musical heights that this child named Johann Sebastian would explore. There had never been a composer whose work summed up all of music history until that point. That there hasn't been such a composer since is perhaps the reason the world is now celebrating the birth of Johann Sebastian Bach three hundred years ago.

Bach was wholly of his own time. He took the forms and ideas available to him and worked with them, exercising no criticism on the media of artistic expression lying at hand, feeling no compulsion to find new musical paths. His contemporaries thought him anachronistic, so conservative was he in his approach to compositional style.

He represents the pinnacle of contrapuntal writing. The essence of counterpoint is simultaneity of voices, preternatural control of resources, seemingly endless inventiveness. In counterpoint a melody is always in the process of being repeated by one or another voice; the result is horizontal rather than vertical music. Any series of notes is thus capable of an infinite set of transformations, taken up first by one voice, then by another, fragmented into submelodies, transposed, augmented. The voices sound against as well as with all the others. Instead of a melody at the top being supported by the thicker harmonic texture beneath (as in most nineteenth-century music), Bach's contrapuntal music is composed of several equal lines, sinuously interwoven, working themselves out according to stringent rules.

The rules of counterpoint are demanding, and Bach made himself their master. Who else would make a musical offering of ten puzzle canons and a six-voice ricercar based on a theme to its composer, the ruler of Prussia, Frederick II? Who else could write the forty-eight preludes and fugues of the *Well-Tempered Clavier* and never once repeat himself musically? Each fugue is its own world, each sufficient unto itself.

Need it be said that he was as prolific as he was masterful? In the keyboard music alone, most of which was written between 1717 and 1722 when he was court composer in Cöthen, we find *six* English Suites, *six* French Suites, *fifteen* Inventions, and *fifteen* Sinfonias, each exploring a different tonality, each bringing to life a motive completely characteristic to the individual work in question. It has been said that once Bach began the process of working out an idea—for example, of the solo violin partita—he was not satisfied until he had worked it out several different ways, exhausting the idea itself by creating musical structures that have lasted for all time.

According to Albert Schweitzer, Bach himself was not conscious of the extraordinary greatness of his work. His sole intent was to offer to his God whatever praise could be contained in his music.

> Music is an act of worship with Bach. His artistic activity and his personality are both based on piety. If he is to be understood from any standpoint at all, it is this. For him, art was religion, and so had no concern with the world or worldly success. It was an end in itself. Bach includes religion in the definition of art in general. All great art, even secular, is itself religious in his eyes; for him, the tones do not perish, but ascend to God like praise too deep for utterance.[1]

Happily, Bach was also quite human. His portraits show him to be a man plain of visage, nearsighted (blind in late life), and rather puffy in a friendly way in the cheeks and smile. He was known to be a sharp man where money was concerned: in a 1729 letter, he cannot help showing his indignation over that unusually healthy year, when the Leipzigers "took so little pleasure in dying that the burial fees brought the cantor a hundred less thalers than usual." He was even prone to

---

1. Albert Schweitzer was a theologian, organist, musicologist, writer, humanitarian, philosopher, and physician. His two-volume biography, *J. S. Bach*, was first published in 1911. He was awarded the Nobel Peace Prize in 1952.

arguments and political maneuverings in Leipzig with a certain Görner, whom Schweitzer describes as an "arrogant but insignificant musician," over which of them would be hired to conduct the university services.

For the performer today, playing Bach's music can be a joy, but it is often a perilous attempt at crossing the veritable minefield of performance practice research, arguments over the authenticity of editions, and that perennial question, Should one play Bach on the piano at all? This last question can absolutely paralyze the pianist. Once again, though, Schweitzer offers a solution that will even give the harpsichord purist pause:

> The characteristic of Bach's piano [*sic*] and organ style is precisely this, that he demands from the keyed instruments the same aptitudes for phrasing and modulation as the strings. At bottom he conceived everything for an ideal instrument, that had all the keyed instruments' possibilities of polyphonic playing, and all the bowed instruments' capacities for phrasing.[2]

Pianists, take heart!

While it has become fashionable to celebrate the round-numbered birthdays of the major composers, I think there is a deeper reason for our particular interest in Bach at this time. The zeitgeist has a way of reminding us of what is not right in our lives. Today we are aware of a spiritual apathy caused by the helplessness we feel in our attempt to affect the world around us. Violence and senselessness are closer to each of us than ever before. It is a far cry from the world of Johann Sebastian Bach and his music.

In 1845, in an attempt to interest the world in Bach's cantatas, Johann Theodor Mosewius, a contemporary of Mendelssohn, wrote the following: "One thing is needful. An inner unity of soul is absolutely indispensable in performing Bach, and every individual chorister must not only have thoroughly mastered the work technically but must preserve his spiritual forces unbroken throughout."[3]

Yes, Mosewius, it is more needful than ever.

---

2. Albert Schweitzer, *J. S. Bach*, vol. 1, 385.
3. Albert Schweitzer, *J. S. Bach*, vol. 2, 468.

47

The Well-Tempered

Out of the Woods

MARCH 2000

Fifteen years ago, in my first year of writing for *Clavier*, I began my column:

> On March 21, 1685, a son was born in Eisenach to Johann Ambrosius Bach and his wife, Elisabeth, née Lämmerhirt. He was the eighth and last child of their union, and like the children of the Bach family for generations, he was to become a musician. No one in the family could possibly have imagined the musical heights that this child named Johann Sebastian would explore. There had never been a composer whose work summed up all of music history until that point. That there hasn't been such a composer since is perhaps the reason the world is now celebrating the birth of Johann Sebastian Bach three hundred years ago.

That final sentence rings as true today as it did fifteen years ago, and so the music world this year will commemorate the 250th anniversary of Bach's death. We are a hero-worshipping species, especially in round-numbered years. It's easy to poke fun at our fetish for anniversaries, but our obsession runs deeper than marketing concerts; our need to honor our heroes is greater than ever. New ones aren't exactly knocking the door down.

Unfortunately, all that honoring takes its toll. Think of the abysmally played Bach you have heard. Recall the mechanical evenness and ugly sound of some, the emotional detachment often justified in the name of historical practice. It's amazing how rude we are to our heroes.

In an effort to make feeble amends in our tiny speck of the musical world, the Weirich studio is currently immersed in the first book of the

Well-Tempered Clavier. On Bach's birthday, March 21, twelve students will present their findings to the public as each plays a pair of preludes and fugues. There will be no attempt at a more-authentic-than-thou performance; the goal is simply to make living music.

This has been a group effort. Rather than learn pieces individually and in a vacuum, we studied the music in weekly group sessions, sometimes analyzing, sometimes singing the fugues *a cappella.* At other times, we listened to recordings of the *WTC* and of cantatas, pieces for organ or violin solo, and even concerto movements. The idea has been to rid ourselves of the accrued dogma of playing Bach. If this music is so good, then let's find out why. Perhaps in the process, we will learn something about all music—which, if you read Bach's preface to the *WTC*, is exactly what he intended.

The first prelude is a case in point. Easy enough to play that a child can manage the notes, it nonetheless challenges the most sophisticated artist. It could serve as a primer for tonal harmony, for the rules of voice leading, for the magic of asymmetry. (All the phrases but one in the piece are four bars long.) Despite the simplicity of the harmonic language, all twelve tones of the chromatic scale appear in the piece. It comes at the beginning of the book, standing like a musical Table of the Elements before the more complex pieces to follow.

Looking now at just such a challenge, the C-sharp minor fugue is astonishingly dense: five voices; three different subjects; at 115 bars, the second longest in the *WTC.* Albert Schweitzer, among others, pointed out that by drawing a line between the C-sharp that begins the four-note subject and the final D-sharp, then drawing a similar line between the two inner notes (B-sharp and E), a cross is visible. Perhaps this is looking too hard for symbolism, but surely it can be no accident that Bach uses the theme later in the crucifixion choruses of the St. John and St. Matthew Passions. The class unearthed many such coincidences in its research, leading to a far greater emotional understanding of these supposedly abstract and scholarly preludes and fugues.

Alongside profundity one also finds lightness, joyfulness, even humor. The world as encompassed in the *WTC* is as many-hued as the one in which we live. We should not, however, imagine an ivory-towered artist creating it above the bustle of everyday life. Bach reused a lot of old material, slightly revising eleven preludes from the little book for Wilhelm Friedemann. In one of his most practical maneuvers, he simply added a key signature of six sharps to a fugue already written in D minor to produce the complement to the E-flat minor prelude (thus explaining that enharmonic curiosity). This is the pragmatic collection of a busy, frugal composer, whose leftovers were too good to throw out. Mixed with newly-rustled-up preludes and fugues for the occasion, this is a meal fit for almost three centuries of students of every persuasion. Beethoven cut his teeth on it. In our humble way today in my studio, we sit at the table tasting its delicacies, savoring its flavors and nourishment.

Unfortunately, the 1722 autograph has not survived. Today, scholars produce urtext editions from a 1732 copy in Bach's handwriting and from copies made by his wife Anna Magdalena, his son Wilhelm Friedemann, his son-in-law Altnikol, and his student Kirnberger. Publication came only in 1800. Imagine the task of copying out the music, seated at a desk with candlelight, dipping a pen into ink, going from the original copy to the one you are making. Contemplate being one of the few people on earth who even knew of its existence. I wonder what it would have felt like to be one of these people.

Imagine yourself copying out the C minor fugue and then having lunch with the man who wrote it. He didn't know he was a hero. Then go to the piano, and play this music as you would the music of a friend. I think Bach would like that.

48

Copland I

The View from the Second Floor

NOVEMBER 1990

At this late date, Aaron Copland hardly needs another article for his bibliography; he was dubbed the dean of American composers fifty years ago. Still, this most honored of our native musical creators has not had an easy time of it. Some of his most significant compositions, especially the works for piano, have achieved only grudging acceptance into the repertoire, and his career has suffered other setbacks, suggesting that even the most successful composers today live with uncertainty.

This month Copland joins the estimable ranks of nonagenarians. The celebrations will be quiet; there were major media events for both the seventy-fifth and eightieth birthdays, and ill health now confines Copland to his home. He has not written a new piece since the early 1970s. Nevertheless, if an average music-lover were asked to name a living American composer, my guess is that Copland would be the first name to come to mind.

Perhaps it is because his music is so, for want of a better word, American. He waves no flag, even in a piece as overtly historical as *Lincoln Portrait*, and uses folk melody only in the ballets to add local color. Most of his music is starkly abstract yet redolent of whatever it means to be an American. It is cleansed of affectation and overrefinement; plain faced, it keeps its distance yet haunts the memory.

Copland's three major works for the piano are masterpieces that more than hold their own on a program of standard repertoire. The earliest of these, the Piano Variations of 1930, still sounds shockingly skeletal, its textures confined to the bare necessities of pitch and rhythm. It seems to invent itself as it goes, using only the most elemental materials. Unlike European music, it forsakes lyrical growth; instead, the piece develops rigorously from a four-note declamatory motive. The variations arise from such abstract compositional techniques as canon, inversion, diminution, augmentation, and transposition of notes to widely separated octaves. There is no accompaniment; the infrequent chords all come from the theme. At the risk of imposing too personal an interpretation, I wonder if Copland used this music to make a philosophical statement about our country and its dilemma in 1930. Reflecting the depths of the Great Depression and a mechanized, impersonal society facing an existential unknown, the music seems to suggest not only that the pleasant melodies of the past were no longer to be trusted but that much could still be made of the spare, raw material, though far from beautiful by traditional standards. Despite the percussive piano textures and the strictness of compositional control, one finds at the heart of the Piano Variations a Spartan nobility, an intensely human courage.

The Piano Sonata, written between 1939 and 1941, represents Copland at the height of his powers, fresh from his first popular successes with *Rodeo* and *Billy the Kid*. While less harmonically ascetic than the Variations, the Sonata is still an uncompromising work. The three movements chart a psychological journey from the tense, predominantly chordal material of the first movement ("Molto moderato"), through the skittering restlessness of the scherzo ("Vivace"), to a final movement ("Andante sostenuto") that seems to absorb and transform the uneasiness of the previous movements into what Wilfrid Mellers called "a quintessential expression of immobility."

The opening chords of the first movement suggest both a blues inflection and the strictness of a Puritan hymn. These mighty harmonies lurch across the page in jerky syncopations; melody is nonexistent. Despite a second theme with a hint of lyricism (marked "with sentiment"), the movement explores a world of unmistakable alienation. Out of the desolation of the first movement's close rises the basic material of the scherzo, a perky questioning motive in five-eight that soon begins to divide and re-form itself like cells gone berserk. This surface rhythmic energy, however, is held in check by an extremely slow harmonic rhythm. Frustration builds as the motives combine and collide, apparently going nowhere. Suddenly the music explodes, only to subside into a trio stuck in reiterations of an ostinato built on sixths. Two fragments of song tentatively emerge, only to disappear with the return of the scherzo material, but a seed has been planted. It flowers in the final movement: both melodic fragments are allowed to blossom, and the relief of tension to both performer and audience is palpable. The hymn theme of the first movement returns with its attendant spiritual unease, but through a long passage, like the swing of some cosmic pendulum, Copland resolves the initial motive, bringing the entire structure of the piece together in the final measures.

The *Piano Fantasy* of 1955–57 is perhaps the most remarkable of all Copland's compositions. It is the least known of the three major piano works, and its lack of acceptance illustrates one of the dilemmas Copland has faced in his career. I will discuss the *Fantasy* and conclude these thoughts on Copland and his piano music in a future issue.

49

Copland II

The View from the Second Floor

FEBRUARY 1991

Aaron Copland died on December 2, 1990. As I wrote the first part of these reflections on his piano music for the November *Clavier*, it didn't occur to me that the second part would be an obituary. He seemed invincible, a rock in uncertain times. His death made front-page news, but it is as if a giant had slipped quietly away, not wanting anyone to notice. Because he stopped composing in the early 1970s, we mourn that his voice will now be forever silent. Who is there left to admire? Can the music world afford to lose many more heroes?

Copland was not always lionized. In the '20s, as a young composer, plenty of detractors abhorred this brash New Yorker who employed jazz rhythms in serious concert music. Later, riding the crest of approval for such works as *Appalachian Spring, Billy the Kid*, and the Third Symphony, he began using the compositional principles of the twelve-tone school. This time he was taken to task by both sides: the conservative public thought he had abandoned them, and the avant-garde shunned him for coming too late to the twelve-tone fold. Leonard Bernstein is quoted in the *New York Times*: "When he started writing 12-tone, I figured it was inevitable. Everybody has to fool with serialism. But still I asked him, 'Of all people, why you—you who are so instinctive, so spontaneous.' And he answered me: 'Because I need more chords. I've run out of chords.'"

A paucity of chords wasn't Copland's only trouble: three days before Dwight Eisenhower's first presidential inauguration, Copland learned that his *Lincoln Portrait* had been withdrawn from the inaugural concert. Congressman Fred E. Busbey had questioned Copland's patriotism in a speech in the House, frightening the event's organizers. A few months later, Copland was subpoenaed by the House Un-American Affairs Committee for his association with the likes of Serge Koussevitsky,

Dmitri Shostakovich, and Marc Blitzstein. Copland spent only two hours before the committee, but the stigma affected his career for years afterward. As late as 1960, the Dallas Symphony received anonymous cards protesting a Copland concert.

The *Piano Fantasy* (1955–57) was conceived during these personal and artistic crises. The work represents a search for new musical expression by a composer who needed more chords, who was not content to rewrite the same piece over and over. Copland's use of the twelve-tone system is entirely personal; most of the musical material of the *Fantasy* comes from the first ten notes of the row, and the final two notes (E and G-sharp, forming a major third) are used only for cadential purposes. There is much that is tonal about the *Piano Fantasy*; curiously, it is Copland's most melodic piano work, more overtly tuneful than either the Variations or the Sonata.

A single movement spanning over thirty minutes, the *Piano Fantasy* is an immense structure in three large sections (slow, fast, slow). In the opening, the notes of the ten-note row peal forth one at a time, as if announcing the elemental participants in the drama to come. Then enormous chords ring out, collections of the pitches in the row. The melodic and harmonic framework of the piece thus established, the declamatory opening gives way to a nagging, questioning motive (marked "restless, hesitant") that signals the onset of the work's journey into uncharted territory. The music develops as it proceeds, not so much through the Second Viennese School's technique of continual variation as by an almost improvisatory process that discovers the row at opportune moments, like a signpost marking the way.

The fast section beginning in measure 296 is reminiscent of the scherzo of the Piano Sonata in its jazzy syncopations and angular, irregular meters. Building to a wild intensity, the music abruptly stops short at the work's halfway point, as if the futility of the mad dash were suddenly obvious. The piece seems to laugh at itself here, nervously chuckling as it wonders how to resume the journey. After briefly recalling the fast section's opening material (marked "sotto voce, 'muttering'"), the music gets back on track, and gradually the color of augmented triads begins to vie for predominance with the row. A battle is soon joined, and the alien material overcomes the row, shouting its temporary triumph in a violent climax at measure 812. A reworking of earlier material in a new transposition leads to a hauntingly quiet passage of great beauty and folklike simplicity. Gradually the row's original melody reemerges, slowly but inexorably building to the return of the opening's clangorous chords. The power of this final climax is shattering, leaving in its wake only the cadential major third and ripples of melody from the earlier quiet passage. The work ends *pppp, da lontano*.

Copland wrote, "An artist can take his personal sadness or his fear or his anger or his joy and crystallize it, giving it a life of its own. The arts offer the opportunity to do something that cannot be done anywhere else. It is the only place one can express in public the feelings ordinarily regarded as private. It is the place where a man or a woman can be completely honest, where we can say whatever is in our hearts or minds, where we never need to hide from ourselves or from others."

We can only be thankful that Copland had the courage to reach for such honesty through his music, and as in all great music, perhaps we can find it there too.

50

Mozart

The View from the Second Floor

DECEMBER 1991

O Mozart, immortal Mozart, how many, how infinitely many inspiring suggestions of a finer, better life have you left our souls.

—Franz Schubert, Diary, 1816

In this late year of the twentieth century, the music world must find itself especially needful, for we have been celebrating the *death* of a composer over a concert season. Mozart is everywhere these days: PBS has broadcast concerts and operas, Lincoln Center will offer every note of his music before the year is out, and commemorative recordings abound in the CD bins at the mall. Not long ago, I walked into a truck stop off one of the interstates to pay for gas and a cup of coffee for the road, and there on a rack with Roy Orbison, Johnny Cash, and Bonnie Raitt was a *Mozart's Greatest Hits* cassette, its cellophane thumb-smudged by curious hands.

There has always been something mythic about Mozart, this man who lived only thirty-five years, born January 27, 1756, the seventh and last child of Leopold and Anna Maria Mozart. Five of his siblings died in infancy; how remarkable that he was the one to survive.

There is no explaining such things. He wrote his first pieces at the age of five. Between 1763 and 1766 he journeyed with his father and sister to the musical capitals of Europe. He appeared before Louis XV at the age of seven. George III of England gave him difficult keyboard tests when his family came to London. He wrote a one-act opera when he was twelve. His five violin concerti were all composed in 1775; he happened to be nineteen.

He succeeded in every genre of composition, from opera to string chamber music to concerti to sacred music to solo keyboard sonatas. His quintet for piano and winds, K. 452, was one of his favorites; he wrote nothing else for that ensemble, but when he turned to it, out came a masterpiece for the ages. That musician's bible of his works, the Köchel catalogue, lists 626 compositions written in roughly thirty years. There is no denying his genius.

Still, he must have worked very hard. How else explain eight piano concerti between March 15, 1784, and March 9, 1785, as well as the aforementioned quintet, three string quartets, two violin-and-piano sonatas, and two of his finest sets of piano variations? The final three symphonies were written one after the other in the summer of 1788. His opera *Così fan tutte* came to life in the last four months of 1789. During the same period, he also completed three concert arias, a set of twelve minuets and another set of twelve German dances for chamber orchestra, not to mention the Clarinet Quintet, a work that alone would make the reputation of any composer.

This bespeaks more than hard work aided by even the most rarefied genius. One wonders what fueled him, what obsession burned within him to produce so much in so little time. The times were fickle; one would think that the composer of *Le nozze di Figaro* (1786) and *Don Giovanni* (1787) would never have to worry about his next commission. Yet he had to wait until 1789—two years in which his career stalled at its apogee, forcing him to move his family from one dwelling to another to avoid his creditors—before *Figaro* was revived in Vienna and the Emperor remembered to ask him for something new. The result was *Così*.

It is tempting to call it a miracle, yet he was flesh and blood with human needs and foibles. He must have worked ceaselessly. My guess is that he had little choice; the music streamed through his creativity, arriving in the reality of eighteenth-century Europe like the birth of Venus. It was very much of its time, the style understood by every listener.

Any of the contemporary composers could have put those notes and rhythms together, yet only Mozart did it...again and again and again.

That the music still has reality to the twentieth century is the miracle to me. Few of us, if any, are born with an understanding of his style in our bones. Furthermore, we live in an age of specialization, where scholars of the authentic-performance movement are searching for a deeper truth about Mozart's music. We tend not to trust our judgment without the approval of the experts.

What interests me is that somewhere out there on the interstates, an eighteen-wheeler is rumbling across the land with Mozart pouring from the cab speakers, and someone who knows nothing about a proper appoggiatura is discovering a beauty that transcends even the incongruity of the situation.

Let there be no doubt: Mozart lives.

51

Chamber Music

Out of the Woods

OCTOBER 1997

In twelve years of writing a column for *Clavier*, I've never written a love song to chamber music. This comes as a surprise, since a lot of my musical attention focuses on the grand and glorious repertoire for piano *and* strings and/or winds. Having just come off a summer immersed in this uniquely cooperative art, the time has come for a valentine, however out of season.

No one will argue with the greatness of the music. The uniqueness comes from the fact that one must have partners to perform the music. The path to a performance requires rehearsing together; when a group of musicians are really making chamber music in the best sense, the rehearsals are more fun than the performance.

But I am ahead of myself. This ode to chamber music must begin with the fact that the repertoire is vast, and that which involves the piano is among the greatest of all. As if the lucky pianist did not have a lifetime's work in the thirty-two Beethoven sonatas for solo piano, the master from Bonn also wrote challenging, absorbing piano parts in his ten sonatas for violin, the five sonatas for cello, and the seven piano trios. The forty-five piano trios of Haydn probably contain more truly great music than the fifty-two solo keyboard sonatas. The two piano quartets of Mozart and the quintet for piano and winds are on the same level as his greatest piano concerti. The trios (five) and quartets (three) of Brahms—not to mention his sonatas for violin (three), clarinet (two), and cello (two)—are superb works, each a masterpiece, and his quintet for piano and strings must rank as one of the great works of music, period. The ode could easily go on to the trios of Mendelssohn and Schubert; Fauré's quartets; the quintets of Schumann, Franck, Dvořák, Shostakovich...How can I stop? There is so much rewarding music to learn and play, and more is being written every day, the implications of which we will return to in a bit.

It takes two to tango, however, and in the case of chamber music, anywhere from two to eight or nine. More than that needs a designated leader, but you'd be surprised how many pieces can be done quite successfully without an actual conductor (Copland's *Appalachian Spring* in the version for thirteen instruments, for example). It is this quality of partnership or teamwork that is chamber music's most intriguing characteristic. Unlike solo playing, you can't go it alone. To be a successful chamber player, one's "interpretation" must take into account both the musical and personal considerations of the other players. For someone who has grown up an only-child soloist, sitting down to dinner with a family of musical siblings can be a shock.

It is difficult to talk or write about these subtleties of working together. If it were easier, we could all name the great teachers of chamber music or give a list of how-to books to our students. The mentors of chamber music are simply more-experienced colleagues; they do not teach so much as invite you along for the ride, and they insist on sharing the driving. Playing chamber music, you switch roles often, sometimes accompanying, other times leading. The joy comes not only from knowing your role and doing it well but from pushing the limits. "Just how slowly can I play the first four bars of the 'Adagio' and still allow the horn to play the next four bars in one breath?…Can I match the articulation of the violin's sixteenth notes when I answer her two-bar phrase?…Will I catch the cellist's change of tone color at the recapitulation and match it instantly?" In chamber music, one needs to constantly be at a peak of musical awareness.

The personal interplay in a chamber group can be intense. Playing a sonata with another person is like an intimate conversation; increase the size of the ensemble to a trio or quartet, and the group dynamics expand exponentially. If one person in the group is withdrawn or gloomy, it affects everyone. Similarly, one giant ego can make life miserable for the rest of the ensemble. At Marlboro, Rudolf Serkin used to put the puffed-up soloist in a group with a couple of hardcore chamber players who could sandpaper the inexperienced virtuoso into submission—a sort of enforced group therapy that he believed served both the music and the musicians.

Much more often, though, playing chamber music creates joyous, long-term friendships.

This summer I played in the Poulenc Sextet, in which the group's biggest problem was containing our laughter at rehearsals. On another occasion, I joined in the Brahms Horn Trio, in which both other players knew the work inside out. The first reading was good enough to be the performance, and with each succeeding rehearsal, the trust and pleasure among us only increased. By the end, we had all learned something new about the piece from each other.

Chamber music is a lovely metaphor for life; we figure out our role(s) and then how to best interact with the people closest to us. If we can discuss and resolve differences of opinion, so much the better. If we meet up with a wise and experienced mentor who makes it all seem easy, then we can really count our blessings.

It may well be that the concertgoing public somehow senses all this because people are flocking to chamber music series and festivals all over the country. I believe it is safe to say that these days chamber music concerts outnumber solo recitals by a significant margin. In the old days, audiences wanted the bigger-than-life personality—the fire-breathing, death-defying, orchestra-conquering titan of the keyboard. The rock scene now provides the theatrics in music; I believe the classical audience has matured in its taste, and while delighting in an occasional dip with the Three Tenors, it has moved on, believe it or not, to chamber music. The corporate and professional world in which the audience works places a high premium on teamwork, the very thing that is on display right there on stage. The product: beautiful music achieved with apparently seamless cooperation. No wonder it's popular. To cement the argument, I offer the fact that contemporary composers are writing more chamber music than pieces for soloists. Why? It is much more likely to be performed.

The ode could continue, but the point is best made by trying it yourself. All you need to do is call a couple friends, set a date, and practice your part. Then the fun really begins; you might even fall in love.

52

Chopin Étude Project

Winds of Change

March–April 2011

In the ongoing effort to stimulate my students, I have occasionally tried an all-studio repertoire project. For example, in the winter of 2009, my students performed two recitals devoted to the complete solo piano music of Maurice Ravel. This turned out to be a splendid choice: two quite advanced students had already undertaken *Gaspard de la Nuit* and *Le tombeau de Couperin*, another had two movements of *Miroirs* scheduled for her recital, and another was working on *Sonatine*. Yet another had played *Valses nobles et sentimentales* the previous year. From there it wasn't that difficult to assign the remaining pieces: difficult shorter works went to graduate students, easier shorter works to undergrads, including three freshmen that year. Ravel's solo piano music fits on two seventy-plus-minute CDs, so it's not like undertaking all the Beethoven sonatas or the complete solo works by Brahms. We learned a lot from the experience and at the same time bonded as a group more intensely than weekly studio classes permit.

This year, the studio's population had changed enough that I thought it time to try another project and, over the summer, hit on the idea of tackling the twenty-four Chopin études contained in opuses 10 and 25. There were thirteen students, two with rather small hands, so my concept was that eleven students would play two études apiece, with the remaining two going to the students who had never before been grateful for petite hands. "How hard could it be?" I thought. With barely more than an hour's worth of music to learn, and everyone knowing the études from years of aural familiarity if not digital experience, and no one having to play more than two études, I thought this would be relatively easy. And with a December 2010 recital date, we'd even get in under the wire of the two hundredth anniversary of Chopin's birth.

The first sign of trouble came in the opening lessons of the fall semester. I had emailed everyone their assignments in June, but curiously, hardly anyone brought their études to the first lesson. In ensuing weeks, they started trickling into the studio, one at a time, at very slow, labored tempos. As optimistic as I had been, I wasn't expecting miracles, and so with each étude we set to work solving the technical problem, developing practice methods, searching for the musical poetry latent in the forest of notes. It was stimulating work, but slow. Progress was even slower. I'm rather ashamed to admit, given my years of teaching experience, that I thought the students would gobble up these études like so many potato chips. Had I given it more thought, I might have remembered that Chris—the kind of student who would be a star in any studio and whose *Gaspard* left jaws on the floor wherever he played it—had only partial success with the first étude (Op. 10, No. 1) when he attempted it.

Chris had moved on to graduate school elsewhere, and Op. 10, No. 1 fell to Daniel, whose enormous hand would have less trouble with it (or so I thought) than anyone else in the studio. Dear JingYi—she of the quick, precise, Chinese-trained fingers—had Op. 10, No. 2. Trevor, the poetic freshman, landed Op. 10, No. 3; fiery Noah caught a break with No. 4 since he had already played it but was determined to play it better this time. And so on—every student, all with distinct stories, matched to études that seemed to have wills of their own. In making the assignments, I tried to be sensitive to difficulty levels. So if a student ended up with a handful like Op. 10, No. 7, which fell to sophomore Kent, the other étude was supposed to be "easier"—in Kent's case, Op. 25, No. 4, one of the least-often played. We discovered the reason for this paucity of performance: it's just as difficult as any of the études—it only sounds easier. Indeed, Kent probably had more trouble with his "easy" étude than with the ever-formidable Op. 10, No. 7.

About six weeks into the semester, I realized we would need a booster rocket if this project was ever to get off the ground. My former Peabody colleague and distinguished Chopinist Ann Schein was in the neighborhood for another residency, and we were lucky enough to invite her to give us an all-day session on the études in mid-November. With her arrival imminent, everyone's practice seemed to go into high gear. Ann knows the études as only someone who learned them all at age twelve can. To say that her seven hours with us was humbling understates the case by a factor of ten. As hard as I had tried to solve the problems in these pieces for my students, there could be no substitute for the years of familiarity Ann had with them. She couldn't solve the problems either— it was simply the years of working on them, of knowing each note in the body, mind, and soul. Everyone but Ann was exhausted at the end of that day. She could have gone on all night!

We had to get up the next morning, though, and push on to the performance. Lessons and studio classes became wall-to-wall Chopin études. Yet another difficulty reared its ugly head as we began to imagine the recital experience itself: sitting down cold and playing the fast études is like diving into an icy, turbulent sea and swimming for your life. There could be no warm-up—just coming onstage and playing two minutes of dizzyingly intricate pianistic patterns…cadence…bow. Then someone else does it all again, through two sets of twelve. This was not a recipe for a delightful recital experience for either performers or listeners. So, with our lemons we made lemonade. I took on the role of genial host, seated comfortably in a chair to the side of the stage, and talked to the audience about the whole project, about what it's like to learn these pieces, about what goes into performing one. This took some of the pressure off since we were giving the audience a glimpse into the process rather than presenting a finished product. I said that mistakes were permitted—everyone had a "Get Out of Jail Free" card. And why not? The impossible demand for perfection every time we step on stage is paralyzing. Perhaps we would have a better connection to our audiences if they were more aware of just how difficult it is to play in public. Perhaps more students of all ages would continue to make music if they weren't afraid of making a mistake.

As it turned out, not many cards were needed. Daniel practically aced Op. 10, No. 1, and was greeted by a high five from his teacher as he left the stage. Noah wailed through Nos. 4 and 5, earning personal bests in each. Chelsea traced the intricate chromatics of No. 6 and arrived safely ashore. Kent nailed No. 7, and Charl delighted with No. 8. I cannot mention everyone but must give Vicky a special honor for conquering her fear of the dreaded "Double Thirds" étude in Op. 25, performing it with great assurance only a few weeks after giving birth to her first child.

Everyone conquered inner demons that day. The project of mastering the Chopin études will continue for years for all of us, but on that one day, we could all say we had at least begun the process.

53

Nobody's Old Favorites

The View from the Second Floor

DECEMBER 1986

This is my tenth year of college teaching. That's not a long time as teaching careers go. In fact, I usually take the attitude that I'm just getting started. There is one thing, though, that makes me feel like I've been teaching since the Paleozoic period, and that is the 13,251st student performance of the G Minor Ballade. The 27,094th "Waldstein" does it, too, and if I never hear the Khachaturian Toccata again in an audition, it will be too soon.

There's a reason we hear pieces such as those so often: they are good pieces (except the Khachaturian, of course, and it is surely a sign of the moral degeneracy of our times that that piece ever became popular). A student, even an artist, learns much tackling the most standard fare in the repertoire. Who would deny that the G Minor Ballade is a terrific piece, loaded with almost everything you need to know about Chopin to get a BM degree? I love the G Minor Ballade—I've played it and taught it, more often than I care to admit.

The same can be said for the top fifty greatest piano warhorses. We all love the Liszt B Minor (well, most of us); *Carnaval* makes us giddy with delight. But isn't it possible that we have had too much of these good things? How many repetitions can the greatest masterwork bear before it wears out? Or more precisely, How many repetitions can our ears bear before they can no longer truly hear?

There is a way around this dilemma, and before recital season starts in earnest, I would like to make a plea for programming works that aren't heard so often. There is nothing new in this idea: the *New York Times* critics propose it once every ninety days or so. Sometimes they even admit that the suggestion arises from the fact that they break out in hives with the mere mention of another Beethoven's Fifth "from one of the world's great orchestras." The amazing thing to me is that we music teachers hear four or five times as much music daily as the busiest music critic, and yet we assign the same pieces over and over. Sometimes I think we have hidden desires to man an assembly line. I am as guilty as the next party, and I hereby shake a finger most scoldingly at myself. A couple years ago, I had three F Minor Ballades going at the same time. That is simply not healthy for me, for the students, nor for the F Minor Ballade. We all needed sabbaticals by the end of the year.

There is much to be said for studying less-familiar music. First, it encourages originality: the students can skip the step of listening to the twenty extant recordings and taking the average. In fact, they might have to make some interpretive decisions based on their own musical ideas. That in turn could lead to a contemplation of musical ideas in general (i.e., whether they have any at all). If these lines lie heavy with sarcasm, forgive me, but I have heard in my ten years too many nonthinkers, too many generic music-makers who do not really listen and hence have no true musical ideas of their own. The fact that the same fifty pieces get played all the time encourages this nonhearing. Playing something new spurs originality and stimulates a sense of mission. Performers who do so acquire a certain responsibility to both the piece in question and to their listeners when they bring to light little-known works. Convictions matter. How else project in one performance a total artistic statement?

Permit me to proselytize for a few deserving pieces. Not all are new by any means. In every stylistic period, there are hidden gems that have either been overlooked or fallen out of favor. Herewith a list of "nobody's old favorites."

Baroque. The mighty J. S. Bach was so prolific that a few pieces have never had the attention they merit, namely the *Overture in the French Style* and the Four Duets. Another favorite of mine is the Fantasy and Fugue in A Minor, S. 904, a worthy alternative to the *Chromatic Fantasy and Fugue* on any program. Scarlatti offers hundreds of possibilities over and above the dozen or so usually played. But to go further afield, how about Soler? Or for the truly adventurous, Carlos Seixas? Both bring fresh, invigorating ideas to the binary sonata. I am also a member of the nearly nonexistent minority that likes to hear an occasional piece by Rameau played on the piano; there are some wonderful musical and technical challenges hiding there.

Classical. A gold mine exists in the lesser-known Haydn; two of my current fascinations are the D major Sonata, H. 33, and the E-flat Sonata, H. 25. I haven't heard many Mozart Variations lately either. All of Beethoven seems to be doing very well, thank you. Poor Clementi, on the other hand, hasn't seen the light of day in some time. C. F. Peters publishes four volumes containing a total of twenty-four sonatas. More than one of them deserves favor. For something completely different, try either C. P. E. Bach—who left no fewer than four hundred works for the keyboard, including 143 sonatas—or Baldassare Galuppi, a Venetian composer of opera buffa, who wrote about ninety sonatas. (For much of this numerical and bibliographic data, I refer you to that guide of all guides Maurice Hinson and his books on the pianist's repertoire.)

Romantic. Actually, a moratorium could be placed on this entire period for a while, but since that would never happen, it will be a long time before the complete genius of Franz Liszt is represented in the standard repertoire. There are those incredible late pieces like "Nuages gris" or "Czárdás macabre." There are the hard-to-find pieces, like the *Apparitions*, and there are neglected masterpieces in the *Années de pèlerinage* and other collections. Yes, I know some are played, but not enough. Even more regrettable is the almost complete neglect of one of the great masters of nineteenth-century France, Gabriel Fauré. Perhaps the music is too understated and refined to achieve mass popularity, but it is music that is satisfying to both the hands and heart as well as the mind. Special favorites of mine are the sixth and thirteenth Nocturnes. I also recommend the four sonatas of Carl Maria von Weber—especially the fourth in E minor, a four-movement work of great dramatic strength. Tchaikovsky wrote a good bit of piano music, some of which is delightful stuff. The same can be said for Grieg. Reger, perhaps like Fauré, has had difficulty outside his own country—it loses something in translation?—but his is a sizable, even formidable body of works that deserves more than passing mention.

Twentieth century. In our time, even the masterpieces are neglected, and I speak here of such giants as Bartók, Schoenberg, Ives, and Messiaen. The only composers who turn up at all regularly on piano programs these days are Prokofiev and Stravinsky, and the latter is represented solely by the *Three Movements from Petrushka*.

So, students, if you've read this far in the sermon, I now freely give a list of ten specific works, any of which will make your senior recital the talk of the school if you give it a good performance:

- Janáček: *In the Mists*

- Griffes: Sonata

- Bartók: Études, Op. 18 (beware, they are tough!)

- Shostakovich: Sonata No. 2

- Copland: *Piano Fantasy* (beware, it's long)

- Dallapiccola: *Quaderno musicale di Annalibera*

- Schoenberg: Suite, Op. 25

- Carl Nielsen: *Chaconne*

- Leon Kirchner: Piano Sonata

- George Crumb: *Gnomic Variations* (beware, it's not all on the keyboard)

Granted, some of these pieces are difficult, but no more so than many of the favorite warhorses that your colleagues line up in an orderly queue to play year after year.

Go ahead—be different! It really would make my day.

54

Modern Music

Winds of Change

MARCH–APRIL 2017

Change has been on our minds a lot lately. When I coined the name of this column in 2009, I had no idea how prescient it was. (Some of these recent changes would have been hard to predict even a year ago.) With the future certain only insofar as there *will* be a future, please allow me some personal ruminations about "modern music" and its role in bringing the great music of the past into the future.

For that matter, what significance does the great music of the past have in today's whirlwind culture?

When Beethoven's music was new, it challenged, contained truths that couldn't be uttered in words, and repaid prolonged exposure and study. When I was younger, modern music's triumvirate was Stravinsky, Bartók, Schoenberg; contemporary composers were people like Copland, Carter, Stockhausen, Boulez, Crumb, and so forth. Much of this music also repaid constant listening, deep study, and connected one to those brave enough to venture into these new sound worlds with a message inexpressible any other way.

However, years have elapsed, and while I wasn't looking, these modern composers became passé or commercialized or in some cases forgotten. For example, Schoenberg's Suite for Piano, Op. 25, was considered groundbreaking, yet when was the last time you heard it performed in recital? You are rare if you can say you *ever* heard it.

Last term I assigned the Webern Variations to one of my students. He had never done an atonal work, let alone something twelve-tone. As I reacquainted myself with it after an almost thirty-year absence, I recognized its inherent romanticism even more than I did when I first studied the work. While this music may sound modern, its roots are in Bach and Brahms (similarly Schoenberg). Communicating that to someone from China, however, was a challenge (a subject for another column—the globalization of world cultures). And this wasn't an assignment of castor oil because a little Webern is good for you. I believed in the piece—and still do—and thought my student would grow if he tried to come to terms with it.

He memorized it—or, better stated, played it by heart. In some ways, I think he understood it better than the "Waldstein" Sonata, which was on the same program. In this case, the modern piece might have helped pull the standard rep into the present. The energy it takes to make sense of the Webern is the same as that needed to bring music two hundred years old into contemporaneity.

Recently I have been reading a biography of the American composer Leon Kirchner.[1] Interestingly, it was in the only year I heard the Schoenberg Suite performed live that I also heard Kirchner's Piano Sonata for the first time, in both cases played by seniors of my esteemed Oberlin teacher, Emil Danenberg. (I was a freshman.) Danenberg studied with Schoenberg at UCLA, as did Kirchner. Modernism was thus in the drinking water.

Kirchner grew up in California, studied with other modernists of a serious vein (Sessions, Bloch), and always had a connection to performing—he was an excellent pianist and conductor. His music, despite its difficulty, made an impact on audiences. From a review of his *Sonata Concertante* for violin and piano:

> [It] is not music that can be absorbed at one hearing. But it is music that stirs the mind, the emotions, and the esthetic curiosity immediately...The idiom is challenging and hard to grasp; the inspiration and power of conceptions are unmistakable.[2]

---

1. Robert Riggs, *Leon Kirchner: Composer, Performer, and Teacher* (Rochester, New York: University of Rochester Press, 2010).

2. Riggs, *Leon Kirchner*, 63.

About ten years after graduating from Oberlin, I had the good fortune to play the Piano Sonata (No. 1) for Kirchner at his house in Cambridge, Massachusetts. After hearing it, he asked me what else I was working on. I said *Carnaval*. He listened to some of that as well, and his comments were every bit as insightful as with his own work.

It is this connection between the past and present that one encounters again and again in Kirchner, an attempt by the composer to write "new" music that is nonetheless rooted in the past. From a program note by Kirchner: "Form-building, Schoenberg called it, that most vital and characteristic aspect of musical art in the Viennese classic and before, that which gave music the possibility of endless revelation in performance…and so my music seemed to recapitulate the past in an effort to empower an alternative future…my fantasy of course."[3]

What of this future, now our present? Please forgive the coming string of rhetorical questions. Show of hands: How many of you know Leon Kirchner's music? Reminder: you are the elite—at least you know Beethoven and Schumann. A related question: Does your neighbor two doors down care if she hears the "Eroica" any time soon? Would your neighbor's life be better if she knew the "Eroica"?

What are you doing about that? What am I doing? It is not enough to work only in the relative safety of academe (or the private studio) with similarly inclined minds. There's a world out there that needs our help.

> What I wanted to achieve and wished to alter when I set forth from the University? The answer was quite clear: to achieve, along with everyone else, a *future*, by altering the *present*— *now*.[4]

---

3. Riggs, *Leon Kirchner*, 217–18.
4. Riggs, *Leon Kirchner*, 276.

X

■ On Competitions

Since Van Cliburn's triumph in the 1958 Tchaikovsky Competition, competitions have been part of the ambitious pianist's life. The first piece I wrote for *Clavier* dealt with competitions. At that relatively early stage of my career (I was thirty-four, just over the age limit to participate in most competitions), I was more familiar with them than I wanted to be. "A Look at the Competition Syndrome" was a cry to put the music first, to rise above the athleticism of pure technique, and to invent noncompetitive performance opportunities, especially for younger students. It was dismaying to see teachers' organizations depending on competitions as the goals to motivate students. Looking back at the essay, I see it now as a window into my prejudices—given the values of my teachers, it is no surprise that my musical ethics favored virtue to virtuoso.

Also, I still felt bruised a bit from my own competition experiences, which had their ups and downs. As a student at Oberlin and Yale, I won my schools' concerto competitions with the Bartók Second Concerto. Although I thought my technique weak, this was not a piece for cowards, given its demanding muscular vigor. I didn't learn it for its difficulty, though; I just liked the piece. Then there was the time I entered a municipal orchestra's competition that required two concerti. I chose the Mozart C Minor to pair with the Bartók. Admitted to the finals, I had to choose which one to play. Going against the grain, I chose the Mozart, even though the other finalists were playing works like the Tchaikovsky, Prokofiev Third, and *Totentanz*. Somehow I won. Perhaps my proudest moment in competitions.

Most other moments were less happy. During that time in Vermont teaching in a prep school (i.e., before graduate school), I entered the 1973 Van Cliburn competition, learning an immense program on my own—on an upright piano—when not in class or minding the dorm. I was fortunate to have as a friend the local pastor who had a Steinway grand in his living room; he kindly invited me to practice there whenever I could. If I'd been less naive, I would have known I had no business in a competition at that level, but I went anyway. I did not advance but had a wonderful time in Fort Worth with my host family.

During graduate school, I entered several New York City competitions that might have led to a debut recital. Again, no dice. I started to develop a phobia—as I sat down to play, all the things that could go wrong crowded my consciousness. While I don't remember any disasters, I know that my playing was skittish, disconnected from the music's forward motion. I played the pieces but inwardly rebelled against the situation. Later, I learned that this was *cognitive dissonance*, a useful psychological term that describes the feeling we get when immersed in a situation that is incompatible (dissonant) with a long-standing personal value. I loved music and playing the piano (long-standing value), and here I was in a competition being judged not for my love but for whether my playing met the judges' criteria.

My one other competition "success" was placing third in an international competition for the performance of American music, sponsored by the Rockefeller Foundation and the Kennedy Center. Here I remember playing well in the semifinal round, eager to share music in which I really believed. I did not play as well in the final round; I think it was because I was too aware of being judged. It was no longer about the music—I was being compared to others for ranking. I let that interfere with the flow of the music. Still, being a finalist led to publicity, to an opportunity to play in New York City, to a few other concerts, and ultimately to a better teaching position. Competitions are not all bad.

The essays that follow cover nearly forty years of thoughts and questions, beginning with "A Look at the Competition Syndrome." Rereading it, I realize it could use some updating; the rules have changed in competitions, and I must admit I've altered my views somewhat as well. So, the text of the article is printed as it appeared in the May–June issue of 1985, but I have added footnotes to explain arcane references.

This early essay is followed by a more recent selection (2013) from *Winds of Change.* Things had indeed changed by then: competitions were designed to be more transparent, but they had by this time become an industry. They weren't going away any time soon. Cognitive dissonance endures. Is it simply a matter of "Can't live with 'em; can't live without 'em"?

As early as 1990, however, competitions were appearing that met my hoped-for standards. I wrote about three of them in a *View from the Second Floor* that year, calling them gifts to the piano world. They represent competitions with a difference and focused on three very different cohorts: young students, would-be recitalists, and an attempt to launch the kind of career that might change history.

The next article explores that third category in depth; it is a report on the first Gilmore Foundation festival, which I cheekily titled "Artistic Absolutes and the Girl from Kalamazoo." Touted as a significant departure from competition business as usual, the Gilmore was a kind of "uncompetition." The article details how the Gilmore Artist was chosen and what his debut at the festival was like. It also explores the effects of inundating a midsize Midwestern city with all things pianistic. The festival has changed a great deal since 1991; it is fascinating to consider its vibrant ambition in its earliest days.

The Gilmore had been the brainchild of David Pocock, who continued his desire to avoid head-to-head combat when he later became artistic director of the American Pianists Association (APA). There, he imaginatively changed the way the fellowship awardees were chosen, leading again to something that went beyond competition. I interviewed him for *Clavier* in 1999. Sadly, Pocock died in 2017.

In 2013, *International Piano* asked me to write about APA's Discovery Week, then under the direction of Joel Harrison. Thus, there is a continuity of intention through these last three articles. I leave it to readers to form their own opinions about the efficacy of "uncompetitions."

No chapter on competitions would be complete without my article for *Clavier* on the 2001 Cliburn Competition, where my student Stanislav Ioudenitch shared the first prize with Olga Kern. I was as swept up as anyone in the gladiatorial aspect of the competition, despite cognitive dissonance. The Cliburn is America's answer to the Tchaikovsky and Warsaw—from the start, it has longed to name a winner who will achieve the fame of Horowitz or Rubinstein in the present day. It hasn't worked out that way.[1] Perhaps the goal itself is unattainable—artists are all different, with different personal needs and abilities. Twenty years later, Stanislav has become a consummate teacher. I believe he was happy to give up the constant requirement to prove himself with every performance and is now happy behind the scenes as his own students win major prizes (Behzod Abduraimov in London; Kenny Broberg at Fort Worth, Moscow, and most recently the APA).

---

1. However, it could be rewarding to follow the career of the 2023 Cliburn winner, Yuchan Lim. He is the kind of pianist who seemingly has everything: a volcanic technique, a poetic soul, and the kind of immediate, devoted audience appeal necessary to become a star. Only time will tell.

55

A Look at the Competition Syndrome

The View from the Second Floor

MAY–JUNE 1984

I've just recovered from a blistering game of recreational tennis. My game is a far cry from professional caliber, but I try not to let that get in the way of my enjoyment. As the game progressed, with points scored and lost, it suddenly became clear to me why we are a nation of sports fanatics. The answer is black and white: there must be a winner. In no uncertain terms, one person will run up a higher score than the other and is therefore the one and only winner. Aside from a doubtful line call in tennis, there can be little question regarding who the better player is. There can also be little doubt that the better player usually wins. Simple. Clean. Uncomplicated. Our national sense of competition and winner takes all is tailor-made to the unambiguous rules of most major American sports.

Piano competitions have winners, too, and though there are usually several prizes, there is only one big winner, who does in fact take all. There is often a lot to win these days, thanks to growing public awareness and to the rivalry among competitions to attract the attention of the young pianistic lions. Substantial cash prizes and, more importantly, a list of engagements and the attention of concert promoters and managers are reason enough to put yourself on the line and serve up your best.

At last count, the *Musical America* annual directory listed 132 competitions in this country alone.[1] Most of those are for advanced performers, the pianistic equivalents of Connors and McEnroe slugging it out on national television.[2] It is probably impossible to estimate the number of competitions available to less advanced pianists, but if you

---

1. This was 1984. In 2013, the count had risen to over seven hundred.

2. Jimmy Connors and John McEnroe were the reigning male tennis stars of the time.

want to try, take the number of community contests available to your students and extrapolate that number to cover the entire United States!

What about a piano competition in which younger students are putting themselves on the line? In my experience, most students have been scared to death knowing that some stranger is going to judge them.[3] They may have come to hate the piece thanks to the incessant drills the dedicated teacher has inflicted upon them. They may even begin to wonder why the teacher seems more interested in this contest than they are.[4] What else explains working on the same repertoire for the past six months?

What about the students who make steady, if unspectacular, progress? They may be reasonably pleased with their accomplishment, but as soon as they enter (or are entered in) a competition, they find themselves up against the whiz kid star of all the studio recitals. Just as in the tennis game, they know they are beaten, even before the game begins.

I think it is time to reexamine competitions from several points of view. The examples above do not apply to everyone. And there are competitions in which the students are simply heard and given comment sheets; they do not compete against each other. There will be rebuttals to many of the points made here. Contests of all sorts, however, are so much a part of our musical life that we must do some strong thinking if we are to understand their place. We are in danger of being controlled by the competition syndrome: the all-pervasive acceptance of head-to-head combat as the best way to find the artists of the future.[5]

Any competition, sporting or musical, involves the pitting of one's own resources against those of others. In a music competition, one's physical, intellectual, and spiritual perceptions of a musical work are compared and contrasted to the perceptions of the other contestants,

---

3. Here my own fears were projected onto the young students. Some children *love* to compete and are not bothered by higher moral issues. They haven't gotten there yet!

4. Teachers often have much to gain from a student's win and are therefore likely to be even more engrossed in the outcome.

5. Here my own involvement with high-level competitions may have colored my words. Competitions can be about more than finding the artists of the future.

letting an omnipotent jury decide the winner. On occasion the contestant is up against the jury's mutually agreed upon concept of an "artistic ideal."

Right away two questions arise. First, how are the points scored?[6] In tennis, you must keep the ball in play. In a piano competition, you must do the same thing; you simply cannot drop many notes. Constant fluffing of technical hurdles is the equivalent of too many double faults. If you know that's the way it is, you can learn to live with it, but as teachers, we are doing a disservice to our students if we put them in a contest for the experience when they have not yet learned how to play the piano on a technical level. Whether competitions have in fact raised the general level of technical accomplishment is a hotly debated issue. After judging a major international competition, Leon Fleisher stated that, at best, the "level of mediocrity" has risen. Food for thought.

The second question that arises is even more provocative: If competitions assume a high technical level of playing, how does the jury decide on artistic excellence?

Therein lies the rub. Trying to make black-and-white decisions about what constitutes artistic excellence is difficult enough. If we are to continue to grow as musicians, we must reassess the nature of our art every time we sit down to work. The decisions we make are often affected by the qualities in music that speak most directly to us. Some of us will be most concerned with sound, others with rhythmic precision, still others with faithfulness to the composer's score. These items as well as numerous others are important, but is one any more important than another? In the competition jury room, such things must be decided.[7] We all have a standard, but the chance of that standard being completely in agreement with another musician's is not a likely occurrence. If we all thought about music the same way, we would all play alike. Perhaps this is the place to mention the fear that contest watchers all over the world have expressed: all the young lions sound alike!

---

6. Nowadays, a point system is not used in major competitions. One still sees grading sheets, however, in competitions sponsored by teachers' organizations.

7. This may have been true in the past, but these days, conversation about such things is not allowed among the jury.

The inherent conflict suggested by differing opinions about music promotes the artistic variety necessary for the continuance of our musical tradition.[8] This same conflict makes the competition jury's task not only difficult but almost impossible. The repertoire requirements often call for the competitors to play the same pieces.[9] To differentiate between the players, the jury must remember Contestant A's gorgeous trill or Contestant B's subtle pedaling. Objective items such as these might be singled out, judged, and rated; a tally is kept, almost like a scorecard. Because the difficult issues dealing with the true nature of the art remain ambiguous, the jury focuses its attention on quantifiable topics. Whose runs are most pearly? Who has the strongest octaves? Whose Beethoven appealed most? Even so, the jury is making the musical equivalent of line calls in tennis—in this case, as they *hear* them. No one has ever written down the rules of a perfect performance.

Juries are really judging *manner* rather than *substance*, to borrow Charles Ives's terms. The substance is the music itself, but because juries must concern themselves more with the manner of presentation, the music becomes secondary to the whole proceeding, having no other purpose than to serve as a vehicle for the performers to show their stuff. Again, if everyone understands what is going on, we can deal with it. There is a need for a respected group of jurors to occasionally reaffirm a standard of excellence in performance.[10] Manner is important, but only as a means to an end, which is the music itself.[11]

Any performer who enters a competition should therefore understand the nature of the game. To do justice to the music, the contestants should remain subservient to the composer and yet, at the same time, be willing to be judged by auditors with differing musical ideas, who for the time being are more interested in manner

---

8. A confusing sentence! It simply means that without diametrically opposed artists (e.g., Rudolf Serkin and Earl Wild), our musical tradition suffers.

9. Another practice that has changed. Free repertoire choice today is the more likely option.

10. I have no idea why I thought this was even a possibility when I first wrote the essay.

11. Here again, my values are showing. I am a grandson of Schnabel, after all.

than substance. They must also remember that there will be a first prize winner, and most people will always assume that number one is "better" than number two. If nonwinners fall prey to this assumption, a particularly destructive kind of depression can set in, adversely affecting future performances as well as their self-esteem.[12] During the competition itself, the contestants must accept having pieces cut off at any moment. They must accept learning a prescribed repertoire, perhaps attempting pieces that are physically or emotionally awkward or even alien to them. By entering numerous competitions, the contestants may come to view the act of performing as an extremely judgmental hurdle that needs to be cleared like the events in a decathlon. They must accept the basically antisocial nature of a competition in which the playing is intended primarily for the judges' ears, even when an audience is present. Much fuss has been made about the presence of an audience in certain competitions, but the sad truth of the matter is that regardless of how loud they shout for a performer who moves them, they must eventually await the judges' decision, having no real power of their own.

Performers who can withstand the pressures and understand the bizarre requirements that a competition puts on heart and mind should give it everything they've got. But let's stop talking about competitions as the only game in town, and let's stop thinking of them as artistic events. They are essentially concerned with the manner in which a piece is presented, and their fascination is really that of a sporting event. Our attention goes to the winner, whose performance may or may not bring forth the substance of the music itself.

And what about younger students? Surely, we can think of other ways to give them performance experience. When average students play in a competition, they are most concerned about the fact that a judge is listening and that their performance had better be good—or else! The last thing in the students' awareness is the musical experience itself. There must be other ways to inspire students to work toward a goal. By using contests to stimulate the student to work,[13] we set up a

---

12. Looking back, I think this happened to me. I imagine most musicians are at least somewhat familiar with cognitive dissonance.

13. This was my main concern in writing the essay for *Clavier* in the first place. Teachers' organizations seemed to accept competitions as the best way to get students to work. I am still concerned about this.

Pavlovian response: the students see the possibility of reward if they do well in the contest, and therefore they work. Is this the best way to build a musically enlightened public in America? I think not.

Music making is a social, communicative activity, and it is successful only in the hands of musicians who understand that they are the vehicle for the music itself, not the other way around. Similarly, audiences should be led to receive the composer's message first, the performer's skills being secondary to the musical communication.[14] Otherwise, a recital is little more than a sporting event. Competitions may not be the best way to find such a musician, because the very act of competing requires an unflappable ego that is unphased about using the music as a means of self-ennoblement. True musicians have emerged from the competition circuit—Murray Perahia and Radu Lupu spring immediately to mind— but they are the exception rather than the rule.

Likewise, audiences are encouraged by competitions to root for the most obvious sort of personality. For emerging artists, we need a system of public exposure like the kind experienced by conductors in the old European opera houses: they had years to grow and develop, to learn music from the inside out. There are pianists aplenty who have talent and something to say, but they need real audiences in real halls, *without judges*, in which to play. They need to test out an interpretation and let it grow instead of honing it to a cold, steely perfection acceptable to the greatest number of judges. They need to make music, and we must give them that opportunity. It is the only way we can all grow.

---

14. Here, my values have tempered a bit. While the music is still central to the experience, the performer's role is not unimportant. See section IX.

56

Later Reflections

Winds of Change

I've found myself thinking a lot about competitions lately. One of my first pieces for *Clavier*, even before I started a regular column, dealt with "the competition syndrome." Rereading it, I'm struck by how little things have changed, other than the fact that I'm more uncertain about things than I was in my thirties.

That early essay decried the heartlessness of piano competitions and the impossibility of picking a winner in anything as subjective as art. As sports-obsessed Americans, we want one winner who's better than everyone else. The illogical conclusion: *American Idol* and its many spin-offs, a veritable industry dedicated to the idea that anyone can be a winner with enough talent and moxie. And people eat it up!

Thanks to the internet, a sizable, passionate audience can now view the major piano competitions, and they aren't shy about posting comments following webcast performances. In the late spring, dedicated listeners from across the globe eavesdropped on both the Cliburn and the Queen Elisabeth competitions, and due to the newfound transparency of the proceedings, those listeners have been quite vocal about their wonder at how the juries came to the decisions they did.

In July, Terry Teachout wrote an article for the *Wall Street Journal* called "Why Piano Competitions Will Never Yield a Superstar." He answers his titular question succinctly:

> Because the winners are chosen by juries. A jury is at bottom a committee—and a committee, as John le Carré famously said in *Tinker, Tailor, Soldier, Spy*, is "an animal with four back legs." They exist to generate and perpetuate consensus views. They can't make great art, and it's all but impossible for them

to agree on great artists. Such disagreement inevitably leads to compromise, which more often than not produces B-plus winners who please all of the jurors but thrill none of them.[1]

While my distaste for competitions resonates with Mr. Teachout's conclusion, I don't think it's that simple. First, he assumes there are great artists to be chosen as winner in a competition, and that simply isn't the case very often. Deserving of attention? Yes. Worth being heard again? Sure. Great artists who change the way we hear music? Highly unlikely.

Second, juries don't talk much behind closed doors these days. In fact, it was forbidden in this summer's World Piano Competition in Cincinnati, where I was one of five jurors. When we had to vote eighteen contestants off the island between the preliminaries and the semifinals, it was a straight vote on multiple ballots. On the first ballot, two people received a majority of the votes. On the next ballot, two more made it. It took four ballots to come to "agreement" on the final person. In the meantime, eleven other contestants received at least one vote at some point in the proceedings.

That suggests a jury with a wide range of values and tastes, not to mention a very interesting set of contestants. Whether we were all pleased with the final result is anyone's guess. The answer is probably not. But is there a fairer way to choose? Would long, drawn-out arguments over the relative merits of the contestants have been better? Again, probably not, since such verbal-sparring matches depend at best on the lawyerly skills of the advocates or at worst on who can go on longest and loudest.

Thus, more and more competitions favor a voting system that prevents arm-twisting and power plays. Does this lead to a consensus (read: mediocre) winner? Perhaps. Mr. Teachout's solution: do away with a multimembered jury and give the job to one famous artist. No consensus needed—just the clear vision of someone to whom the world should pay attention. Teachout admits this probably wouldn't work either.

---

1. Terry Teachout, "Why Piano Competitions Will Never Yield a Superstar," *Wall Street Journal*, July 4, 2013.

There are now more than 750 piano competitions worldwide.[2] Thirty years ago, the number was maybe 200. It doesn't take a genius to notice that the rounds of the majors open to the public are much better attended than a typical piano recital, even one by a big-name artist. The audience tends to be less experienced with classical music and more excited by the event; they are there for the thrill of victory and the agony of defeat.

Alas, competitions are not going away. They are an industry unto themselves, and perhaps we should thank them for keeping solo piano playing alive in some form. Finding the next superstar may be beside the point when young pianists can make careers of sorts going from one competition to the next, finding bigger audiences than playing the awards concert they might receive for winning. The catch-22, though, is lethal: age limits mean that eventually competitions are no longer open to you, just as you are maturing enough to have something worth saying.

I do wish we could come up with a better way. The Gilmore and the American Pianists Association have a good idea in taking some of the competitive heat out of the mix, and the Gilmore has removed the age limits. As for the head-to-head combat in the typical competition, it belittles the music. After all, when Contestant A plays Mozart and Contestant B plays Liszt and Contestant B almost invariably wins, isn't there something wrong here?

Adding insult to injury, the *Harvard Gazette* leads the curious reader to an article published in the *Proceedings of the National Academy of Sciences* titled "Sight over Sound in the Judgment of Music Performance." Its author, Chia-Jung Tsay, who has a PhD in organizational behavior with a secondary PhD field in music, studied the role of the visual in identifying the winners of competitions by having participants— including highly trained musicians—watch silent video clips of contestants. The abstract is worth quoting in full:

---

2. *Cincinnati Enquirer,* July 8, 2013.

Social judgments are made on the basis of both visual and auditory information, with consequential implications for our decisions. To examine the impact of visual information on expert judgment and its predictive validity for performance outcomes, this set of seven experiments in the domain of music offers a conservative test of the relative influence of vision versus audition. People consistently report that sound is the most important source of information in evaluating performance in music. However, the findings demonstrate that people actually depend primarily on visual information when making judgments about music performance. People reliably select the actual winners of live music competitions based on silent video recordings, but neither musical novices nor professional musicians were able to identify the winners based on sound recordings or recordings with both video and sound. The results highlight our natural, automatic, and nonconscious dependence on visual cues. The dominance of visual information emerges to the degree that it is overweighted relative to auditory information, even when sound is consciously valued as the core domain content.[3]

Mr. Teachout, meet Ms. Tsay. Why don't the two of you go out for coffee and keep working on that better way? It must be there somewhere.

---

3. Chia-Jung Tsay, "Sight over Sound in the Judgment of Music Performance," *Proceedings of the National Academy of Sciences*, September 3, 2013, http://www.pnas.org/content/early/2013/08/16/1221454110.full.pdf+html?sid=6dc63bac-60ff-4e0a-a970-flaf4fd041b8. See also http://news.harvard.edu/gazette/story/2013/08/the-look-of-music/.

57

Competitions with a Difference

The View from the Second Floor
DECEMBER 1990

Last year during the holiday season, I wrote about gifts: a performer's gift to an audience, a teacher's gift to a student. Anyone who spends a life in music is giving and receiving in every season of the year. One thinks as well of the gift of talent: may the lucky recipient be humble enough to thank nature for such a blessing. As Pablo Casals once told a student, "Do not brag about your talent—it is not your fault."

Focusing this year on the more tangible, I'd like to describe three organizations that are gifts to the young and not-so-young pianist. All are concerned with providing opportunities. We often rationalize the burgeoning number of competitions as opportunities to perform, hoping that such a worthwhile goal would erase the negative aspects of artistic battle. Among these organizations, only one is a competition; their intentions lead the participants to a broad and lasting musical experience.

In the Pacific Northwest, there exists a wonderful organization called the Seattle Young Artists Music Festival. Each spring, any music student in town can take part in a weeklong series of events that combine playing opportunities with lessons from guest teachers. A fifth grader playing a work of Bach, for example, might enter the "fifth and sixth grade Baroque" event and, at the appointed time, appear with three other youngsters of the same age, all playing Baroque pieces, performing on a good piano in a real concert hall for an audience of parents and other children. A mini recital takes place, and all the while, a guest teacher (I avoid the word *judge* or *clinician*) writes comments on the performances that the students take home if they wish. Following the recital, complete with applause and bows, the guest teacher joins the students on stage and shares thoughts and experiences with them in such a way that the students often perform the pieces a second time in an even more relaxed, supportive atmosphere. For those with first-time nerves, this is a second chance. For the solid performer, this is a chance to explore and stretch. The festival offers many repertoire categories for ages ranging through high school. Over a thousand students take part each year in piano and all the orchestral instruments. It is a private organization, relying on volunteer help, and my hat is off to them for their hard work that yields so many positive results.

New York City is full of piano competitions, but one stands out in my mind for its humane sanity. Much is due to its founder, Frinna Awerbuch, whose name graces the Frinna Awerbuch International Piano Competition. Sponsored to a large extent by the Piano Teachers Congress of New York as well as several foundations and private donors, the competition looks on paper like any of several smaller events held in New York—cash prizes, a recital to the winner, a finalists' recital for those not taking the first prize. However, none of the recitals are given the full media spotlight attendant on a major debut; expectations are kept reasonable. In a sense, it is making a debut without really making a debut, an experience of no small importance. Frinna is very good to all her finalists. She often finds small venues for them around New York. Even the competition is a good experience— the repertoire requirements are both sane and useful, and a large jury hears all three rounds, giving the finalists plenty of experience under competition pressure. Finally, everyone involved shares in the most rewarding gift of all: getting to know Frinna, a tireless and enthusiastic supporter of young talent who should be spending her golden years in something less strenuous than running a piano competition. Instead, she chooses otherwise, to the great fortune of those who know her.[1]

New to the scene is the Gilmore Foundation, whose first piano festival will occur this spring and will include concerts by notables as diverse as Claudio Arrau and Chick Corea. A new concerto for the left hand has been commissioned for Leon Fleisher. Most interesting of all will be the naming of the first Gilmore Artist. If all goes according to plan, some unsuspecting pianist will be awarded a sizable chunk of cash, concert engagements, New York management, and a great deal

---

1. Sadly, the competition no longer exists. Frinna died in 2001 at age one hundred.

of media attention. The new wrinkle is that no one can apply for the award. Instead, a panel of musicians nominates pianists who are then screened by a second panel that observes the finalists without their knowledge. The nonwinners will never know they "lost." It works much like the MacArthur Foundation "genius" grants, or those of you with a long memory may be reminded of the 1950s TV show *The Millionaire*. The foundation will also award four $20,000 scholarships to promising pianists under the age of twenty-one. Again, they do not apply. It all represents a fascinating and daring experiment, and obviously a lot of money stands behind it. It is made possible by the late Irving Gilmore, a Kalamazoo businessman who loved the piano and created a foundation with his estate that would support and nurture all things pianistic. One eagerly anticipates the late April festival and how it will all turn out. This is clearly the largest infusion of money and manpower to promote pianists and piano music in recent history. Let's hope it works! It's quite a Christmas present, whatever the season.

Artistic Absolutes and the Girl from Kalamazoo

A Report on the First Gilmore International Keyboard Festival

Clavier

SEPTEMBER 1991

Last spring the ever-ailing piano world received a shot of vitamins worth about $2 million. Chances are good that anyone reading this article has at least heard about it. Whether the patient survives is anyone's guess.

On April 27, 1991, the first Irving S. Gilmore International Keyboard Festival got underway in Kalamazoo, Michigan, where a full house of three thousand people in Miller Auditorium turned out to see what all the fuss was about. Electric-green and yellow banners along the city streets heralded the festival, while local television carried news stories at noon, six, and eleven. A grand piano graced the arrival gates at Kalamazoo Airport. For months, ads had been appearing in magazines such as this, proclaiming "The Whole World Is Listening." For the next nine days, a series of thirty-four performances promised Kalamazoo quite a bit more keyboard music than Carnegie Hall would hear in its one-hundredth-anniversary year.

In fact, the Gilmore Festival was all this and more. There was music for every taste—classical, jazz, and pop—but everywhere there was a piano or one of its relatives. Two new piano compositions— including a Concerto for Left Hand and Orchestra, written for Leon Fleisher—were commissioned and received first performances. The concerto's composer was Curtis Curtis-Smith, a Kalamazoo resident whose music has had performances here and abroad. The legendary Van Cliburn was on hand to bring the festival to a newsworthy close. On consecutive evenings, listeners were treated to the unlikely succession of pianist Alicia de Larrocha, harpsichordist Igor Kipnis, and avant-garde jazz keyboardist Chick Corea. Matti Raekallio played the Beethoven sonata cycle in eight noontime concerts, which had been sold out for weeks before the festival. Malcolm Bilson played the Mozart sonata cycle to packed houses in four afternoon recitals. The Kalamazoo Institute of Arts hosted an exhibition of museum-quality instruments called "The Vibrant World of the 19th-Century Piano." Nine master classes—given by such well-known teachers as John Perry, Nelita True, Adam Wibrowski, and Aube Tzerko—were liberally sprinkled into the calendar. No one went away hungry.

As if this were not enough, the festival set about finding a pianist who deserved an international career but didn't have one, a pianist who, as one insider put it, "somehow fell through the cracks." Additionally, the festival wanted to provide up to four awards to young pianists under the age of twenty-two with the potential to become important artists in the future. David Pocock, the festival's artistic director, decided that a full-blown competition was *not* the way to go and devised what the festival's press releases called "a humane way to find talent." To quote from the release:

> During 1989 and 1990, an anonymous, virtually invisible process was under way. It involved two distinct committees of distinguished performers and teachers, one to nominate and one to evaluate candidates. The Nominating Committee, its members drawn from around the world, privately recommended candidates for both the Gilmore Artist and Young Artists Awards. Nominees had no knowledge [that they had been nominated]. Recordings of performances by the nominees, their identity concealed to ensure impartiality, were then reviewed by the Artistic Advisory Committee.
>
> After a first selection was made, biographies and other pertinent information were provided to the committee which then narrowed the field to the finalists for the Gilmore Artist Award and made its final selection of the Gilmore Young Artists. [To make a final selection of the Gilmore Artist] members of the Advisory Committee as well as the Festival's Artistic Director David Pocock traveled incognito, to hear each of the candidates perform in scheduled recitals and concerts. In the spring of 1991, although one of the most

substantial awards in music will have been made, there will be no losers. In fact, only the "winner" will ever know he or she has taken part.

"Musicianship, rather than competition skills, should, for once, have the last say," remarks David Pocock, who researched piano competitions around the world before conceiving the Gilmore selection process. "When musicians can be observed unobtrusively, under unforced, more natural conditions, their true quality would seem to stand a better chance of manifesting itself."

All that music (not to mention the committees and fancy PR) costs money. Luckily, the Gilmore is loaded, thanks to the legacy of Irving S. Gilmore, a wealthy Kalamazoo department store owner who died in 1986. Gilmore set up a foundation in 1972 to assure that his philosophy of giving would continue after his death, and the $100+ million now in the foundation coffers supports human services, health, education, and community-development programs in addition to music. Gilmore was in love with the piano and its music; some people who knew him think he cared more about it than his business. He found ways to help people from all walks of life, from the poor to the visually impaired. Anonymously he paid for the education of a promising music student. When composer C. Curtis-Smith asked him for a loan to help him buy a grand piano, Gilmore found a way to make it a gift.

In a time, then, when arts budgets are being slashed, when even well-known pianists find it hard to fill their engagement books, the Gilmore launched itself with confidence and no little fanfare. It invited music critics from all over the world to attend, fitting a Music Critic's Institute into the proceedings. As a writer for *Clavier*, I was lucky enough to be invited, and I went with eyes and ears wide open, wondering what real money and good intentions could do in the name of music.

* * *

People were arriving an hour early for opening night. The program promised a double portion of excitement: in the second half of the concert, Leon Fleisher would give the first performance of Curtis-Smith's new concerto with the Kalamazoo Symphony under the direction of Yoshimi Takeda. The big event, though, was the orchestral debut of the Gilmore Artist, whose name had been announced in a press conference almost two months before the festival's opening. Curiosity abounded this night about a thirty-eight-year-old Englishman named David Owen Norris who had just had the most substantial prize in music fall at his feet.

According to the Gilmore's executive director, David Hook, Owen Norris will receive professional artist management and the services of a publicist. He is provided with some sixty concert engagements on both sides of the Atlantic, and he will receive direct financial assistance, the festival covering all career-related expenses for at least two years. So far, that has meant a new piano and a nanny for the children. "In short," says Hook, "anything it takes to launch an international career." The prize is estimated to be worth more than $250,000.

On opening night, everyone wanted to know why David Owen Norris deserved this kind of attention. Unfortunately, his biography in the program booklet dealt with the Gilmore selection process more than the artist. The critics, however, had been given a press release that described Norris as a "diverse, eclectic musician—concert pianist, professor, repetiteur, recording artist, radio personality, organist, writer and lecturer, authority on authentic performance, festival director." No one could call him inexperienced. Before he came onstage to play, Hook and Pocock introduced him to the audience with more expertly crafted publicity prose and a short film of the artist talking about music. When the film ended, the lights went out. An amplified voice announced, "Ladies and gentlemen, the 1991 Gilmore Artist...David Owen Norris!" The spotlight came on, and there he stood.

What followed was a very decent performance of the Britten Piano Concerto that could not possibly have stood up to the hype that preceded it. The Britten is an early work, atypically glitzy and lightweight. Norris played it cleanly and with energy. On this occasion, he proved himself a performer of cultivated intelligence, with a strong sense of musical time and a wry appreciation of Britten's acerbic wit. He is outgoing on stage but lacks charisma in the usual sense. Although there was much to like about his playing, the picture seemed incomplete; the piece's interpretive demands were too narrow to prove convincingly that Norris was, as one of the members of the Artistic Advisory Committee put it, "The kind of pianist who is strong enough to change the outlook of the musical world."

He certainly changed no one's opinion of Leon Fleisher, who took the stage for the second half of the program and the premiere of the Curtis-Smith Concerto. Fleisher can turn a page with more drama than many pianists find in an entire program, and his playing on this occasion was the embodiment of communicative immediacy. From the first notes, his sound was deeper, more enveloping than anything Norris produced with two hands. The Concerto is an invigorating, colorful excursion into bell-inspired sounds, which on first hearing elicited a long, cheering ovation from the audience. The first movement is especially powerful; Curtis-Smith has an uncanny sense of the piano's resonance, combining pitches in long pedals for extraordinary effect. It is a piece that cries out for recording. Here is a composer with something to say, capable of reaching a wide audience.

The opening night hoopla raised the first of many questions about pianistic careers as they occur in the late twentieth century. While the festival wanted to spare its Gilmore Artist most of the tribulations of winning a major competition, it saddled Norris with the curse of living up to the publicity that had been generated for the express purpose of crafting interest in him. Our culture suffers the numbing effects of too many choices; a large and wealthy advertising industry exists to help us make up our minds. Hype is nothing new, of course—Liszt certainly knew its uses. The unfortunate consequence, though, is that the actual experience is seldom as good as its buildup. Too many expectations were in the air concerning Owen Norris to be satisfied by one Britten concerto.

Ironically, the festival addressed many of these career issues in some of the Music Critic Institute workshops. The morning after Norris's debut, Stephen Wigler, music critic of the *Baltimore Sun*, chaired a session called "Whatever Happened to the Pianists of the 1950s— and Why?" He had the assistance of Harold Schonberg, author of

The Great Pianists; Joseph Horowitz, author of the recent book about the Van Cliburn competition titled *The Ivory Trade*; and Leon Fleisher, one of the pianists in question. Their often-spirited exchanges raised even more questions about performing careers. Wigler, a real piano aficionado, pointed out that the two hottest tickets in New York right now are a pianist who is not yet twenty (Evgeny Kissin) and a pianist who is almost one hundred (Mieczysław Horszowski). He named a dozen pianists who exhibited real promise in the '50s who were no longer playing or had not grown to the musical preeminence of the pianists of a generation before. Fleisher suggested that there had been so much emphasis in those days on playing one hundred concerts a year that anyone who didn't felt like a failure. He wondered how any pianist could rise to the upper reaches of artistry burdened with that kind of grueling schedule. Schonberg, who has made a career writing about careers, thought that the pianists of the '50s were the last to show the kind of magnetism that could lead to the "big career" because they had studied with teachers who were born in the nineteenth century and were therefore connected to the spirit of Romantic pianism in a way that today's younger pianists could not be. Horowitz felt that the concertizing specialization we take for granted is in fact something new, that the pianists of past generations avoided becoming performing machines because they also composed, or taught, and were physically unable to perform so much because of the pre-Concorde lifestyle. He also pointed out that Liszt, the progenitor of the species, retired at thirty-five. If the "big career" actually exists, who would want it?

Horowitz spoke the next day on piano competitions, noting that there are twice as many today as in 1970 and ten times as many as in 1950. He noted that part of our fascination with competitions stems from what he calls "the democratization of attainment in art." Competitions permit a young pianist the dream of instant stardom, of rising from obscurity to a hard-earned, albeit well-deserved, place in the pantheon. That they seldom provide this kind of career celebrity is becoming increasingly clear. He also noted that public participation plays a large part in competitions like the Cliburn. The "horse race" thrill of who will finish first contributes more than a little to the elation felt by audience and winner alike. Once the excitement passes, the young artist is thrown onto stages from Dubuque to New York, and before long, another winner comes along to grab the spotlight. It is a system remarkably like planned obsolescence. Horowitz praised the Gilmore for developing the noncompetitive Gilmore Artist Award, which avoids the head-to-head battle prevalent in so many competitions. He also cited the idealism inherent in the Gilmore's decision to open the award to nominees of any age, since the artist manager's predilection for youth practically guarantees early burnout.

The Gilmore's Young Artist Awards, designed to support the most promising of the fledgling pianists nominated, are another step in the right direction. Four Americans split over $70,000, which can be used in any way the recipient sees fit. According to one of the winners, the festival keeps an account for each of them, and they need only call the office to have tuition bills, a new gown for an important performance, or an airline ticket to a distant competition taken care of. With this kind of financial assistance and prestige behind them, they may find those trips to Warsaw, Bolzano, and Fort Worth unnecessary. The lucky winners were Wendy Chen, 18, of South Pasadena, California; Brenda Huang, 17, of Northbrook, Illinois; Peter Miyamoto, 20, of San Francisco, California; and Christopher Taylor, 20, of Boulder, Colorado.

Taylor played a recital at nearby Hope College on the first Sunday afternoon of the festival, and I hitched a ride with two highly experienced music critics to hear him. His program was quite serious (Bach Fantasy and Fugue in A Minor; Beethoven Op. 31, No. 3; Liszt Petrarch Sonnet No. 123 and "Funérailles"; and the Brahms F Minor Sonata), and he favors what I call the postmodern approach to interpretation: basically Bauhaus with a few personal kinks. The playing is accurate, intellectually controlled, and personal to the extent that a planned surprise now and then can keep things lively. At the very least, his playing held my attention. I liked the Bach and the Liszt a lot; the Beethoven and the Brahms were another story. However, one of my partners that day had the opposite reaction: she found the Beethoven interesting and the Brahms quite engaging, while the Liszt actually annoyed her. Our third colleague retired after the first half to a bench on the shady campus to read a book he had brought along.

Our reactions bring up another question posed by the whole Gilmore enterprise—namely, that of artistic absolutes. What does it mean to say "I liked that" or "That playing moved me"? The related questions are "What does it mean to award one pianist out of seventy-five an award totaling $250,000?" and "What does it mean when the *New York Times* says it's bad?" One almost hopes that something absolute is involved. If it moved me or the Gilmore Artistic Advisory Committee, should it move someone else? Our threesome went out to Hope College wanting to like the recital, and yet we responded so differently. It may be that the most experienced listener is the hardest to reach, having a more strongly defined artistic absolute, in some cases, than even the performer. Is it the performer who comes closest to our own ideal that pleases us most? If that were the case, the listener would never learn anything from a performance. The only way that permits the performer freedom and the listener the opportunity for growth is to be open to an artistic experience that leaves the absolutes to history. Artistry must remain indefinable; as soon as it can be labeled, it becomes the stuff of textbooks.

All of which brings us back to David Owen Norris: he *is* different. One of the Artistic Advisory Committee (AAC) members remembered hearing his tape for the first time and how it was the only tape among seventy-five that created an individual impression with every piece played. Of course, the pieces chosen were not exactly standard fare: Bax, Byrd, and Butterworth, according to the AAC, were his version of the Three Bs. There was a Brahms Op. 117 that was "decidedly left of center, but it made you listen."

Norris has always favored neglected repertoire and has had plenty of time to explore it in his various professions. He pursued it in Kalamazoo in two more formal appearances, first as a chamber musician and then as a soloist. With the Blair String Quartet, he performed the Elgar Piano Quintet, a long, rambling work that is not without effect but decidedly off the beaten track. The piano plays a relatively subservient role in the work, so once again I left the concert feeling a bit at sea as to just what David Owen Norris was all about. I found the program note he wrote for the Elgar more revealing than his playing, but again blamed it on the piece. In all his appearances, he emerged as an eminently likeable fellow, quirky and inquisitive, fascinated by the vastness of music's reservoir.

His solo recital on April 29 assayed similarly unexplored territory: two short works of William Byrd, the Arnold Bax Second Sonata, and a suite of transcriptions by Liszt of twelve songs from Schubert's *Die Winterreise*. Other than one of the Liszt transcriptions, I had never heard any of it. Word had it that Owen Norris discovered the Liszt suite lying about in a European collection, and his performance in Kalamazoo was the first ever in the United States. Even the encores were unfamiliar—and surprising: two jazz novelties by Billy Mayerl (one of which included a quotation of the old popular song "The Girl from Kalamazoo," giving the natives a good laugh) and a setting of a Scottish folk song by the avant-garde composer Peter Maxwell Davies. The hall was jammed for the recital, and it is no small compliment to the Kalamazooans that they hung on every note. Once again, the performer did not play to the gallery; he is demonstrative on stage but in no way histrionic. He plays the piano extremely well; technique is not an issue other than as a means to a musical end. He plays these works as their champion, as a fond collector would show off the curiosities discovered during years of patient searching. His individuality, what the publicity calls his "unique voice," seemed not so much a function of his artistic imagination as the approach of a kindly uncle to these prodigal relatives he rescued from oblivion. Since he played not a note of standard repertoire in three days, I find it hard to be more specific. But abandoning artistic absolutes as I must, who cares if I liked it?

The press response thus far has been favorable. Nancy Malitz, music critic of the *Detroit News*, called Norris "a musician with an original viewpoint, who not only argues a solid case but also sweeps people along in his enthusiasm for the offbeat repertoire he loves." The English press had a field day, cranking out their superb vocabulary to gloat over a native son beating the Yanks at their own game. As Alan Rusbridger put it:

On the one hand, the professional American piano world, where the repertoire is pre-ordained, the keyboard techniques are electric, and the critics sit with pens, notebooks and voltameters. On the other hand, an unorthodox Brit ("please don't call me eccentric") who cheerfully confesses to a less Semtexian technique and who loves to explore the B-roads and farm tracks of the pianistic canon.

Without a doubt, the Kalamazooans loved him. Who can say what will happen next for the eminently different David Owen Norris?

It is wonderful to know that an organization exists that is seeking out young pianists to support as well as older pianists with something to say who may "have fallen through the cracks." This same organization is bringing a biennial festival of keyboard music to a medium-sized Midwestern town, creating any number of converts to Irving Gilmore's true love. It is nothing short of amazing to contemplate the amount of money in the Gilmore treasury and the good it could do the entire piano world. One hopes that it will be spent wisely. (Rumors of the fee paid to Van Cliburn for his recital are nothing short of scandalous; however, in these days when merely average major-league baseball players receive $1 million a year, perhaps we should be glad that a pianist can command a truly hefty fee.) It remains to be seen whether a major career can be launched from such a platform, or even needs to be. What is important is that someone is, indeed, listening.

59

Taking On the Competition:
An Interview with David Pocock

Clavier *Magazine*

JULY–AUGUST 1999

RW: *Clavier* readers may know you as the first Artistic Director of the Gilmore Festival, and there are probably quite a few people around Philadelphia who recognize you as the education director of the Philadelphia Orchestra from 1993–97. What's going on at the American Pianists Association since you've become artistic director?

DP: The American Pianists Association has been an elegant, though largely well-kept, secret for over twenty years. The dramatic recent successes are built on its wonderful history. In the past two years, the endowment of the APA has grown from $20,000 to over $1 million, and we are nowhere near finished with that campaign. The money spent on the selection processes and the various programs has more than tripled; recent winners of the fellowships have played more than fifty concerts around the world. I feel pretty good about that. The big news, though, is the change in the selection process itself.

I think that many readers of this magazine know of the work I did at the Gilmore. As a brief refresher, the Gilmore employed a jury to travel around the world incognito to listen to deserving pianists in a totally noncompetitive fashion—so noncompetitive, in fact, that the winners didn't even know they had been "competing" until they were told that they had won. The Gilmore, of course, has changed and, in their last go-around, awarded the prize to an already-established superstar, Leif Ove Andsnes.

The APA's new method keeps the best aspects of what was originally intended to be the Gilmore process. It is designed to identify and reward musicianship and communicative ability rather than competitive skill. In a nutshell, we are going to run our competition like an elegant concert series that will culminate in a festival.

First, we solicit nominations—from pianists, music schools, other competitions and festivals, and others—to identify a pool of outstanding American pianists between the ages of eighteen and thirty. We then put together tapes of live performances from these candidates and choose a group of five as finalists.

These five pianists will come to Indianapolis one at a time, separated from one another by at least a month. This series will be called the Premiere Series. Each residency will have a concerto performance with the Indianapolis Chamber Orchestra, a solo recital, another concerto with a high school orchestra, and a series of performances and visits to area community centers, schools, and retirement complexes. Each pianist will spend about a week in Indianapolis, receiving a good fee, at least one review, and in general will be treated as a visiting artist: fêted, wined, and dined!

In the spring of 2000, the five pianists will return for Discovery Week, during which they will share programs of lieder, chamber music, solo piano music...will engage in workshops and master classes and immerse themselves once again in Indianapolis. Everything in both series will be evaluated, and at the end of the Discovery Week, two of the five finalists will be named Fellows of the American Pianists Association. I love this, and I think the pianists chosen to participate will love it as well.

RW: That should be fascinating. Why did you feel you had to rethink the traditional competitive process? Why are some competitions more successful at identifying winners who go on to performing careers?

DP: My first concerns about standard piano competitions were largely pragmatic. I had been hired by the Gilmore Foundation as a consultant, and my task was to tell them how to organize and produce a new major international piano competition, something that would out-Cliburn the Cliburn. The Gilmore Foundation had the resources to do just that, but the first red flag went up as I considered the mind-numbing number of competitions already in existence.

Just think: Cliburn, Leeds, the Queen Elisabeth, Warsaw, Tchaikovsky, Naumburg, Rubinstein, Bachauer, Honens, Montréal for starters, and then a seemingly endless list of very good competitions—Hamamatsu, Dublin, Scotland, Palm Beach, Busoni, Beethoven, Liszt, Santander, Cleveland, and on and on. Then there is a truly endless list of "international" competitions in places such as South Carolina and Missouri and Sicily. I found more than sixty "international" competitions just in Italy! Who could keep track of all these competitions, let alone the winners? Remember that terrifying book called *15,000 Pianists* that came out a few years ago which listed competition entrants and winners?[1]

Next, I tried to understand why so many competitions were producing so few real careers. Long ago, by and large, were the days when great artists—musicians such as Pollini, Ashkenazy, Argerich, and Fleisher—were discovered and launched through the competitive process.

Were competitions themselves the culprits? Certainly, there were a lot of theories floating around. Many people felt that the very process of having to eliminate some competitors in the winnowing process assured that strong artistic profiles would fall by the wayside and that inoffensive, middle-of-the-road candidates must necessarily prevail. Some complained of unethical, politicized judging. Many felt that piano contests were going the route of ice-skating competitions and that judges were making decisions based on the equivalents of easily quantifiable (and audience pleasing!) triple jumps and perfect landings, as opposed to the more mysterious and infinitely more difficult-to-quantify realm of artistry.

In short, I could not in good conscience recommend another standard competition, and I have been lucky that both the Gilmore and the APA allowed me the chance to come up with interesting and workable alternatives.

RW: Do you think the Gilmore "winners" and the soon-to-be APA artists are somehow more viable as musicians than the standard competition winner?

---

1. Gustav A. Alink, *International Piano Competitions, Book 2: 15000 Pianists* (Music Library Association, 1990).

DP: I do think so. Certainly, the first two Gilmore Artists—both of whom are musical polymaths extraordinaire—are far more interesting than most traditional competition winners. Both compose, conduct, and play absorbing repertoire to perfection. They have overactive brains and imaginations attached to their fingers! I would still go far out of my way to hear either of them play, a claim I could not make for many of today's laureates.

The APA's new format is designed to cast a wide net for the most interesting American pianists and to give them the chance to be evaluated based on their work in actual concert situations. Even though the APA has a good track record in finding and helping some of America's pianistic gems, I didn't want to be limited to pianists who just happen to apply in any particular competition cycle. Above all, I didn't want future candidates to duke it out, as it were, in musical gladiatorial combat. Rather, I wanted to feel confident that we would issue invitations to the most stunning young talents out there to come to Indianapolis and give them a series of rewarding and stimulating experiences. I know that, based on the nominations we received and the decisions which have been made thus far, we are well on the road to doing precisely that.

RW: What of all the fine young pianists who aren't selected for this process? Aren't you relying a lot on your nominators, creating in the process an elite club of "name" teachers nominating their own students?

DP: Perhaps, but the membership roster for the club is pretty large. Remember, it is not just an "elite" group of pedagogues making the nominations and suggestions—it is also other piano competitions and festivals plus the rather large group of APA counselors who serve on the Artistic Advisory Board. I spend part of every day on the phone with musicians around the United States and the world trying to keep informed about the music business in general and the piano world in particular. I feel confident that the APA "tentacles" are spread far enough that the appropriate names will all come to our attention. The invitational aspect of our selection process provides a clear advantage since we are not forced to consider only the names of those pianists who choose to apply.

More to the point is the fact that some nominators were hard-pressed to think of American candidates at all. In this excruciatingly competitive and complex business, there are few American pianists who should realistically contemplate performing careers, or who distinguish themselves in important competitions, or who, for that matter, are even accepted these days to prestigious schools such as Curtis and Juilliard. Those few Americans who do stand out came quickly to the minds of the musicians responsible for making nominations. We asked nominators to set the bar as high as it would go as they contemplated names to put forward. As a result, we ended up with a relatively small group of nominees, but some of those names were put forward by three, four, or five different sources.

RW: What qualities should be sought out and developed in the pianists any organization chooses to assist?

DP: The critical factor—the quintessential factor—for which we should all search is, simply, an ability to communicate. Competitions that look for the next great pianist, for someone to take over where Horowitz and Rubinstein left off, are doomed to failure. Competitions that reward ivory gunslingers—quick-draw artists good for one brilliant, speedy shot—are increasingly irrelevant in today's marketplace. Competitions that superimpose repertoire or dress codes—or, for that matter, most anything else—are dinosaurs. Let me be very clear: I have no interest in finding and helping someone go out and play the Tchaikovsky Concerto thirty times a season.

Rather, I want to work with artists such as J.Y. Song, who wants to produce a video featuring some late Liszt, or Anthony Molinaro, who plays classical and jazz and who improvises. Jim Giles plays first performances of music by Curtis Curtis-Smith and William Bolcom and gooey transcriptions by Earl Wild. Too many competitions "advance" the general state of the performance art by rewarding speed, accuracy, and correct performance practice. Should every young musician go through the regimen of playing a Mozart concerto and a Romantic concerto and an étude and a Bach suite, and so on? At the highest levels, we must look for genius and the ability to share that genius, and we must convince audiences that these people are worth hearing.

60

Report on the 2013
American Pianists Association Awards Finals

International Piano

Indianapolis is a quintessentially American city—capital of the Midwestern state of Indiana; site of the Indy 500 race on Memorial Day; current home of the football team formerly known as the Baltimore Colts; and birthplace of such notables as late-night television personality David Letterman, author Kurt Vonnegut, bank robber John Dillinger, actor Steve McQueen, industrialist Eli Lilly, and a US vice president, best known for misspelling *potato*, Dan Quayle.

The piano world should take note, though. Indianapolis also supports a unique organization dedicated to discovering, promoting, and advancing the careers of young, world-class American jazz and classical pianists. The operative word here is *American*, since US citizenship is required for participation, and while jazz may be the more American art form, the American Pianists Association is equally intent on assisting classical pianists at a crucial time in their early careers.

Since its founding in 1979, the American Pianists Association has identified forty-three winners, the large number due in part to selecting more than one fellow with each competition. In the past five years, the six most recent classical and jazz Fellows have given nearly two thousand performances on six continents in thirty-seven countries and forty-one states. That's a lot of assistance. Collectively, they hold twenty-seven prizes and awards from other national and international competitions, in addition to the APA award. That's also a rather good record of success.

The APA Fellowship Program is much more than a competition, however. It does its best to avoid the hoarier aspects of gladiatorial combat—indeed, one cannot apply for the competition. Participation requires a nomination from a wide network of concert pianists, conductors, teachers, and artistic administrators. A panel then sorts through the aspirants, selecting only five as finalists. The lucky five in 2013 were Sean Chen, twenty-four; Sara Daneshpour, twenty-six;

Claire Huangci, twenty-three; Andrew Staupe, twenty-eight; and Eric Zuber, twenty-seven.

Then begins a seven-month sequence known as the Classical Premiere Series. Each of the five finalists is invited to Indianapolis for separate weeklong residencies that include an adjudicated solo recital and concerto performance with the Indianapolis Chamber Orchestra and an innovative engagement with local high school orchestras in which the finalists prepare and perform another concerto movement with the school musicians. APA's full resources are poured into these events, essentially treating the finalists as artists-in-residence. All these events are fully produced concert opportunities, giving the performers real-life experience in front of varied audiences. The pianists are thus treated as true professionals. They never even see the other finalists during their individual weeks in Indianapolis. Hidden among the audience, however, is a second judging panel that rates the finalists one to five over the course of the series.

With Classical Discovery Week, held April 15–20, 2013, the five finalists finally "compete," participating in several adjudicated events spread over six days and heard by yet another jury (Charles Hamlen, former chairman of IMG Artists; Anthony Fogg, artistic administrator of the Boston Symphony Orchestra; and the noted international pianists José Feghali, Murray McLachlan, and Christopher Taylor, who won APA's Classical Fellowship in 2000). Every weekday at noon, a finalist performed an hour recital at the intimate, reverberant Christ Church Cathedral on Monument Circle. In addition to solo works, the pianists were joined by the Linden String Quartet in a piano quintet of the finalists' choosing. On Monday evening, five new piano works commissioned by APA for the occasion (from composers Lisa Bielawa, Margaret Brouwer, Gabriela Lena Frank, Missy Mazzoli, and Sarah Kirkland Snider) were premiered at Butler University. On Thursday evening, the pianists became vocal collaborators, accompanying the stunning soprano Jessica Rivera in a wide-ranging evening of song. Friday and Saturday evenings comprised the grand finale: the finalists performed the concerto of their choice with the Indianapolis Symphony Orchestra, conducted by Gerard Schwarz.

When asked why so many facets of musicianship are tested,

APA president and artistic director Joel Harrison said, "The competition process includes all the various skills a professional pianist might encounter in the world today. The finalists leave Indianapolis with some serious performing credentials they did not have before coming here." Indeed, one might credit APA with nudging the young pianistic lions toward a well-roundedness that typical competitions eschew.

The song recital proved particularly telling as each finalist appeared onstage alongside a singer of great charisma and musical projection. Jessica Rivera's collaborators almost instantly differentiated themselves from her accompanists. Eric Zuber's Debussy exhibited subtlety and flair equally, balancing Ms. Rivera's intensity in every phrase. Andrew Staupe missed a chance to shine in four songs of Richard Strauss, while Sean Chen made up for the relative simplicity of songs by Joaquín Turina in a lovely solo interlude. Claire Huangci disappeared in songs of Mompou, while Sara Daneshpour sounded heavy-handed in songs of Samuel Barber.

Of course, the concerto finales drew the most attention, with sellout crowds both nights at the Hilbert Circle Theatre. Daneshpour led off on Friday night with Chopin's First Concerto in an anonymous performance that found little help from Maestro Schwarz. Huangci followed with the fastest Prokofiev Third imaginable, which impressed for brilliance even as it lacked musical substance. Zuber's Rachmaninoff Second was thoroughly professional, again overwhelmed by a conductor whose ears seemed to be everywhere but with the pianist. The following night, Sean Chen opened the program with Bartók's Second Concerto. Schwarz was more in his element here, and the performance blazed with color and excitement. It was Chen's first time playing the complex work with orchestra. Andrew Staupe's Rachmaninoff Third was rock solid, alas lumbering when it should have soared. To this listener, the competition was between Chen and Zuber.

For the first time, only one fellow was chosen. To general acclaim, Sean Chen was awarded the Christel DeHaan Fellowship worth $100,000—including a $50,000 cash award and career assistance for two years involving publicity, performances, and other opportunities worldwide. The other four finalists each took home $10,000 and performing experience for a lifetime.

61

"And Then There Were Two..."

The 2001 Cliburn Competition

Clavier

SEPTEMBER 2001

This story begins for me in Cleveland on a wet December day in 1998. Through a remarkable series of serendipities, I was recommended as a teacher to an immensely talented twenty-six-year-old pianist from Uzbekistan named Stanislav Ioudenitch. We met that day over lunch at the Marriott Hotel to discuss the possibility of his studying with me at the University of Missouri in Kansas City's Conservatory of Music. Neither of us knew much about the other, but by the time dessert came around, we shared the sense that this could work. Within three weeks, Stanislav moved his wife and child to Kansas City to begin doctoral studies.

On June 10, 2001, Stanislav was named a cowinner of the gold medal at the Eleventh Van Cliburn International Piano Competition. While this account cannot claim journalistic objectivity (like everyone on earth, I am entitled to my opinions), I invite the reader to join me in my seat at the competition. There is much to tell of tension and triumph, and the coming to terms with both.

PRELUDE

The Cliburn is without doubt one of the handful of truly important piano competitions in the world today. Its substantial prizes, the media attention it receives, and particularly the long list of engagements awarded to the finalists make competing in it a goal for ambitious young pianists everywhere. This past winter, the competition received over two hundred entrance applications; 137 of these aspirants were granted forty-minute recital auditions heard by a five-member screening jury in Utrecht, Budapest, Moscow, Lugano, New York, Chicago, and Fort Worth. Interestingly, these recitals were open to the public, and thanks to good publicity, achieved overflow audiences in several locations.

The screening jury chose thirty pianists to compete in Fort Worth. They ranged in age from nineteen to twenty-nine, with the gender division favoring the males, twenty-three to seven. There were twelve Russian (or old–Soviet Bloc) pianists, seven from the Far East, four Italians, and a smattering of other nationalities that included only two Americans. It should be noted, however, that eleven of the thirty studied in the United States. The preliminary round, in which each contestant played a fifty-minute recital, began on May 25 and ended late on May 29.

Although I did not attend the preliminaries due to other commitments, the Cliburn website provided daily updates via links to reviews in both the Fort Worth and Dallas newspapers. The prelims may be the most exciting—certainly the most interesting—part of any major competition. Where else can you hear thirty different pianists from all over the world, playing as though their lives depended on it? Dazzling pianism abounds. One encounters some fascinating repertoire choices as well, whether from personal commitment to a composer or style, or simply to create an effect. Quite a few contestants took the serious approach: Maurizio Baglini chose to play only Schubert's G Major Sonata and Liszt's *Après une lecture du Dante*, a risk that paid off in his advancing to the semifinals. Others were not as fortunate: both Paavali Jumppanen (with the "Eroica" Variations and the Chopin B Minor Sonata) and Amir Katz (with the "Waldstein" Sonata and *Kreisleriana*) were heard no more. The two Americans in the competition performed newer American music to great critical acclaim: Andrew Russo made history as the first pianist in the history of the Cliburn to play on the *inside* of the piano in George Crumb's *A Little Suite for Christmas, A.D. 1979*, and Roger Wright's performance of Frederic Rzewski's *Winnsboro Cotton Mill Blues* brought the audience to its feet. Alas, neither of them made it to the semifinals.

In nearly all the programs, the display of virtuosic technique is the common denominator. In a competition at this level, the pianist simply must play the piano extraordinarily well, and the best way to demonstrate that is by wailing through a certifiably difficult piece (usually more than one) with all guns blazing. For that reason, pieces like the Liszt Sonata, Ravel's *Gaspard de la Nuit*, the Brahms *Paganini Variations*, and Stravinsky's *Petrushka* were heard frequently. Rachmaninoff's Sonata in B-flat Minor, Op. 36, won the popularity contest, offered by nine of the accepted contestants. If you think that feats of pianism have reached the limits of possibility, think again; I heard several young pianists accomplish feats of derring-do during the Cliburn that still boggle my mind. Roll over, Horowitz!

MAY 31, 1:30 P.M.

My wife Karen and I had long planned to attend the competition, should Stanislav make it to the semifinals. Upon receiving the good news, we had twenty-four hours to get to Texas. Driving into Fort Worth, billboards proclaimed the Cliburn, and along the downtown streets, banners flew from streetlamps. Traffic clogged the entrances to parking garages near the hall. A large and buzzing audience nearly filled the two thousand seats of the Nancy Lee and Perry R. Bass Performance Hall, which opened its doors in 1998 and was hosting the competition for the first time.

The twelve competitors selected for the semifinals each perform twice: once as soloist in a seventy-five-minute solo recital without intermission, and once in a chamber music setting, performing a piano quintet by Brahms, Schumann, Dvořák, or Franck. These twenty-four events are squeezed into eight ticketed concerts, each lasting well over three hours, scheduled in the afternoons and evenings of four consecutive days. Three different pianists are heard in each concert: afternoons feature two solo programs bracketing a quintet, and evening concerts are the opposite. While this system may be difficult to describe, the result is simple: the semifinals are the most intense, nerve-racking, challenging part of the competition.

The first semifinalist we hear—twenty-one-year-old Vassily Primakov—belies all the clichés about successful competition playing. His was a big, risky, vibrantly personal *Carnaval* that broke with tradition even as it established its own inevitability. He was also the first to play Lowell Liebermann's *Three Impromptus*, one of five new works offered to competitors this year instead of the single commissioned work that all semifinalists had to perform in previous years.

Primakov's recital is followed by a performance of the Dvořák Piano Quintet by Oleksiy Koltakov, a twenty-two-year-old Russian studying in Australia, with this year's quartet-in-residence, the Takács String Quartet. The performance never quite gels, and one wonders if Mr. Koltakov has played much chamber music in his short career (and whether an international competition jury can expect such). The second soloist of the afternoon, Maxim Philippov, plays an obscure Haydn sonata with perfect correctness, two pieces from Ravel's *Miroirs*, and repeats the Liebermann, this time from memory. Now well into our third hour of listening, Karen and I retreat to the exit before the complete Rachmaninoff Preludes, Op. 32, could drain us of our last energy. The next morning's review calls it the highlight of the afternoon; an acquaintance in the audience calls it "thick."

Opinions swarm at a competition like locusts over a cornfield. On the short trip to the refreshment bar in the lobby, one could hear reviews of the previous competitor ranging from "talent of the century" to "latent axe murderer." The critics of the *Fort Worth Star-Telegram* (Wayne Lee Gay) and the *Dallas Morning News* (Scott Cantrell) covered every concert during the seventeen days of the competition and disagreed with each other as often as audience members. Above it all, in the boxes to the right rear of the hall, sat the jury, whose collective opinion was the only one that mattered.

The word in the papers—and on the lips of the audience at intermissions—is that there are three front-runners after the preliminary round: Antonio Pompa-Baldi, a twenty-six-year-old Italian who won the Cleveland International Competition in 1999; Olga Kern, also twenty-six, a statuesque Russian with a Meg Ryan haircut who plays, in the words of Scott Cantrell, "as though she ate earthquakes for breakfast"; and Stanislav, who many say had won the longest ovation of the preliminaries. All three will play the next afternoon.

FRIDAY, JUNE 1

Both Olga and Stanislav had been in the 1997 Cliburn. Olga, playing under a different surname and hair color, didn't make it past the first round. Stanislav was advanced to the semis, but early on the morning before they began, he poured boiling water over his left hand while making tea, causing second-degree burns that forced his withdrawal from the competition. In 2001, both have something to prove, and the audience hangs on every note they play.

Stanislav's solo program opens the Friday afternoon lineup. The hall is well filled as the Cliburn's stage announcer, Steve Cumming, begs the audience to turn off alarm watches, pagers, and cellular phones. He then announces Stanislav and his program. My palms are sweating as if I were the one about to play. Stanislav is enigmatic onstage—he walks on quietly, unhurried, bows politely, and sits down. The audience's applause is barely finished as he attacks Prokofiev's *Sarcasms*, which he plays with an extraordinary range of moods and color. He seems totally focused and in command. I relax enough to enjoy the music, but my palms sweat on. Next comes Liszt's *Spanish Rhapsody*. Stanislav possesses a technique capable of taming any virtuoso showpiece; what is so fascinating about his playing is his musical imagination—he finds and projects a psychological complexity in everything he plays, even such fluff as the *Spanish Rhapsody*. The audience responds with a roar of approval.

The centerpiece of his program is Schubert's *Moments musicaux*, twenty-five minutes of pure music with no virtuosity to hide behind. It is risky to program something like this at the Cliburn, where the audience wants fire and dazzle, and the judges reward technical accuracy and personal charisma—perhaps the only two indisputable quantities they can all agree on—more readily than imponderables like artistry and musicality. Everything, it seems to me, is riding on the Schubert. As I had hoped, he plays it simply, honestly, and does not try to sell the music, as other competitors have with their so-called easier selections. Aside from a little memory bobble in the fourth piece, it cannot be faulted, in my opinion. I'm hoping the judges agree.

Then without intermission (he has been onstage for fifty minutes at this point), he launches into his choice for the contemporary commissioned piece, Judith Lang Zaimont's *Impronta digitale*. It is a nine-minute tangle of notes—a vibrant, exciting piece, almost a *moto perpetuo*, with occasional tonal leanings amid its blazes of color and dynamism. Stanislav makes a convincing case for it, despite two glitches on the part of the page turner. The composer, who is present, rewards him with a standing ovation. I sense he is tiring, however, and his final piece—Stravinsky's *Three Movements from Petrushka*—is not all that it could be. At his best, Stanislav owns this piece; it never occurs to the listener to miss the orchestra. When he played it in Kansas City last winter, visiting critic Joseph Horowitz said privately that he'd never heard it better. In his hands, the music dances, and the execution of the technical difficulties leaves listeners open-mouthed in disbelief. Today, it is good, but I can tell he is exhausted.

We rush around the corner to the Bass Hall stage entrance. Security is tight at the Cliburn—there are simply too many fans who would clog the stage wings if access were granted to everyone. We wait in the sweltering, close heat for Stanislav to emerge. After what seems an eternity, he appears, trailed by a cameraman, a mic bearer, and Peter Rosen, the director of the competition documentary. Other reporters, with portable tape recorders slung over their shoulders, vie for position. As the crowd pushes toward him, we embrace briefly as he tells me, "That was catastrophically difficult."

As eager as I am to talk with him, there are fifty people behind me. Pompa-Baldi's chamber music is already underway, and Olga's solo program will end the afternoon session, so we head back to the hall for more listening.

The sound monitors in the lobby indicate that Pompa-Baldi is already into the scherzo of the Schumann Quintet. Amazingly, seven semifinalists have chosen this piece, even though it offers the pianist little opportunity to shine. The piano is seldom heard alone and often merely doubles the string writing. It is a glorious piece, of course, but once the tempo is set, it basically plays itself.

After hearing seven performances of the piece in four days, I discover that many competition pianists think that "faster and louder" will work as well in chamber music as it does in virtuoso repertoire. Pompa-Baldi's scherzo is frantically fast—while pianistically impressive, it makes no musical sense. The Takács string players sound as though they are lashed to their bows, forced to play faster and faster by the unrelenting, domineering piano. At one point, the five derail briefly. The finale receives the same flogging; I wonder how Pompa-Baldi can retain his front-runner status with playing like this.

Still, during the intermission that follows, the lobby is buzzing with words like "brilliant," "electrifying," and "he's so handsome." The excitement mounts: Olga is next.

When she was in Fort Worth for the 1997 Cliburn, Olga Kern was known as Olga Pushechnikova. She fell in love with another competitor that year, Dimitri Teterin, and they married soon after. Back home in Russia, Olga gave birth to a little boy, Vladislav, but the marriage didn't last. She wanted to start all over, so she changed her name, her teachers, and most importantly her attitude. She shares a two-room apartment with her son and her parents in Moscow. Her story has won the hearts of many Texans—the newspapers soon dub it "Olgamania."

She comes onstage in a sleek black gown trimmed in gold, cut off one shoulder. She is strikingly tall, her blonde hair catching the light. Her long arms swing nonchalantly as she strides toward the piano. She smiles as she enters, and her face lights up with joyous wonder as she bows to the audience. In short, she makes a dazzling connection before she plays a note. Her program (two Schubert Impromptus, both books of Brahms *Paganini Variations, Impronta digitale*, the Scriabin Ninth Sonata, and the Barber Sonata) highlights her strengths, which is—quite simply—her strength. She is a formidable pianistic athlete; technical difficulties disappear one after another under her hands. The octave glissandi in the Brahms sound like child's play. She attacks *Impronta digitale*, played by memory, with a take-no-prisoners assurance—Zaimont is overwhelmed. (Later she tells me, "I used to think I could play the piano.") Aside from the Schubert, the program has been one weight-lifting feat after another, and with the final notes of the Barber, she is still going strong. The audience goes wild.

INTERLUDE I

At this point, the semifinals are only half over. I feel as though I've been in Texas for a month instead of forty-eight hours. "Intense" barely begins to describe what goes on. With the best of intentions to stay through all the evening performances, Karen and I wilted before the final recital. Thursday evening, Xiaohan Wang's Schumann Quintet suggested a unique voice, but one not ready for prime time. Maurizio Baglini's recital started promisingly with Bach-Busoni Chorale Preludes, but the Scriabin Third Sonata proved an ill-advised choice for him, *Impronta digitale* seemed blurred, and his *Carnaval* was not nearly as interesting as Vassily Primakov's. We missed Alessandra Maria Ammara's quintet completely. The next night, Masaru Okada turned in a decent Schumann Quintet, but Davide Franceschetti's decision to play Beethoven's "Diabelli" Variations as the bulk of his recital program struck me as noble but nuts. The last semifinalist, Sergey Koudriakov, went on without my ears in attendance.

Despite the tension, there have been lighter moments, such as the cell phone going off in the hall, despite all the warnings, that played "Raiders of the Lost Ark." Steve Cumming subsequently lectured the audience with a visual aid: a comically oversized score titled "Grave silencia"—with an indication that the silence be repeated ad infinitum. "The performers pay attention to their music; this is *your* sheet music," intoned Cumming. "Unlike a graphic artist or a sculptor, a musician uses a palette of silence," he continued. "Silence is your music. All the musicians have memorized their music. Please memorize yours."

Downtown Fort Worth offered many distractions for competition attendees. With free parking after 5:00 p.m., the streets are full into the wee hours most nights. Bass Hall has no doubt added to the downtown's allure; with its two imposing angels trumpeting from on high, the building proclaims itself a Parnassus of Art. Nearby, bars and clubs do a thriving business, and outdoor cafés and restaurants beckon those who like to dine in an ambient temperature hovering around ninety degrees. While the crowds in Bass were impressive, the revelers carousing through the streets, even on weeknights, suggest that classical music need not worry about becoming *too* popular. On any given night, there were more people in downtown Fort Worth who knew Chopin as a vodka rather than as a composer.

Most competitors eschew the nightlife in favor of practicing, so their domestic situations mean a lot to them. Since its inception, the Cliburn has arranged for the pianists to stay with host families in Fort Worth. This organizational element of the competition produces at least two benefits: it guarantees that the community comes into close contact with the musicians, and it helps keep the competitors sane. It is not uncommon for lifelong relationships to develop.

Stanislav's hostess in Fort Worth is a sixtyish woman with sparkling eyes and a determined set to her jaw named Judy Needham. In '97, it was Judy who rushed him to the emergency room. In '98, when he came to UMKC to study with me, it was she who signed a financial statement promising to make up any insufficiency should Stanislav find himself in need. (Thankfully, such a shortage never occurred.) This spring, she welcomed him to Fort Worth two months before the competition began to give him the solitude and moral support he felt he needed to train for the marathon of performances to come. Upon our first meeting, we had an instant rapport. Within hours, we called each other "Coach."

Marty Leonard is another true believer in Stanislav. Seldom have I met a person who made a stronger first impression than Marty: ageless, with perfect posture, more at home in jeans than a business suit. Her radiant blue eyes meet your gaze with total directness. She is completely without affectation and, in partnership with Judy, has cornered the Fort Worth market in generosity. While Stanislav slaved away at Judy's, Marty hosted his wife, Tatiana, and their five-year-old daughter, Maria. I feel fortunate to know these two extraordinary women.

SUNDAY, JUNE 3

The last day of the semifinals again pitted the three front-runners against each other. On the previous day, Koltakov gave blistering accounts of the ubiquitous Rachmaninoff Sonata and the Liszt-Horowitz *Second Hungarian Rhapsody*, but his Liszt Sonata meandered like a ship adrift in a boundless ocean. Primakov's Brahms Quintet was often beautiful, but his youth was betrayed by music of this order. Xiaohan Wang's solo recital was interesting but lacked consistency. Philippov's Brahms Quintet that evening showed this twenty-nine-year-old's maturity and experience; the playing was again thoroughly professional, if perhaps dull.

At 1:30 p.m. on Sunday, Antonio Pompa-Baldi took the stage with a curious solo program that opened with Debussy's *Suite bergamasque*. Here is a pianist whose fingers can do anything his mind commands and a piece that doesn't require much in the way of special effects. The resulting combination produced a rhythmically distorted performance in which uninteresting inner voices were brought to the fore. It was as though he didn't trust the music to speak for itself. Lowell Liebermann's *Three Impromptus* were played with complete confidence and control. These are facile, ingratiating pieces that break no new musical ground, even as they challenge the performer with their deceptively simple pianistic intricacies. Next came Rachmaninoff's B-flat Minor Sonata in its final performance of the competition; Pompa-Baldi may be a perfect pianist for this piece, in that he has both the technique and the imagination to clarify the texture. I was nevertheless left a bit cold since there was never a hint of struggle or pathos. As a palate cleanser, the pianist played Poulenc's "Caprice italien" from the suite *Napoli*, an inspired repertoire choice. The program ended with both books of the Brahms *Paganini Variations*, but in a daring move, Pompa-Baldi rearranged the order of the variations, following the cue of pianists such as Backhaus and Michelangeli. Since I am not fond of these variations in any order, I simply let myself be swept away by the avalanche of conquered difficulties. I was not alone in finding Pompa-Baldi a perplexing artist. Scott Cantrell of the *Dallas Morning News* wrote of him, "He sometimes plays beautifully, sometimes too aggressively. His Chopin Sonata [from the preliminaries] and Schumann Quintet were too pressed and pressurized, but his best performances arguably merited a continuing place in the running."

Stanislav's Franck Quintet followed. The chamber music segment of the semifinals is, depending on your view, either that which separates the wheat from the chaff or that which adds two days to the whole without telling much of anything. Admittedly, very few young, fire-breathing virtuosi have had the time or the inclination to play a lot of chamber music while still in their twenties. Then, given the tight schedule at the Cliburn, they are given one seventy-five-minute rehearsal with the quartet the day before the performance. Nothing of substance can be done in the way of rehearsing; the competitors are at the mercy of the seasoned members of the quartet-in-residence, who have played these pieces many times and are such savvy chamber musicians that they can follow (usually) a veritable Tasmanian devil through the score. The jury knows within five minutes if the pianist has a clue about real chamber playing; unfortunately for the inexperienced player, these pieces last a lot longer.

Truth be told, Stanislav had not played a lot of chamber music. The Franck was new to him, and surprisingly, the Takács had never played it either. Nerves were running high at the rehearsal on Saturday morning when Stanislav arrived ten minutes late, retrieving his specially constructed bench (he sits very low at the piano) from Judy Needham's trunk as the cameras rolled and followed his breathless rush to the stage. Brief pleasantries gave way to a reading of the first movement. At first, Stanislav tried too hard, overwhelming the strings with the piano part's lush figuration. I made notes for later discussion, and those of us in the hall gave him the "softer" sign whenever he looked out for an indication of balance. Soon all five players found a groove and produced some ravishing moments. Throughout the rehearsal, the first violinist asked detailed questions about specific points, and the other quartet members chimed in with requests for attention here, some freedom there. Given the shortage of time, Stanislav had to depend on osmosis; being a highly intuitive musician, he could absorb what he needed just from hearing these fine musicians play and meshing it with what he already knew and felt about the piece. The quartet was equally attuned to his ideas; 95 percent of the rehearsal was nonverbal. Despite the rough beginning, the rehearsal ended with good feelings all around.

I was nevertheless extremely nervous for the performance. I had the deepest conviction that Stanislav was musically gifted enough to win; it was his inner resolve that worried me. Only two days before, he had played a grueling program that exhausted him. His left wrist was bothering him, and the cameras dogged his every step. Wayne Lee Gay's reviews in the *Star-Telegram* had been favoring Kern and Pompa-Baldi as the two stars of the competition, glossing over Stanislav's performances with supercilious condescension. By now I knew my student well enough to recognize his late arrival at yesterday's rehearsal as a psychological protest. Anything could happen today.

Such circumstances can give birth to great art, or madness and destruction. You can't plan to give a great performance; one comes about in a crucible of uncertainties. On this particular day, the gods smiled, and the Franck Quintet emerged as a glorious pinnacle of Romantic expression. It was a performance that no one in the audience will soon forget. The *Dallas Morning News* called it "a performance of both unbelievable power and tenderness. There was passion at the very edge of hysteria, but never over, and also moments of sweet soaring lyricism… This may have been the most compelling chamber music performance of all."

Even Wayne Lee Gay admitted, "Ioudenitch turned in an energetic, passionate performance within the necessary constraints of the genre… [making] a slightly stronger impression in his chamber music than in his solo recital of the semifinal round."

The rest of the day's performances were essentially anticlimactic. Masaru Okada's disappointing recital eliminated him from contention for the finals, and Olga's Schumann Quintet contained no surprises. The *Dallas Morning News* called it "a hyperactive performance that might have benefited from a dose of Ritalin." Gay, on the other hand, continued to thump his Olgamania drum: "The return of Olga Kern to Fort Worth may well be the introduction of a major star to the American concert circuit."

The announcement of the finalists, scheduled to be made at 10:30 p.m., came near midnight. Richard Rodzinski, the executive director of the Cliburn, explained that the jury had taken extra time to decide several special prizes, which would be given at the final awards ceremony. In the meantime, well over one thousand people, as well as dozens of reporters anxious to make their deadlines, waited breathlessly in Bass Hall for the announcement of the finalists. At last it came: the front-runners were all included (Kern, Pompa-Baldi, and Stanislav), as was Maxim Philippov, whose steady, middle-of-the-road performances could not be faulted. The final two were surprises to many: Oleksiy Koltakov and Xiaohan Wang, both young, relatively inexperienced, and rough around the edges. Monday morning, jurists complained of the absence among the finalists of Alessandra Maria Ammara, whose gentle musicality seems to have been ignored, and Vassily Primakov, whose individuality may not have been to everyone's liking but who played with more technical and musical consistency than either Koltakov or Wang. Nevertheless, the power rests with the jury. On to the finals!

INTERLUDE II

The three-thousand-seat auditorium of the Tarrant County Convention Center, scene of past Cliburn finals, had been turned to rubble in the name of progressive improvements to the facility; no one connected to the Cliburn was too upset, given its shoddy acoustics. Knowing that demand for tickets would run higher than the two-thousand-seat capacity of the new Bass Hall, the decision was made early in the 2001 planning process to repeat each of the three finals concerts. Even with top ticket prices of $125, the finals were essentially sold out before the first note was played on June 6.

Finalists are required to play two concerti: one with chamber orchestra (Mozart, early Beethoven, and a few other possibilities) and one with full orchestra (Liszt, Brahms, Tchaikovsky, Rachmaninoff, i.e., the usual suspects). The order of performance follows that of the preliminary round; hence, Koltakov and Wang would play Wednesday and Thursday evenings, Pompa-Baldi and Philippov Friday evening and Saturday afternoon, and Ioudenitch and Kern Saturday evening and Sunday afternoon. The jury would hear all the performances, taking the second into account as much as the first. The critics wrote of both as well.

Unfortunately, there were duplications of repertoire. Ioudenitch and Philippov both played the Mozart C Major Concerto, K. 467; Pompa-Baldi and Wang both chose the same composer's Concerto in A Major, K. 488. The Rachmaninoff Third had no fewer than four proponents (Koltakov, Wang, Philippov, and Kern) and was therefore heard eight times in four days. In the period of a week, the members of the Fort Worth Symphony more than earned their overtime, performing seven different concerti in six public concerts with six different pianists, each of whom received two rehearsals per concerto. Only the extraordinary vitality and musical empathy of James Conlon, the conductor/ringmaster who held it all together, matched the orchestra's stamina and dedication.

Another change to the competition's format had even greater consequences. According to a program essay ("The Subjectivity of Ranking") by executive director Richard Rodzinski, for the first time in the history of the competition, the rules allowed the jury to award "its top winners three medals in any combination of gold, silver, and bronze that most correctly reflects the final vote." The medalists would receive equal prize money ($20,000 apiece, whatever the medal's metal) and share in the coveted engagements over a two-year period. If the numerical vote were close, ties could be awarded. Rodzinski went on to say, "We hope that the voting system will help dispel the notion of 'the best,' which in the arts, is a spurious concept. More importantly, it will help promote more than one promising artist of relatively equal merit, affording each member of the jury the leeway to be more inclusive and reward a wider spectrum of artistry."

The notion met with mixed reviews around town—a lot of people wanted to know who was *best*, period. I heard the sentiment "Someone has to win" spoken more than once. Others were more sanguine, and a few, myself included, applauded the idea. I believe it was Charles Ives who said, "Competitions are for horses."

Meanwhile, my horse was tired. His composure as depleted as his energy, Stanislav worried about the upcoming rehearsals, his sore wrist, and the consequences of losing—or perhaps worse, of winning. With the finish line in sight, he realized his life could change beyond recognition.

THE FINALS

According to one longtime observer of the Cliburn, the finals are the least interesting part of the competition. "Whoever plays fastest and loudest wins," he said. As we settle into our seats at 7:30 p.m.

Wednesday night, my sole concern is Stanislav, who will not perform until Saturday night. Perhaps by then, his confidence and zeal to play well will return.

Oleksiy Koltakov leads off, with a performance of the Second Concerto of Beethoven that lacks focus. Xiaohan Wang's Mozart A Major is schizophrenic: moments of musicality giving way without warning to clumsy scales and ugly tone. Matters go from bad to worse when the two attempt back-to-back performances of the Rachmaninoff Third. Final score: Rach Third 2, Contestants 0. The merciless reviews made one pity both contestants, who had to go back out the next night and play again. Of course, the jury who put them in the finals had to listen a second time as well.

Friday night, Antonio Pompa-Baldi and Maxim Philippov raise the stakes considerably. Under Pompa-Baldi's hands the Mozart A Major seems a tad perfunctory, but the Prokofiev Third blazes to life, giving the pent-up audience a well-deserved opportunity to shout its approval. Philippov's Mozart, the C Major Concerto, K. 467, has grace and balance but remains earthbound. He is in his element, though, with the Rachmaninoff Third, delivering a performance of nobility and warmth in which he never overplayed. Final score: two medal contenders and a much happier audience.

Still, everyone knows that the big showdown, the gunfight at the O. K. Corral, has been saved—through the accident of their initial drawing for performance order—for the final two concerts: Stanislav and Olga will bring the Eleventh Van Cliburn International Piano Competition to a close.

With everything riding on these performances, my palms are veritable Niagaras as Stanislav takes the stage Saturday night, walking on with nary a smile and sitting down to a cool audience reception. At his first entrance, I hear immediately that he is not projecting as he should. In the scale passage to the second theme, he takes a wrong turn and nearly loses the thread of the music. The cadenza is messy; another memory mishap occurs in the third movement—come on, Stanislav, snap out of it! The performance ends with a decidedly mixed impression; there has been much to cherish, but it's all a bit distant. My heart sinks.

Olga's Mozart, the B-flat Concerto, K. 595, while hardly a musical revelation, is at least solid. She comes on in a vibrant red dress with a little white jacket, and her smile alone wins the audience over. She plays gamely, without much subtlety, but at least she appears to be enjoying it. Stanislav looks as if he were attending his own execution.

After intermission, Stanislav returns with the Tchaikovsky First—"Van's concerto," the papers remind us. To my amazement, Steve Cumming announces that the concerto has not been played in the Cliburn finals since 1985 (by José Feghali, who won the gold that year). The familiar opening strains sweep through the hall, and for just a moment, I relax: Stanislav has known this piece since he was sixteen. His playing is better but does not have the energy it should. Again, he suffers a slight memory slip. What is good is very good, but you can't win a major competition with slips like these. The concluding ovation does little to assuage my worries.

Olga's Rachmaninoff Third is everything I expected: tireless, note-perfect, fast, and loud. Through it all, she glows; the audience adores her. In an inspired fashion move, she has doffed the little white jacket, revealing spaghetti straps and shapely shoulders. Her charisma, a combination of glamour and gawkiness, approaches force-of-nature power. "No matter how this comes out," I think to myself, "she will have a very nice career."

Judy Needham, Marty Leonard, Karen and I, and a group of other friends accompany Stanislav and Tatiana to a late dinner at Mi Cocina, his favorite Mexican restaurant. He knows he must play better the next day. Over the course of the meal, I see his utter dejection transform into something akin to acceptance. Perhaps it is the fact that there is only one more performance, or perhaps his fierce desire to win—whatever the case, by the time we part a couple of hours later, he seems stronger.

Sunday afternoon, the real Stanislav is back. The Mozart soars with elegant lyricism; the Tchaikovsky roars with power and romanticism. He even smiles to the audience. His second performance is the only one by a finalist that is markedly different from the first. He accepts the final ovation with exhausted grace, savoring the moment for what it is—the end of a four-year journey to prove he could do it.

7:00 P.M., JUNE 10

The Awards Ceremony at the Cliburn is a black-tie affair, with champagne before and a huge reception after. Speeches and introductions take up the first fifty minutes, and then James Conlon steps to the podium to announce what everyone wants to know. First come the special awards: the jury has made four discretionary awards to promising nonfinalists: Davide Franceschetti, Sergey Koudriakov, and Masaru Okada (all semifinalists) and Alexandre Moutouzkine each receive $4,000. The Phyllis Jones Tilley Award ($5,000) for best performance of a new work goes to Antonio Pompa-Baldi for his interpretation of the Liebermann *Three Impromptus*. The crowd cheers. Van Cliburn himself gives three awards of $1,000 for best performance of a chamber work: Davide Franceschetti, Stanislav Ioudenitch, and Maxim Philippov take the honors. The crowd cheers again, as much for the performers as for the jury, which clearly shows its reticence to compare performances of three different pieces: the Schumann, the Franck, and the Brahms.

With nothing left but the ranking, the tension escalates in the hall. First, Conlon announces Koltakov and Wang will receive $10,000 apiece and two years of concert engagements.

Then comes the first surprise: he reads the list of prizes to be awarded to the bronze medalist and says, "Not awarded." The audience buzzes, and even Richard Rodzinski goes to the podium for a word. Over the microphone, the audience hears Conlon say, "I know." Rodzinski sits down. He then reads the silver medalist's prize and announces, "Antonio Pompa-Baldi." The crowd roars its approval, and Antonio takes the stage. After the requisite handshakes and the placing of the medal around his neck, he returns to his seat down front. Conlon continues, as if he had never left off, leaning on the first word: "*And*...Maxim Philippov."

The stunned crowd roars again, while Maxim, looking slightly dazed, follows in the steps of his co-medalist.

Now the excitement is even more tangible. Conlon reads the gold medalist's prize, drawing out the suspense. After an expressive pause, he reads the name. "Olga Kern."

Pandemonium erupts. Olga stumbles onto the stage, completely undone by joy. She embraces Cliburn, Rodzinski, and Conlon, anyone in sight. She receives the medal and a huge silver trophy bowl, which she holds aloft for the audience to see. The applause is deafening for the first woman to win the gold since Cristina Ortiz in 1969. When she finally returns to her seat, the audience realizes one name has not been called. What does this mean?

Conlon savors the suspense, looking out over the podium. He then says, "*And—*"

But the audience swamps his last words with another huge roar. Stanislav proceeds to the stage, a distinctly less demonstrative presence than Olga, but his face is bathed in relief. I see the first genuine smile I have seen in months—he has won after all.

The next morning, the papers quote various jury members about the decision. Jury chair John Giordano said the new ranking system worked as expected. "Kern and Ioudenitch had very different styles of playing, yet both deserved gold medals," he said. "People want to have a winner, but in music it isn't so simple. You have different, subjective approaches to making music, and all are valid."

Rodzinski said it best in his program essay. "No intelligent person would dare pronounce Bach a 'better' composer than Beethoven, or Rubinstein a 'better' pianist than Horowitz. However, anyone has the right to say they *prefer* Bach to Beethoven, or Rubinstein to Horowitz."

The Cliburn jury has offered the concert world two very different pianists, both with merits that warrant attention. To my mind, it is an inspired decision. The pressure on past Cliburn winners has been extraordinary—it's simply not possible for a twenty-year-old pianist to be all things to all people. With two gold medalists, the burden is shared.

During the competition, the critics, particularly Gay, wrote repeatedly of the need for the Cliburn to discover a superstar. It is a ludicrous notion—he confuses pop celebrity with artistry. Cliburn himself had both, but his instant fame in 1958 following the Tchaikovsky Competition was more a result of the Cold War than his superb playing.

With one sweeping statement, the jury has essentially challenged the classical music business to grow up. The only winner in art is the recipient of the artists' gifts. Let there be more artists, and those capable of hearing what they have to say.

CODA

On the winner's side of the finish line, Stanislav realizes that a whole new journey is beginning. His doctorate on hold for the time being, he has played since June at Aspen, Interlochen, the Kennedy Center, and with orchestras in Texas and California, and spent three weeks in Europe, with recitals in France, England, and Italy. All the Cliburn winners will be busy for the next two years.

In the meantime, I've lost the best assistant I'm ever likely to have. A teacher must say goodbye to every student at some point. This bird leaves the nest in a more spectacular fashion than most, perhaps, but my feelings are the same: "Stay well, Stanislav, and play like you mean it!"

XI

■ Fighting the Good Fight

It has been a privilege to have enjoyed the career I've had. Growing up in rural Ohio in the 1950s, the oldest child of parents who had not gone to college, my life changed completely when Mrs. Getz came on the scene. While there was some uncertainty along the way, it was basically a straight shot to Oberlin, Yale, the White House, performances, and good teaching positions. The previous chapter on competitions may have expressed reservations about head-to-head combat, but I should pinch myself to think that one of my students would win the Cliburn.

This chapter considers the costs. I remember Claude Frank telling someone that Bob is a very hard worker, but he will not win a major competition, so he'd prefer not to write a letter of recommendation. I can now see he was right, but I always thought if I worked a little harder, I'd get there.

There are limits to how hard a person can work. This section collects some of the columns I wrote when I thought trying harder was the answer, but more work only led to doubt, frustration, and finally burnout. My career could have derailed in the early 1990s. These columns offer some insight into how that almost happened.

The section opens with two pieces I wrote on the tyranny of memorization. The first admits that an upcoming recital was not safely memorized and goes on to examine the pros and cons of playing from memory no matter what. I reached a conclusion I never thought I'd reach, even though the second piece reports that I played that recital by memory despite the workload. That program took place twenty years ago; I am even more convinced today that memorization is an entirely unnecessary evil.

Eventually, something crumbles. Will it be the pride of the soloist who fails in public? Everyone has a memory slip now and then, but it is mortifying to have bomb after bomb explode, destroying the carefully wrought composition, not to mention the reputation of the ostensibly incompetent performer. Will the audience be disappointed that a sacred tradition has been violated if the score sits on the music rack? The musical snobs will complain, but memorized recitals are simply tradition. If the tradition changes, a new norm will take over. The bottom line: Who cares if you can memorize a full program! I'd like to think that audiences are much more interested in hearing great music than seeing pianists perform without scores. From the start, it was a circus trick. (Thank you, Franz Liszt.)

This led to another realization that I had avoided for many years: the need for the artist-teacher to serve two masters. On the performing side, one accepts the constant practice, but there is also the requirement of self-management, finding the engagements, planning the travel, sending publicity materials, and thinking on a multiyear basis. In the meantime, the university expects its performers to maintain a full-time teaching load, committee service, student recruiting, and general university citizenship. It also wants those recital dates to be professionally significant. It's really two full-time jobs. I finally came to see it as unhealthy, if not downright dangerous.

Other columns discuss our society's penchant for criticizing. Here I refer not so much to interpretation or commentary as to disapproval and judgment. In school, grading starts early. Most teaching is about what *isn't* right. Perhaps my hide is not tough enough, but I believe that criticism can inflict real damage. I still remember being yelled at more than fifty years ago by an assistant band director in front of the whole marching band. He shouted that I should never forget there is always someone better than me. Wasn't there a kinder way to get the message across?

Another column wonders if it's easier to relish something if you don't know too much. If enjoying music is the ultimate goal for both performers and listeners, perhaps there are times when the cognoscenti must swallow their surfeit of knowledge in order to avoid the quick, negative judgments that an abundance of learning can inspire.

Competition comes up again, this time going beyond gladiatorial conflict to the struggle for opportunities, for an audience, even rivalry with the dead! The end of this essay addresses the level at which an artist tries to operate. Despite my shortcomings, I would like to think that I have always tried to make music at the highest level I could. Yet there have been many disappointments; these personal sacrifices are part of every artist's life. Perhaps the only answer is to be less demanding?

The last two essays discuss burnout, which was certainly close in the fall of 1989. I was just starting my first leave of absence from Peabody, awarded because I received a National Endowment for the Arts Solo Recitalist Fellowship. As it happened, I was also homeless due to a house renovation. No wonder I was frazzled. Four years later, I decided to leave Peabody, to redirect my career, to give more time to family and occasions like visiting Mount Rainier. The essay from 1993 relates the end of *The View from the Second Floor* and the start of *Out of the Woods*. Nevertheless, I was still trying to juggle too many things at once. I taught for a semester at Eastman, subbed for Bob McDonald at Peabody a year later, became artistic *and* administrative director of the Skaneateles Festival, and took up conducting (performing an all-Gershwin program with the Syracuse Symphony). Again, I rarely took time off.

I still needed more talent. I define *talent* as "something for which you do not have to work." It is an innate aptitude, a felicity, a natural ability that is a gift. It is hardwired. You don't do anything to deserve it—it's just there.

Ultimately, most talented people probably feel they aren't talented enough!

62

Memorization Part I

Out of the Woods

NOVEMBER 2001

By the time you read this, I will have played a solo recital. It may or may not have been performed from memory. As I write, the program is not memorized, although I am working frantically toward that end. The performance date will be here in no time at all. For now, I cannot say how it will turn out; the only thing I know for certain is that I will play the recital, whether from memory or from score.

There has been much debate in recent years about pianists performing from memory. This magazine had a lively exchange about the subject several years ago; even the chief music critic of the *New York Times*, Anthony Tommasini, has weighed in. (He thinks it is not necessary.) Tradition has it that Liszt himself started the tradition. "*Le concert, c'est moi,*" said he as he became the first musician to put forth an entire program on his own. Until that time, concerts were shared affairs. Clara Schumann was another early proponent of performing from memory, but whether this was her idea or her father's, we will never know.

Whatever the case, for nearly two hundred years, audiences have expected pianists to perform solo recitals from memory. Those mavericks who have resisted are rare and known to everyone with an interest in pianists: Myra Hess, Sviatoslav Richter in his later years, and Gilbert Kalish throughout his career. It's likely that memorization arose as a trick, an attempt to fool the public into thinking the pianist was making up the music on the spot. At the very least, all performers wish to leave the impression of oneness with the music, a noble and worthwhile goal indeed. But is the absence of a score necessary to accomplish this goal?

For the first time in my professional career, I am questioning the tyranny of memorization, and it has thrown me into a maelstrom of self-doubt and conflict. Having memorized even the most complex contemporary scores in my youth, I tell myself that it should still be possible today, despite a full-time teaching position. Nevertheless, I recognize that the hours required to memorize a score to my own satisfaction go far beyond the number it takes to give a very fine performance of the piece while reading from the score.

Even with the necessary hours at the piano, the price of memorization under the best of circumstances is the haunting, continuous fear that a memory slip is just around the corner of the next phrase. We are certain that the entire audience knows our every missed note. However, we do the composer no favor by giving a less than ideal performance of a work when memory deserts us. How do we reckon the cost of memorization, whether it be to the performance itself or to our peace of mind?

I can rationalize playing this recital from the score on several levels. First, it is a program that I am not likely to play often; the repertoire is somewhat esoteric, and I chose it simply because I thought it presented an interesting musical combination to a hometown audience that has not heard this music in a long time, if at all. For the record, the program is the "Lord of Salisbury" Pavan and Galliard by William Byrd, the Copland Sonata, the Webern Variations, and Beethoven's Sonata, Op. 111.

Immersing myself in such a program to the exclusion of everything else in my life could seem a curious use of my time. Don't get me wrong—I love this music and want to give it the best performance possible, but my other obligations are no less important. All my students have programs underway, and these engage me almost as much as my upcoming concert. My university imposes other obligations that this year include chairing the dreaded Promotions and Tenure Committee. I also have obligations to two professional organizations, both with important deadlines approaching. This dear magazine has its own deadline, and I am already past it. Let us not forget that musicians have home lives, too, and spouses and children need time. As my wife said only this morning at breakfast, preparing a recital is like taking on another full-time job.

At some point, something has to give. In the last ten years, I have done a good deal of chamber music, and as a result my reading at the piano has improved. I absolutely adore playing chamber music concerts because the score is right there in front of me. I know the music very well, but it is not memorized. The merits of the performance have nothing to do with the presence or absence of scores.

Last year, I learned and performed the Stravinsky Concerto for Piano and Winds at my university. Early on, I decided I would not try to memorize it. We gave only one performance, and it was not likely that I would play the piece again anytime soon. The performance was good if I do say so myself. To have played the piece as well by memory would have taken months of additional preparation. I don't regret the decision.

The important thing is to play well regularly, and not necessarily by memory. Those of us who are primarily teachers do not have the benefit of multiple performances of the same program. If we wish to continue performing, we can either play the same program year after year or vary the programming and admit that we may need to use a score now and then.

My first teacher referred to memorization as "playing by heart." Indeed, it *can* be if one has time for the heart to truly absorb the music. When we don't have the time, we need to put our hearts into the playing, not into the memorization.

For this concert, I want to play by heart. I have promised myself that I will do so, whether the score is in front of me or not.

63

Memorization Part II

Out of the Woods

In the November issue, my column could have been called "To memorize or not to memorize...?" That was indeed the question as a solo recital loomed without sufficient time to prepare. I shared my feeling that playing the recital well, even if I had to use the scores, was more important than following protocol and performing badly from memory.

As it turned out, I managed to memorize the recital. There were about three weeks from the time I finished the column to the recital date; I cleared the decks and worked hard, letting several other responsibilities go in the process. I didn't memorize because I had to; as I wrote in that column, the music meant a lot to me, and I wanted to immerse myself in it. Somewhat to my surprise, the memory came as it did in days gone by. Despite the hurried preparation period, the performance that day was probably better than some I've given with far more lead time. I give all credit to the music and its power over me.

Let's not leave the memorization issue just yet, however. Given the number of letters and calls that came as a result of that column, it's a sore point for many. One caller told me he thought memorization was merely a macho holdover from the nineteenth century, a vestigial weapon designed to elevate the "truly gifted" from the "not quite good enough" in the scheme of things. It was, in his opinion, more about competition and survival of the fittest than getting close to the music and subsuming the performer's ego in the composer's ideas.

He has a point, but as I've debated with myself and others over the last few months, it seems to me that the whole subject boils down to two real issues. The first is that memorizing is a trade-off. On the one hand, committing a work to memory can lead to a higher degree of musical freedom or inspiration in performance. On the other, playing without the score usually fosters at least some degree of anxiety over the potential for a memory slip. That concern can lead to a performance that lacks the very spontaneity we had hoped to achieve in the first place. We find ourselves on the proverbial horns of a dilemma.

My experience—and I dare say that of most professional pianists—is that given enough time, memory settles in as the happy result of good practicing and a thorough immersion in the music. We work on the music as long as it takes and eventually try it out for relatives, teachers, and other captive audiences. Perhaps we record ourselves and at last feel confident enough to take the program onstage without the safety net of the score.

The second issue is time. I used to think that I simply didn't have enough of it, but then I took a time-management seminar. The first thing the leader said was, "You have all the time in the world." That's a great line: all the time there is in the world is already yours. No one can give you more time, nor can they take it away. It's up to you to decide how to use all that time. So, I learned about basing my time commitments on the things that matter most to me. I keep a book with daily to-do lists neatly prioritized, and I try not to schedule myself so heavily that I can't possibly get it all done.

The problem is that the task list is usually exceedingly long. I may put "memorize the Beethoven" into the daily schedule with a high priority, but Op. 111 will fill all the time I give it. There is no rushing a masterpiece. Either I give it the time it needs and ignore other things, or it doesn't get memorized. I look into my heart and ask which is more important, and while the answer comes back "Op. 111," the bill collector says otherwise.

Perhaps if Op. 111 paid my bills, I wouldn't be so conflicted. The truth is, the bulk of my living comes from teaching; lessons and all that goes into being a good citizen of the university consume most of every day. Granted, I could say "no" more than I do, but for the most part, I do things I want to do. It's when I tell myself that I should play more concerts at a very high level that I get a little crazy. All the time in the world is simply not enough.

Unfortunately, I'm not the only one saying I should have a busy concert schedule. Universities and conservatories everywhere hire artist-teachers based on their success onstage. Without résumés filled with significant concert dates, played by memory, those seeking college teaching positions aren't likely to make the first cut in a search process. Yet as soon as the ink is dry on the contract, new performance faculty are told they must teach a full load (minimum eighteen hours a week), recruit more and better students, serve on all manner of committees, and turn in their faculty activity reports on time. They are also expected to perform just as much as before, preferably more, and unless a major venue is included in their schedule, they should not count on receiving tenure. They should travel and perform without missing more than two weeks of teaching per term, and of course all lessons must be made up. Oh yes...and be sure to file your absence-request form in triplicate at least two weeks before leaving campus.

Something's got to give, and it's not just playing from memory. I'd like to suggest that university administrators everywhere take a reality check: if you want your performers out playing concerts, give them some load credit for doing so, and don't ask them to fill up their time in menial paperwork duties. If you want them to teach full loads, base their raises and tenure cases on their teaching success instead of their performance schedule. It's time to stop expecting the impossible.

64

"Friendly Criticism"

The View from the Second Floor

APRIL 1990

I recently had an exchange with a reader who was quite upset over my use of a five-letter word. The word was *socks*. As it appeared in last September's column: "There is value in remembering that pianists are human beings who get hungry and have holes in our socks even when we are preparing a major performance and most of our students need extra lessons simultaneously." The reader felt *socks* was sexist and wrote to me in no uncertain terms: "There is value in remembering that pianists are not only human but *female*, too, on occasion, when given the chance!"

Actually, I'd noticed. Some of my best friends are female pianists, and I've probably taught more female piano students than male. Most of them wear socks, at least sometimes. The point of this column, however, is not to prove my innocence as a male chauvinist pig; what I really want to talk about is criticism.

Most of us already know a lot about criticism. We've been hearing criticism since we were old enough to stand up and toddle over to the end table to reach for that pretty purple vase. "Don't! It will break." At the hardened age of six, we are bundled off to grade school, where we learn to arrange letters in the correct order, thereby forming words. We receive a grade, not for our little stories but for our spelling facility. The die is cast early.

Blessed are those who are surrounded by nurturing instructors. It is a rare teacher who informs and enlightens, opening us to the wonders alive in a subject. More of us are more familiar with the critics, the judges of our merits and demerits, the nitpickers who can't see the forest for the trees.

A pianist absorbs several metric tons of criticism during a typical education. Our well-meaning teacher corrects our hand position, scrawls several layers of warning into our music, tells us not to slouch, asks us when we are going to cut our fingernails, and urges us to practice more so we can enter a competition. When that great day arrives, we are measured according to the "standard," whatever that is. We are compared to others. We learn to be cautious. Why risk exposing our true selves in such a hostile environment? Rather than play the music for our own enjoyment, we try to avoid mistakes. The teacher quotes authorities: "Badura-Skoda says the trill must go this way; my teacher Pompositsky said that octaves must be played like this." As a result, most pianists carry around a veritable landfill of criticism, much of it toxic.

It's a miracle that they live to tell about it. They survive by becoming anxious, timid, constricted, dependent perfectionists who have lost the creative spark that once excited them. The music critics in the press are right when they complain that many young pianists sound alike; they, and unnumbered critics before them, have made it so. Sadly, the next step is that these frightened pianists start teaching students of their own.

My quarrel is not with sincere instruction that aims to enrich the talent that is there. At some point, a student can benefit from knowing Badura-Skoda's thoughts on a trill in Mozart, but not before that trill comes from the thrill in a student's heart. If playing octaves is not a technical problem, why fix it?

Imagination is a fragile thing, and often the most creative souls are the ones most easily damaged by criticism. The healthy few are lucky enough to find the caring instruction that can partially counteract criticism's negative effects. A strong ego also helps.

It's no wonder we become our own worst critics. For example, when I write a column, an internal editorial board holds a noisy, fists-in-the-air meeting in the back of my head. There are fights over word choice, punctuation, sentence structure, form, and tone. You name it—we've fought about it. The louder the fight, the less likely I am to say anything. There was a big committee battle at the juncture of the second and third paragraphs of this column over whether to use the word *criticism* three times in three sentences. The nay-sayers favored *it* the third time around, but the yeas argued that the first two paragraphs amounted to a digression and that by using *criticism* three times, I would counterbalance the opening and focus attention on the real subject. I hope the reader will agree that the effort—which took several chocolate chip cookies and a cup of coffee to work out—makes a meaningful difference.

Then the magazine's editors take over. Only rarely can an editor resist changing a word or two, even though the writer has sweat blood over every syllable. I must admit, though, that on occasion they've gotten me out of some dreadful verbal fender benders. Unfortunately, no one foresaw the fatal accident involving *our socks*. This is partially the consequence of the magazine's editorial policy: *Clavier* does not use such constructions as *s/he* or *his/her*, so to avoid the masculine singular I opted for *our*, and then had to think of something both men and women wear. *Socks* was about as universal as I could get in a family magazine.

So, to the irate reader who took the time to write, I thank you for the inspiration for this column. My self-critic goes to bed at night safe in the knowledge that whatever it misses, someone out there will find it.

65

Mixed Criticism

Out of the Woods

APRIL 1998

Back in the spring of 1978, I played a recital in an Atlanta church; afterward, a little girl and her mother came up to me, and the girl gave me a present. It was a pencil drawing she had made during the recital of a grand piano, the perspective of the legs delightfully askew, its pedals colored yellow. She inscribed it (almost spelling my name right):

> "To Mr. Robert Weirch
> I enjoyed it
> From Leslie Peterzell"

I still have that piece of paper; it is framed and hangs on the wall above my desk. Recently it occurred to me that Ms. Leslie Peterzell is now an adult, and I am wondering if she still enjoys it. The question is not an idle one.

Last fall, I played a different recital, this one in Pittsburg, Kansas. Several weeks later, I received a young student's prose description of that recital, forwarded by his teacher to the department chair, who passed it on to me. I'm glad they went to the trouble—I'll probably frame this too. Among other things, Mr. Will Blessent wrote:

> I really liked all the music, but the Fantasia in C Major by Schubert was my favorite. Mrs. Lyerla brought the music. There were lots of pages and one student was following along. I couldn't see the music that well, but it looked very hard. Mr. Weirich had all the music memorized and he played for 1½ hours!!

Modesty prevents me from sharing more of Will's story. Suffice it to say that while I've received some good reviews in my day, none has meant more to me than this one. He *really* liked it.

Contrast these stories with the following, again taken from personal experience. About six weeks after the recital in Kansas, I played the same program in my hometown. A lot of my friends and colleagues were there. A close acquaintance of many years, who is not a musician, called a few days later and said, "I enjoyed your recital..." (Pause.) "Of course, it wasn't your best." I was too stunned to say anything. She then went on to ask me for a favor, which I had no trouble turning down. She was right: it was not my best night. But why was it so important to her that I know she knew?

Then I remembered another recital I had attended not so long ago in which I watched a pianist in the receiving line ahead of me struggle to avoid saying anything congratulatory to the performer. He was distinctly uncomfortable, seemingly convinced that saying anything nice might cause the sky to fall. His pride won out: not a word of praise passed his lips. He escaped with his inner purity intact, armed and ready for the next imagined battle.

Usually at this point in a column, I draw a bead on resolving and head for a conclusion in another page and a half. This situation, however, stumps me. Perhaps it is unresolvable because the act of perceiving music is so personal. My concern, though, is less with what one perceives as with the enjoyment with which one experiences the perception.

In his book *Music and the Mind*, Anthony Storr writes of scientific experiments comparing the listening experiences of nonmusicians and musicians. When an electroencephalogram is taken of brain activity during listening, nonmusicians show a more active right-brain hemisphere. For musicians, the activity of listening is centered in the left brain, the location of critical analysis. This comes as no surprise. However, most neurologists place emotional response in the right hemisphere. A musician may have to work harder to have an emotional response to music than a nonmusician!

Storr also mentions the theory of Wilhelm Worringer, who believes that one's aesthetic appreciation is based on whether the listener has a natural inclination toward either "empathy or abstraction." If the listener (whether musician or nonmusician) is empathic, he loses himself, becomes one with it. If on the other hand the listener is more concerned with discovering the form or structure of a work, there must be a certain abstraction, a bit of distance, to reach a different kind of aesthetic appreciation. Both approaches have value. Like extraversion and introversion, one or the other attitude is usually dominant. Empathic immersion in a work may so involve the listener that critical judgment is impossible. Similarly, an exclusively intellectual approach may make it difficult to appreciate the music's emotional import.

To understand a piece of music completely, though, we need both empathy *and* abstraction. While I am delighted that Leslie and Will enjoyed, in the truest sense, my recitals, they didn't have the sophistication necessary to comprehend the music on the level of abstraction. On the other hand, my critical friend and the rival pianist who found it necessary to make their high standards known were not able to enjoy the music on *any* level. Why do so many of the musical literati feel that a concert must be perfect before they can enjoy it? I recently came across a review of a pianist famous for her emotion-charged performance in which the critic took her to task for playing certain melodic sixteenth-note upbeats as thirty-seconds. My goodness—better not buy that recording!

I'll share my personal conclusion: life is too short. I want to enjoy the music I play and hear, even if it means missing a few thirty-second notes. And Leslie Peterzell, wherever you are, thanks for helping me learn to enjoy it.

66

Frustration

Out of the Woods

Just down the hall, a student concerto competition is about to start. One of my wife's students, a twelve-year-old girl, is taking part. Both student and teacher are nervous. The girl's parents hover anxiously in the hallway: the father carries a video camera; the mother paces. The girl complains of cold hands.

It is a scene we've all witnessed; most of us have participated. We know firsthand the empty feeling in the pit of the stomach, the tingle of adrenaline coursing through the veins. We check the list of contestants, looking for names we may know. We start the piece in our minds, wondering if we will remember the first notes on stage.

We've come to accept competition as a way of life. "It is a necessary evil," we say. Competition serves to motivate us and offers playing experience. We convince ourselves that we become stronger because of it.

Competition takes on many guises, however. A few weeks ago, I attended a symphony concert led by a pianist-turned-conductor whom I admire. On the program was the Ravel Concerto in G Major, which was to be conducted from the keyboard. My favorite recording of this piece has always been the one Bernstein did as pianist-conductor back in the 1950s. As a child, I was in awe of this man who seemed capable of doing everything in music: he played the piano, conducted like a god, wrote music for both the concert hall and the popular theater, and even appeared on television in concerts for young people. I wanted so much to be like him when I grew up. So, perhaps, did the conductor about to play.

The stage was reset for the concerto, the piano lid removed with the keyboard facing the audience. The conductor returned to the stage, took his seat at the piano, and gave a mighty head cue to the orchestra, and off they went. Almost immediately, one heard problems: the piano sound seemed unprojected, given its position on stage, and there were ensemble difficulties for the instrumentalists toward the rear of the platform. Without a baton to follow, they could only rely on their ears to play with the musicians in front. The second movement meandered; the third was simply sloppy. It really wasn't the conductor's fault: both his hands were on the keyboard, and the orchestral musicians couldn't hear him. It's as if Bernstein raised a scepter challenging succeeding generations to do what he did. I know the feeling, having played and conducted from the keyboard. The music suffered. Perhaps we are so competitive that we even take on the dead.

The applause was polite, but the sizable audience went home without really hearing all the piece has to offer. It was just another day at the symphony.

Down the hall, the concerto competition is now underway. While my wife's student runs through the piece with her accompanist in a studio, her father positions himself in the audience where his camera has a clear shot of the stage. I attend the performance as well, curious and a little nervous myself. The piece is Beethoven's First Concerto. She looks small on stage, a little girl trying to look grown up in a long, black dress. She plays efficiently, correctly, somewhat dutifully. There are no major mistakes. It is, in fact, good playing, exactly what you'd expect of a talented but not exceptional twelve-year-old. One judge wrote that he enjoyed it—the only thing missing was the *brio* from the tempo marking, *Allegro con brio*. Most twelve-year-olds haven't lived long enough to comprehend that, no matter how many times the teacher might tell them to play with more life.

The girl received an honorable mention for her efforts that day. She was disappointed. She had done everything her teacher told her to do but still hadn't won. My wife and I went home that day wondering if the girl would lose her love for music if she thought she had failed. She might think, "Competition is part of life, but I'm not good enough." It was just another day in the life of a student.

On another recent night, my wife and I attended a concert by the young German baritone Matthias Goerne, who some call the heir apparent of Dietrich Fischer-Dieskau.

His program consisted entirely of unfamiliar lieder by Robert Schumann. The concert took place in the same hall in which the symphony had played, which is to say a room far too large for a lieder recital. It was perhaps a quarter full. When he began singing, it was immediately clear that we were in the presence of a great artist whose only intent was to bring the songs to life. He was selfless in his dedication to the music; he disappeared in the service of the texts and their settings. Contrary to all the other musical experiences I had witnessed in these weeks, here was art at its highest level. "It doesn't get better than this," I thought.

Then it occurred to me that, as beautifully as he sang, he was still competing. He may have had my rapt attention, but the couple next to me fidgeted uncomfortably in their seats. Distracting coughs echoed around the cavernous hall. The texts were entirely in German, so people noisily flipped program pages to read translations as the singer performed his miracles, despite a printed plea at the bottom of each page requesting that the audience turn only at the end of a song. Many in the audience seemed bent on destroying the exquisite intimacy of the songs.

The vocalist competed not only *with* the audience but *for* one as well. The same night, thousands of people stayed home to watch television or went out to the movies. These incredible songs of Schumann were up against every other element of our culture. Last Sunday, I read an article in the *New York Times Magazine* where a quote caught my attention:

> This song by Nine Inch Nails, called "Broken," came on the radio. It's an amazing song. It's enlightening and at the same time it's terrible—it assaults you with sounds, as though you'd put a conch shell up to your ear to listen to a jet engine warming up. As you listen to it, it undoes all the music you ever heard before. It erases it.

With *that* as the competition, no wonder only three hundred people made it to the Goerne recital in Kansas City, and even fewer heard it.

Competition is a way of life; there is no changing it. Nevertheless, somewhere there must be a place to stand up and make music as beautifully as our ability allows, where others find value and worth in that alone—without competing.

67

Burnout Part I

The View from the Second Floor

NOVEMBER 1989

Sitting by the lake at the end of the summer, I watched the water ripple lazily in the breeze as the clouds shifted overhead without apparent hurry. I was relaxing after a summer of moderate teaching followed by three weeks of chamber music with genial people on the shores of said lake. It had been a delightful summer, full of the pleasures of seeing old friends and meeting new.

The reality of the situation, though, was that my nerves were a frazzled mess, and the unruffled lake only made this more obvious. As the summer progressed, each lesson became more difficult, and each performance arrived at the double bar by an ever-thinner layer of the proverbial skin of the teeth. Were it not for the upcoming partial leave of absence Peabody granted me, you would not be reading this column.

The problem is simple: you can't tell your students that you are too tired to give them a good lesson. They will throw you that puzzled look of eternal youth and assume you don't like them. You can't tell your audience that this performance is not your best. They will make loud coughing noises and rattle their programs, and never come to hear you again. After too many consecutive months or years of this situation, a pianist develops a bad case of burnout, a malady that teachers over the last decade have begun to acknowledge.

You have probably seen magazine articles on the subject or noticed sessions addressing it at national conferences. If you are like me, though, you are too busy to read or attend something that doesn't pertain to the next recital or lesson. Then when the trouble begins, you feel it's your fault, and you summon up the willpower to work even harder. You start taking vitamins; before too much time has passed, you are a certifiable wreck.

I surveyed seven friends and found that six of them had at some point experienced the symptoms of burnout. Talking with them helped me clarify the ways we walk into its traps.

All of us are jugglers and keep several things in the air at once: performing, teaching, a family, and the usual list of other suspects. If this were not bad enough, emergencies in each have a way of demanding our immediate attention and can threaten the balance of the entire act (e.g., the dean wants you to serve on another committee, or you find out the IRS is auditing you).

Another invitation to burnout is the sheer amount of energy we expend. Pianists accept that they must work hard playing the instrument, making a career, and becoming effective teachers. We pour ourselves completely into one or all of the above, and when we meet with less than complete victory, we try harder. At some point, we come up against problems beyond our control: a student we care for who defies our best efforts, or a piece our hands refuse to play. Still, we keep trying. Visions of ships sinking in rough seas flash before our eyes.

Most of the respondents to my survey admitted that, like me, they rarely took time off. Their years went by without a break; workdays stretched from early morning until long past dinner. When they finally took a vacation out of sheer desperation, some bounce returned to their steps within a few days; by the end of the time set aside, all reported a rejuvenated outlook. Sometimes it lasted a few weeks before it disappeared.

People with money know that they shouldn't live off their capital. They guard it vigilantly and add to it every chance they get. Musicians should learn from this. If we spend our energy and knowledge on everything that comes along, we will eventually run out. We must spend wisely and take every opportunity to add to our capital.

I found the survey helpful, but the seventh respondent taught me the most important lesson. After hearing my sob story about how burned out I was, he told me in no uncertain terms that he thought the whole issue was trite and self-indulgent. Unbeknownst to me, he had been suffering from a physical problem that wouldn't go away and for the past year had been unable to play at all. He had seen doctors, physical therapists, and acupuncturists without success and still didn't know how it would turn out. He said that compared to the potentially irrevocable loss of his voice through the piano, he would take a case of burnout any time.

Humbled into silence, I resolved to count my blessings. Somehow though, I knew my problem wasn't over.

68

Burnout Part II

The View from the Second Floor

SEPTEMBER 1993

This is probably the last *View from the Second Floor*. If I continue to write for *Clavier*, I'll have to change the title of the column, because last April I resigned from my teaching position at Peabody. I have not taken another teaching position, so any subsequent views will be those of just another ground-floor musician.

Before the reader jumps to conclusions, please be assured that (1) I really did resign—my departure from Peabody was entirely amicable, although terribly painful in many ways; (2) I still love teaching; and (3) I have not taken a leave of my senses, or at least not all of them. The fourth conclusion—anything having to do with independent wealth—could not be funnier.

I'll probably go back to teaching at the university level at some point—if I can get a job, that is. This decision has been a long time coming, though, and since I've shared perhaps too many personal things with the readership over the years, I may as well write about this.

The official explanation is that I want to pursue several opportunities for musical and personal growth: I have a chance to learn conducting; I have two file folders full of notes for a couple books I want to write; and I'd like my son, not quite two years old, to know who I am before I reach retirement age.

Yes, but give up a job at Peabody—great students and superb colleagues—in *this* economy? Can't you do all that and teach too?

Nope. Sorry, I really tried, and maybe someone else can do it all, but I've come to realize that music making and academia may not go together as well as I always wished it could.

Doing it all, just for the record, meant teaching a full studio, classes in twentieth-century piano literature, pedagogy, and chairing the prep piano faculty at Peabody, playing twenty-five to thirty concerts a year, directing the piano program at the Eastern Music Festival for six weeks each summer, serving as music director of the Skaneateles Festival (four weeks of concerts but year-round planning concentration), and writing this column. I had a manager once, but she quit to become a nurse. At the rate I was going, I could have been her first patient.

The career combining teaching and performance is in essence two careers, each requiring a full-time commitment of time and energy. It can be done successfully if (1) the performer is satisfied with five concerts a year or (2) the teacher has only five students. I exaggerate for effect, but not by much. If there are more of either, the teacher-performer had better be either (1) single with no other interests or (2) married to a mate with no other career than making life possible for the busy teacher-performer. If you don't believe me, read last month's interview with Menahem Pressler.

For a long time, I thought it was a question of working harder. More hours, more concentration, more energy. Perhaps what I really need is more talent, but I think the problem is one any workaholic must eventually recognize: there *are* limits.

My epiphany came in a rental car as I approached Mount Rainier National Park last March. I had stolen a day to unwind after six days of nonstop judging and teaching in Seattle, which I had agreed to because it fit into my spring break. I even gave a recital in there somewhere, because after all, I want to perform. As I drove along, the mountains, clear streams, and forests seemed to absorb my tensions, restoring a sense of balance and perspective. Around the next bend, though, the landscape changed drastically, and I realized that I had come into a section of forest that had been clear-cut. It was simply gone, nothing left but the uprooted stumps and debris. The earth had the look of a mortal wound, desolate and pained.

It suddenly occurred to me that here I was, aged forty-three, seeing a part of the country that I'd always wanted to see for the first time in my life, and already it was partially gone. Nothing lasts forever, not even nature. Here I was in the prime of life, with no time for anything but work.

So, I have had to make a choice. I've chosen to use the time left to see Mount Rainier while it's still there. That means simple things like getting up from the desk to have dinner with my family instead of finishing the *Clavier* column, or writing a letter to a friend instead of writing the umpteenth letter of recommendation that will be scanned and summarily discarded.

It also means looking beyond the limits of a teaching position; maybe there are better views than from the second floor. So far in my career, I have docilely accepted many things about academia, but it seems I can't ignore the questions that have always plagued me. Russia and the United States have stopped making nuclear weapons, but conservatories the world over are still training soloists. Yet where are the concerts? Universities present hundreds of free concerts every year to nearly empty auditoria, yet just down the street the public-school kids have nothing but the sounds coming from their Walkman headphones.[1] Symphony managers and concert presenters complain of dwindling attendance, citing the need for education, yet they hire only itinerant soloists and conductors who must catch the plane to their next engagement. In my "retirement," I'd like to do something about some of this.

If humankind can wreck Mount Rainier's environment, art doesn't stand a chance. Perhaps I am only jousting at windmills, but I don't think so.

---

1. The Sony Walkman was a portable audio player that sold over two hundred million units before it was discontinued in 2010. Think of it as the precursor of the iPhone.

XII

■ On Writing and Self-Reflection

Why write? To communicate. Communicate what? Many things, not the least of which is inner experience.

Why share self-reflection? To find out what you really think. To be honest with yourself, and in so doing, perhaps lead a reader to a bit of self-evaluation.

The word *communicate* has appeared often in previous chapters. It has usually dealt with musical communication, the passing on of the performer's experience of a composition to an audience of one or many. One hopes for revelation—for performers, that the music can be revealed in a public situation; for listeners, that something might touch an inner nerve previously unknown to them.

Writing is not so different from what musicians hope for in performing. I have previously admitted to a strong, early inclination toward literature, so communicating by the written word has for me at its root the same desire for interpersonal communication as music making.

The first essay in this section is a paper I gave on the place of writing in the music curriculum. The College Music Society holds annual national meetings in various locations throughout the country, attended by members in all fields of music study—performers, composers, theorists, historians, ethnomusicologists, and music educators. The major points of the paper centered on how writing allows us to find out what we know and how the act of writing leads to learning.

I can see now that the *Clavier* essays were attempts to learn—about self, career, teaching. Sharing them with the magazine's readership required a willingness to say "I don't know, but I'm trying." It's not unlike a performance that hasn't quite gelled yet.

The rest of the essays in this section reflect my personal journey from 1986 to 2000: job changes, long-distance moves, inner uncertainties. I wrote to learn what I really thought. I was also searching wiser minds, hence mentioning the name Alfred North Whitehead in the 1986 essay. A mathematician and philosopher, Whitehead's book *The Aims of Education* somehow found its way to my awareness and impressed me for its thorough and wide-ranging thought. Its first paragraph summarized what I hoped for in my own growth as well as for my students:

> Culture is activity of thought, and receptiveness to beauty. Scraps of information have nothing to do with it. We should aim at producing people who possess both culture and expert knowledge in some special direction. Their knowledge will give them ground to start from, and their culture will lead them as deep as philosophy and as high as art. We have to remember that the valuable intellectual development is self-development.

A good musician faces a lifetime of developing the self—there is never a moment to say, "I've made it." There are moments to enjoy, however.

I could have included more essays along this line than you will find here—*Clavier* was very generous to let me ramble on as much as I did. Instead, I have excerpted the parts that still seem relevant.

For example, you'll find thoughts on planting a garden, on trying new things in midcareer, on the difficulty of reaching people without an iota's interest in classical music, and on the progress of life's inevitable odometer.

The final essay from 1990 is one of my favorites. Written near the end of a summer in North Carolina at the Eastern Music Festival, I allowed myself a deep dive into the ephemerality of our work, which in the end we must accept as the best we can do.

69

Some Thoughts on Encouraging Young Musicians to Write

A Paper Read at the 1989 College Music Society Annual Meeting

St. Louis, Missouri

The figure of musician as writer strikes a false note in many hearts, musical or otherwise. Performing musicians are to be seen, not heard. Or rather, an audience will accept the sound of their music, but no one expects a musician to function successfully in anything as commonplace as written language. We omniscient music professors know better, of course: the student musicians presently in our care will eventually have to write, among other things, job application letters, biographies suitable for printing in programs, and grant proposals, and some will even attempt doctoral dissertations. Eventually, they may be required to take on that most difficult of all prose forms, the interdepartmental memo. They will never reach such an exalted height unless they can put words on paper in such an order that meaning is conveyed to the reader.

I would like to discuss the role of prose writing in general education, how we might deal with the fear of writing that we all have known at one time or another, and how we might usefully incorporate good writing into the music curriculum.

Let me assure you, I begin this paper with no little fear and trembling. I still remember the disillusionment I felt upon reading the first student papers submitted in my piano literature class several years ago at Northwestern. This was, after all, Northwestern, and these were, after all, mostly master's students, but not to put too fine a point on it, the papers were abysmal. An even profounder grief befell me when I found myself a dissertation adviser. It is hardly news to you that the prose of today's college students will never be confused with that of George Bernard Shaw.

What is missing in their earlier education is anyone's guess. Given our system, some of it has to do with English teachers. If they don't teach the students how to write, who will? However, with the recent "writing across the curriculum" trend, the responsibility to teach basic writing skills has widened. We all need to be able to communicate effectively in writing. Passing on the ability to communicate with others should belong in every course.

There is another fault in our system regarding English teachers: they are not always trained to teach writing per se. For most of them, their real subject is literature. They specialize in reading, not writing. When they do give a written assignment, it's based on the literature the class is reading. I remember my high school English teachers returned papers with two grades: one for content, and another for style. Often, their main concern was the content, which is unfortunate for the poor students' writing instruction. It seems to me that the two should not be separated, since style is the carrier of content.

Writing is, in fact, a record of thinking. It is more permanent than speech and must do without any cues from the speaker's vocal inflection or body language. Writing forces us to say what we mean. If we can think, we should be able to write. What's needed is the motivation (a reason to write) and the means—the vocabulary, syntax, and grammar, which are part of speaking.

I can think of no better motivation for writing than to find out what we know. The act of putting our thoughts down on paper serves to crystallize and clarify; ideas can have value in themselves, but they are of little use to others unless we can articulate them. By writing, we take half-formed ideas and make them concrete and understandable, to ourselves even more importantly than to others. In effect, we write to learn.

I wish I had invented that last phrase, but as is often the case, someone else got there first. This time it was William Zinsser, formerly a teacher of writing at Yale University, and more recently a general editor of the Book-of-the-Month Club. Zinsser has written a book called *Writing to Learn*, and I cannot recommend it too highly. To quote Zinsser:

Writing is how we think our way into a subject and make it our own. Writing enables us to find out what we know—and what we don't know—about whatever we're trying to learn. Putting an idea into words is like defrosting the windshield: the idea, so vague out there in the murk, slowly begins to gather itself into a sensible shape. Whatever we write—a memo, a letter, a note to the baby-sitter—all of us know this moment of finding out what we really want to say by trying in writing to say it.

If writing to learn is our motivation, the pain eases somewhat. Professors, however, in their eternal quest to test the student thoroughly, too often assign papers to find out what the student knows, instead of creating a forum in which the student will learn. This was my mistake with the piano lit papers I spoke of earlier. The assignment was to choose a topic from a list of subjects I gave them and write a paper. Unfortunately, they had no particular interest in those subjects other than how I would grade them. It took me three years to figure out the problem. After another batch of dreck in the second year, I let them choose their own topics, stipulating only that it be something they wanted themselves to know more about. I also took away the grade. It worked; the papers were better, and the students seemed to learn more.

We usually assign writing that is explanatory in nature, concerned with existing information or ideas. Equally valid as a learning tool is exploratory writing, which is concerned with finding out what we want to say. I have used this kind of writing with my applied-piano students. One example: this past spring, I asked them to write how they felt about the performer's responsibility to play music of our own time. Again, I said there were no grades, and I heavily emphasized that I wanted to know *their* feelings, not what they thought I wanted them to say. My only qualification was aimed at the conservatory denizens that I teach: I explained that music of our time did not mean Stravinsky or Bartók. The results were fascinating. I read some of the papers to the weekly studio class meeting, and we spent the rest of the hour in stimulating discussion.

We all ended up learning from that assignment. The problem remains, though: How do we pass on the habits of *good* writing? If an

English teacher can't do it, how can a mere musician? To answer that, I invoke the pedagogical tool used by music teachers for centuries—imitate! When I, as a piano teacher, run out of ways to tell a student how to do something, I play it for them. I am not asking them to slavishly copy me; I simply want to put the music out there on a musical plane where they can use their own powers of deduction to comprehend the end result. The same can be done with writing and has been for centuries. Even Shakespeare had models.

What we need are some models of good writing about music. Happily, there are some wonderful examples out there. The authors are often musicians first and writers second, a fact that should give inspiration to students. To name just three books we might all emulate if we had the ability: Jacques Barzun's biography of Berlioz; Arthur Loesser's scintillating social history *Men, Women, and Pianos*; and Charles Rosen's extraordinary *The Classical Style*. By the way, do not be surprised if your students are unaware of the fact that a literature on music even exists. Unless they've had a bibliography course, they are often completely in the dark. Indeed, my experience has been that most music students are not big readers of anything. The piano department at Peabody once took the bull by the horns and devised a general reading list for our students of books chosen simply because they had given us such enjoyment in our own reading. The subliminal message was that if your teachers found things like *Walden* and *Bleak House* stimulating, maybe you'll like them too.

Back to the modeling idea, there are also some abominable examples out there, too, and we should make clear to our students what's bad about the bad. The books I mentioned earlier were chosen because, to use my old English teacher's terminology, the content comes across all the more clearly thanks to the writer's style. If students experience a bit of literary osmosis with any of these books, they will become better writers. We should make it clear that they should not feel guilty about this modeling process, although a word on plagiarism is never out of place. They will eventually move beyond imitation, just as my piano students do, and find their own voice. Writing successfully and making music are remarkably similar; neither goes well until the students absorb into their very being a sense of how the language works and sense that there is something important out there that only they can say.

From that point on, it's not unlike practicing an instrument. You have to work on your technique, and even with decent chops, you have to rehearse and rehearse and rehearse. In writing terms, this is called revision. If we are really going to help our students improve their writing, we must work time into the teaching schedule for this revision process. Most are discouraged if the writing doesn't just flow. They need to remember H. L. Mencken's dictum that "0.8 percent of the human race is capable of writing something that is instantly understandable." Zinsser thinks that's a little high.

70

Inner Voices

The View from the Second Floor

SEPTEMBER 1986

Time must be flying faster than usual. This month marks the beginning of this column's third year. Wasn't it only yesterday that Barbara Kreader and I talked about a monthly column freewheeling in subject matter and viewed from the standpoint of a conservatory piano teacher? Three years later, I wonder, "Why did she so readily agree?" Little did I know how difficult it would be to regularly come up with ideas that fit neatly in the space between method book advertisements. There were times when I wanted to deal with subjects of Brucknerian expansivity but had to condense and simplify to the point of top-forties pablum. There were other times when the blankness of the typewriter page resembled Schubert's manuscript paper for the third and fourth movements of the *Unfinished Symphony*. What on earth could I write about that would interest the readers that hadn't already been said better by someone else?

To be honest, I almost called it a day with the April 1986 column. When I looked back on past writing, I noticed many of the clichés I intensely disliked, and oh my, how I generalized on topics that deserved the breadth and wisdom of an Alfred North Whitehead. Furthermore, where had all the time gone? Was it really easier and faster in the old days when I had access to a word processor? A real-man writer like Hemingway would laugh in his beer over such a wimpy complaint. Even Andy Rooney swears by his ancient Royal.

This train of thought led me to take a hard look at my teaching. I started to hate that too. The little voices inside began a running commentary: "Oh, come on, can't you think of anything better to say than 'Use more arm'? That's the tenth time you've said it today." Or "I'm sick of hearing you explain Baroque dances. Why don't you switch to Spanish music for a couple of years? A fandango or two would do you good." As soon as I'd get the voices to quiet down, a memory of a long-ago conversation with a teacher of great experience would float up. He said something to this effect: "I really only say about six different things to my students. It's all a variation on those six things." With eagle-eyed hindsight, I now wish I had asked him what those six things were, because so far, I've only come up with five.

As gloomy mood accelerated to full-fledged depression, the little voices tore into my playing as well.

"You call that a beautiful tone? I call that generic cardboard."

"You call that an even scale? Man, that scale has more potholes than Main Street after a hard winter."

"*What*? You have the gall to program *Gaspard*? Do you have any idea how many dewy-eyed, peach-befuzzed teenagers can sight-read that piece?"

Everywhere I turned, there were little voices, critics whose full-time job was to pass judgment on my sense of judgment, experts who had all the solutions for any given problem. Ask them, and they'd tell you just how extensive their knowledge was, how refined their taste; they'd even tell you if you didn't ask.

Nevertheless, here stands *The View*, volume 3, number 1. Has my pitiful ego survived those little, albeit loud, voices? Has self two vanquished self one?

Nope. Nothing as exciting or trendy has occurred in my beleaguered psyche. The scenario of encroaching madness described above was exaggerated for effect. I will, however, admit to a simple yet profound realization that comes in two parts.

First, the little voices will always be there. No amount of *Inner Game* strategy will make them go away. It's wanting them to go away that gives them their power. As soon as you accept their presence, they lose a lot of their ability to drive you nuts. Once you start ignoring their destructive advice, they might even come up with things that can be surprisingly helpful. At the very least, they can keep you from becoming complacent.

That leads to the second part of the realization: we are getting paid (however meagerly) to be musicians who are supposedly experts at what we do. We are the outer voices, as it were, the authorities in our field. To accomplish this, we must take a stand. In fact, we are taking stands all the time. Every sound we make at the piano represents a position, an attitude. The programs we choose similarly reflect an inner belief. Persisting with a musical detail in a chamber music rehearsal requires taking a stand. As teachers and performers, we must be very insistent people. It's no wonder we have inner voices.

This column is beginning its third year because I take stands all the time. I might as well do it in print, or so goes my lopsided reasoning. Writing, as this month's column convincingly proves, is a therapy for me. There are still subjects I need to think about, so I will continue to write. I hope some of these thoughts will strike a responsive chord in you, providing a little therapy along the way. While we may rather be practicing, the process of thought never fails to deepen our music making.

In the meantime, please reassure me. You have little voices, too, don't you?

71

Planting a Garden

The View from the Second Floor (excerpt)

SEPTEMBER 1989

There is an old Chinese proverb that says, "If you would be happy for a week, get married. If you would be happy for a month, kill your pig. But to be happy for a lifetime, plant a garden." It seems to me that playing and teaching the piano are a lot like planting a garden. With apologies to Chance the gardener in *Being There*,[1] consider:

> *You have to wait for things to germinate.*
> *The young plants are so vulnerable in their fragility and tenderness.*
>   *Some don't make it.*
> *The mature plants will grow and thrive and even produce little shoots of*
>   *their own.*
> *You have to tend all the plants, watering, feeding, keeping the bugs off.*
> *The perennials come back year after year if you take care of them.*

How poetic. But don't forget you have to shovel the dirt and rake the beds, hoe the weeds, and get blisters on your hands. You have to face the morally difficult environmental question of using a pesticide. You have to chase away the rabbits, moles, and deer, lest they harvest your bounty before you do. You have to know which plants will do best in your soil, then pray for rain. You have to be knowledgeable, patient, and ferociously determined.

Some interesting similarities, wouldn't you say? There are so many "have-to rules." How can one decide about pesticides without looking at the whole picture? How does one end up a pianist when it's so forbiddingly difficult?

The answers aren't all in a textbook.

---

1. Floating around popular culture at the time of writing was a movie adaptation of Jerzy Kosiński's novel *Being There*, starring Peter Sellers as Chance the gardener. As I wrote this essay, it was clear I was looking for answers anywhere they presented themselves.

72

Report from the Woods

Out of the Woods

MAY 1995

With spring coming on, in more of a hurry than usual, it seems a good time for a progress report on these last two years "in the woods." If the reader imagines my days have been blissfully living out a hermit fantasy, guess again. The woods are cold and lonely, and there are bugs under the leaves.

One early lesson—learned the hard way—is that there is no more time in the woods than back in town. The hours here speed by inexorably, leaving me with almost as many unfinished projects as before. After two years, it occurs to me that I have too many projects.

It has never been easy for me to choose. Rather than do one thing well, I've had a compulsion to do everything—just as well, thank you. After two years, it occurs to me that choosing might be easier in the long run.

As for the experiments I set for myself in the woods, most are at least out of the box. Since I was eight years old and first saw Leonard Bernstein on television, I've wanted to conduct. Rushing in where angels know better than to tread, five years ago I rounded up a chamber orchestra and tried it for the first time. It was a frightening thrill, and I was hooked.

During these past two years, I've conducted several programs; each time brought an addictive adrenaline rush, but with it came the increasing realization that this wasn't as easy as it looked. The moment of truth came in the winter of 1994 when I conducted the Syracuse Symphony in two Gershwin pops programs. I realized that to get really good at it, I would need about twenty years of regular experience, not to mention hours a day to study scores. As reality set in here in the woods, I realize that such time is not likely to materialize in ripe middle age.

Since the world does not need another mediocre conductor, that's one project down.

In the meantime, something that wasn't on the schedule caught me completely by surprise. I wrote a piece of music. Again, I had little business trying; childhood pipe dreams, a few courses in college, and several short tidbits over twenty years do not a composer make. But a poem written by a friend seemed to cry out for music, and last spring I took the leap and started writing. Two months later, a twelve-minute piece for soprano, clarinet, cello, and piano existed on manuscript paper, and I still don't know how it got there.

I'll make no claims for its artistic value, but one thing I know is that writing this piece changed me. There is great joy for a pianist to learn or perform acknowledged masterpieces, but it doesn't compare to the mystery of entering into a creative world where you find never-before-discovered sounds and phrases that you then return to the real world so that others might hear them. As you think and feel your way into the space that will become the piece, there are so many possibilities. Gradually the notes find their way to the one shape that seems right. I do not delude myself of this piece's profundity, but writing it has given me a satisfaction I've never known before. It's amazing what you can find in the woods.

To pay the bills, I've taken on more responsibility with the Skaneateles Festival. My duties have expanded from music director to "artistic and administrative director," which means the buck stops here. I do everything from program planning to writing thank-you notes to volunteers. If you've never had to raise money for a musical purpose, I highly recommend it as the ultimate reality check on your dedication to your art. After years on Alma Mater's dole giving faculty recitals free of commercial taint (or necessity), it is a bracing experience to go out and find the cash to put on concerts that people pay to attend. Surviving in the marketplace will not necessarily improve your art, but I guarantee it will make you a stronger artist.

Throughout this time of questioning and experiment, teaching has never been far from my mind. Before retiring to the woods, I was increasingly concerned that the main purpose of higher music education seemed to be self-perpetuation. What other conclusion would one draw from a system that rewards student recruitment, retainment, and graduate placement above all else? I needed to get away to rediscover my original love of teaching.

It was difficult for me not to teach. Without a regular outlet for my inclination, I found myself inventing situations for teaching: lecture-recitals, master classes, even an occasional speech. I accepted a nine-year-old boy as a student whose mother I met at a party. Through the Skaneateles Festival, I came up with an Arts-in-Education program, which auditions college music students from the area, trains them to do programs for public schools, and then places them in classrooms all over central New York. We even raise part of the money, an enticement for supervisors whose budgets are already stretched to the limit. My plate of projects overflowed—again.

All this taught me, finally, that teaching is about people. So is playing the piano or conducting; composition is perhaps the most fundamentally human expression in that we use our creativity to invent something that wasn't there before. Without other people to listen, to learn, to feel, all the hard work means nothing.

The irony is that I had to go to the woods to discover people. Surrounded by them in the daily rush of existence, I didn't see them. What is that old line about not seeing the forest for the trees?

As I gradually escape my own blindness, perhaps it's almost time to come out of the woods. I still need to pare down the project list, but a light is beginning to appear at the end of the tunnel.

73

Algae in Kansas

Out of the Woods (excerpt)

SEPTEMBER 1999

As I scribble the beginnings of this column in longhand, I'm sitting in the pool area of the condo complex where I live. Warren, an older man who is the resident super, is fussing around the edge of the pool. Eventually he comes over to me and with a worried look says, "Well, we had quite a surprise this morning." My heart beats faster as I wonder who drowned.

"Algae," he says.

I look at him in confusion.

"The sun, you know. Water heats up, and the next thing you know, algae."

Warren is a laconic midwesterner, built close to the ground, a devoted warrior against rust, wood rot, and algae. I wonder if he's ever heard a Beethoven sonata. There we are, in the bright Kansas sunshine, two human beings attempting to communicate, one awash in the effects of chlorine on algae, the other searching for words to put on paper for other pianists to read. I listen and nod my understanding of what he's doing. I don't mention anything about what I'm doing. Perhaps I should invite him to my condo for a mini recital. It would be nice to have a nod of understanding, however slight.

74

Time's Odometer

Out of the Woods (excerpt)

January 2000

With an inevitability that Beethoven would have envied, the cadence of the calendar resolves to January 1, 2000, this month. Every new year, we take stock, make resolutions, and promise to do better. This year, facing a triple match point of year, century, and millennium, I find myself attempting to justify the past as well as plan the future.

A decade ago, I plotted the timeline of the professional pianist and didn't like what I saw. The first pianists emerged about two hundred years ago, celebrating birth and early childhood in the classical period. They roared into red-blooded adolescence and early adulthood in the mid- and late-nineteenth century and settled into productive middle age in the early- and mid-twentieth century. According to my timeline, the profession entered its autumn years in the 1960s. There weren't as many concerts; the same old pieces were played repeatedly; young people ignored us, just as they do the elderly in the population. The piano's hallowed place in the parlor has given way to the home theater, complete with projection television and Dolby sound system. I would guess that 98 percent of all piano recitals occur in the music schools, where we play for each other. As we approach the new millennium, we may not know it, but we've already moved to the retirement community.

If that be the case, perhaps we should diversify. If the piano recital is on its way to intensive care, it is time to take up the musical equivalent of hang gliding. Dylan Thomas said it best: "Do not go gentle into that good night."

I realize, as life's odometer rolls over with zeroes, that it's the effort that counts. Public recognition—or for that matter, one's place in the pecking order, or timeline, of pianists—matters little. The important thing is the quiet dialogue of pianist and score, for in that colloquy is the potential revelation of truth and beauty. Forget about the money; if you want to get rich, there are lots of better ways to accomplish that.

If piano playing is in its last days, perhaps there is some advantage to participating in this incredibly rich twilight. The Dylan Thomas poem goes on: "Old age should burn and rave at close of day." Let's light up the sky with a sunset the world will never forget. The young may be chained to their entertainment systems and never notice, but we will have known—and told—of better glories.

75

Ruminations

The View from the Second Floor

SEPTEMBER 1990

Summer retreats reluctantly this year, still singing like the serenading swain who refuses to acknowledge the closing window of the beloved. So much left undone. Each year one is more aware of the music unlearned, the books unread, the flowers overlooked. September signals new beginnings, and as soon as school starts, we are swept up in the excitement of youth's boundless potential, dizzied by what might be. All that talent, a clean white canvas aching for the fine oils of education and experience. Our summer's idylls are soon forgotten.

Before leaving it all behind this year, I want to linger in one of those humid ruminations about what we do. Sometimes on long cross-country drives, lulled by the hum of the car's engine, seduced by interstate meditations, I almost think I understand it. We make music. We teach others to make music. We move back and forth between these two worlds as our schedules require. Why can't it be that simple?

Scene one: You are at a party, and another guest asks what you do. You start to talk about being a classical musician but quickly give up, frustrated not only by your tied tongue but by the guest's quickness to categorize or, worse, smugly dismiss. You wish you were a stockbroker.

The scene changes: A student asks for some time to talk about the future. You've heard this before—he wants to be a concert artist. You explain that very few make a living from performing only, that there are many other fulfilling careers in music, such as teaching. He interrupts to say there's no way he would teach; you wish you could wring his insensitive neck.

One more hallucination: You have just played a recital at your school. It is a substantial, musically challenging program that seems to excite everyone in the small but enthusiastic crowd. You have played well and allow yourself a modest satisfaction. In the receiving line, the town's music critic shakes your hand and praises the recital, then apologizes that he won't be reviewing it since the paper's policy forbids coverage of in-house university events. Never mind that the community concert association hasn't brought a pianist to town in three years.

Still, there are times when it almost makes sense. Immersed in practicing, you summon the intensely specialized skills developed over many years to address the musical moment. You feel the concentration centering, the merging of consciousness and action. Intention flows directly into sound that instantaneously returns to the ear. You work with a lyric theme, carving the sound from silence, experimenting with touches that release the sound from Earth's tethers. You work with a virtuosic passage, choreographing the hands to move through the obstacle course with grace and apparent effortlessness. As you practice, the circle of intention-action-sound is all-embracing; you lose track of time. On occasion you become the music. When you finally tear yourself away from the piano, you know you could never be a stockbroker.

Working with students is easier to describe to the party guest but infinitely more difficult to negotiate. Suddenly you must wrestle with a set of intentions entirely different from your own. When the student's mind enters the feedback loop—a mind as complex as your own but far less familiar—anything can happen, and often does. Still, you rifle through your file of interpersonal skills and begin to lay a foundation of understanding that will lead to growth on both sides. It takes time, and because that other mind is essentially a wild card, you never know if you'll get there. Sometimes on the way, the most rewarding moments are in the discovery of a new word, a piece of the puzzle that the teacher finds and the student puts into place with the eagerness and relief of someone who knew something was missing but couldn't find it alone.

September's return to school symbolizes for me an acceptance of both the pleasure and the pain of what we do. We will practice and perform, despite the disinterest of the vast majority. We will teach young people to carry on this tradition, even though the invitingly open canvas of their talent may ultimately contain little more than vaguely promising doodles. Our mind's vacation ends, and with it the freer schedule, the pirouetting daydreams. Summer slips away, touching us with regret.

Lingering a moment longer, let T. S. Eliot have the last word (Part V of "East Coker" from *Four Quartets*):

> *So here I am, in the middle way, having had twenty years—*
> *Trying to learn to use words, and every attempt*
> *Is a wholly new start, and a different kind of failure*
> *Because one has only learnt to get the better of words*
> *For the thing one no longer has to say, or the way in which*
> *One is no longer disposed to say it. And so each venture*
> *Is a new beginning, a raid on the inarticulate*
> *With shabby equipment always deteriorating*
> *In the general mess of imprecision of feeling,*
> *Undisciplined squads of emotion. And what there is to*
>   *conquer*
> *By strength and submission, has already been discovered*
> *Once or twice, or several times, by men whom one cannot*
>   *hope*
> *To emulate—but there is no competition—*
> *There is only the fight to recover what has been lost*
> *And found and lost again and again: and now, under*
>   *conditions*
> *That seem unpropitious. But perhaps neither gain nor loss.*
> *For us, there is only the trying. The rest is not our business.*

XIII

■ Food for Thought

Whenever I have questions, I tend to look elsewhere for answers. That other source had better be authoritative, one that leaves no doubt in a skeptical mind. As a child, I often looked to the *Encyclopedia Americana*, whose volumes lined a bookshelf next to the mantel. I'm sure my parents stretched their budget to purchase these tomes as I entered grade school; little did they know that their offspring would eventually leave childhood's boundaries thanks to these windows into the world. At first, I was fascinated by the photographs of things bigger than anything in my Ohio backyard: tall waterfalls, skyscrapers, mountain peaks. Soon I read details that I still remember: the Empire State Building was 1,250 feet tall; Angel Falls in Venezuela was the highest waterfall in the world, at 3,212 feet.

My third-grade classroom had a *World Book Encyclopedia* set. During lulls in the teacher's instruction (remember rest periods?), I would take a volume off the shelf and browse for something to grab my attention. One day I came upon an entry on Vladimir Horowitz that must have contained his photo at the piano; otherwise, I would never have known he was a concert pianist. It also included a copy of one of his recital programs that intrigued me so much I transferred it to notebook paper, imitating the font and spelling out words I didn't know. For that matter, I had never heard of Vladimir Horowitz either; I had only been taking piano lessons for a year at this point. The fact that the *World Book* would include something about a concert pianist was enough for this eight-year-old to take notice. Mrs. Weisgarber, the teacher, eventually came over to interrupt my reverie and return me from Carnegie Hall to Moffitt Heights Elementary School.

Whenever I had a column due and didn't have a topic in mind, I often turned to other people's books. Sometimes these were inspirational—when I needed a boost of confidence, I was not shy about consulting writers who knew secrets I didn't. In a previous section, I wrote of William Zinsser's *Writing to Learn*; his book *On Writing Well* is one I can also recommend highly. More heartening encouragement came from Brenda Ueland in her book *If You Want to Write*. Similarly, Natalie Goldberg's *Writing Down the Bones* promised to "free the writer within." I return to these whenever a mental block emerges to obliterate clarity of purpose.

Sometimes, I simply need a grammar refresher; the musical equivalent might be "Hey, dummy, count out loud!" *The Elements of Style*, first written by Professor William Strunk Jr. for a Cornell English class in 1919 and revised by E. B. White in 1957, attempts "to cut the vast tangle of English rhetoric down to size and write its rules and principles on the head of a pin." I must constantly remind myself of rule number fourteen: "Use the active voice." My inner editor has tried to remove passive constructions from this book, but a few probably remain.

Style remains harder to define:

> There is no satisfactory explanation of style, no infallible guide to good writing, no assurance that a person who thinks clearly will be able to write clearly, no key that unlocks the door, no inflexible rule by which the young writer may shape his course. He will often find himself steering by stars that are disturbingly in motion.[1]

Some might criticize White's first sentence above containing multiple commas as too long or find the masculine pronouns near the quote's end sexist. Are there solutions? One could make more than one sentence out of that first rambler, but the repetition of the word *no* emphasizes the frustration of defining good writing. To avoid the masculine pronoun, one can choose *one* if the word is to remain singular (with obvious depersonalization) or make *writer* plural (*writers* and *themselves*), throwing the reader's imagination to a field of

---

1. William Strunk Jr. and E. B. White, *The Elements of Style*, third edition (Boston: Allyn & Bacon, 1995), 66.

people rather than an individual.[2] Less than ideal choices, you'd agree. Writing isn't easy.

The essays that follow are examples of times I turned to others for inspiration. The attention to verbs arose from the imposed hunger resulting from a diet of too many academic papers. Arthur Plotnick says of verbs in his *The Elements of Expression*:

> Verbs power sentences. Energetic verbs rocket them. In expressing the nature of things, we can tell what they *are*, what qualities they *have*—or we can show what they *do* and *do to* something. The doing is usually more forceful, and it is done with action verbs.[3]

Suddenly I longed for more active verbs at the piano. The essay offers a few with the hope that when we "play," we are in fact *do*ing something *to* our world.

Another writer whose work profoundly influenced me was Anthony Storr (1920–2001), a British psychiatrist who became a successful writer in his later years. He produced twelve books in twenty-six years, including pithy explanations of the thinking of both Freud and Jung. However, music was his true, lifelong love. As a child, he attended performances in Westminster Abbey of such works as Bach's *St. Matthew Passion*, thrilled to be allowed to sit in the organ loft. As a student, he sang in the choir and played the viola in the orchestra and piano solos in concerts. He always maintained that he would much rather have been a professional musician than a psychiatrist or writer, had he been blessed with the necessary talent and training; he freely acknowledged that his friendship with artists of the caliber of Alfred Brendel and the musicologist Hans Keller meant more to him than would equivalent

---

2. In his book *Finishing the Hat*, Stephen Sondheim addresses the gender pronoun problem on the first page of his introduction (p. xvii) with this footnote: "Rather than hacking my way through the jungle of convoluted syntax every time I want to refer to people of both genders, by 'he' and 'his' and other assorted masculine pronouns I mean 'she' and 'her' as well, unless I'm referring to a particular person."

3. Arthur Plotnick, *The Elements of Expression* (New York: Henry Holt & Co., 1996), 67.

friendships with Freud, Jung, or Adler. His book *Music and the Mind*, written in 1992, was his favorite.[4] In it he wrote:

> Let me end by affirming that, for me, as for Nietzsche, music has been 'something for the sake of which it is worthwhile to live on earth.' Music has incomparably enriched my life. It is an irreplaceable, undeserved, transcendental blessing.[5]

In nine chapters, Storr explores music's diverse roles in human existence. My essay from 1994 asks the question "Why music?" and consults Storr for a more learned explanation than I could provide. Every time I dip into this book, I am enriched.

Much has been written about the artist's need for deep experiences of life, yet the hours in the practice room can isolate musicians. To avoid the trap of being merely an executant, we must find knowledge somewhere, and this leads us to Harold Bloom, a scholar of the highest attainment. I came across his book *How to Read and Why* while browsing in a bookstore, and here allow me to lament the closing of so many brick-and-mortar establishments. Yes, we can browse online, but seldom do we happen upon something we weren't looking for that has tremendous value to us. For the same reason, I also mourn the loss of library card catalogues. In times gone by, we might search for a particular book and find it in the catalogue, only to find another even more interesting item related to our search right beside that first card. Adieu, serendipity.

But back to Bloom. The blurbs on the cover jacket alone suggest the magnitude of his work. "He is a colossus among critics…His enthusiasm for literature is a joyous intoxicant," shouts the *New York Times Magazine*. The American poet Anthony Hecht raves, "Harold Bloom is brilliant, outrageous, headstrong, witty, heterodox, full of charm, immense learning, and tremendous zest."

---

4. Anthony Stevens, *Manchester Guardian*, March 20, 2001, accessed January 8, 2022.
5. Anthony Storr, *Music and the Mind*, (New York: Free Press / Macmillan, 1992), 188.

Such is the reader/critic who uncovers the multiplicity of human experience found in literature, laying it out for his readers to consider, to wrap their minds around, to delve more deeply into their own experience as they compare themselves to the work's characters. The book made me think of the musician as reader. How do we disclose the deeper meaning of the music we present to our listeners? We can't do it by reading about the music; we must internalize its deeper message and read the music itself ever more deeply until we connect to the truth that we find unique to ourselves, not to the truth as told by someone else.

Ultimately, this is where teachers cannot go; they can only show the student the doorway.

76

The Verbs of Piano Playing

Out of the Woods

MAY 1994

I listened recently to a speech extolling the virtues of studying music. The speech was full of nouns, mostly of the multisyllabic, conceptual variety. After a while, I longed for verbs—nice, juicy, active verbs—that I could feel with my body. If I were the parent of a prospective piano student, I would want to know what my child would *do* at the piano, and while we're at it, let's talk about how the piano fits into her life once she is grown. While the phrase "collect dust" contains an active verb, it is not what most people have in mind.

When I think of the verbs we associate with piano study, my pulse sags. We have drained the blood from once-useful words like *play*, *practice*, and *perform*. We *play* the piano, which at least suggests some fun, but most of us long ago forgot that connotation. We *practice*, whatever that means. We *perform*, which usually means repeat the practiced piece once more, this time in front of people. If we are ever to convince society that what we teach is worth attention and honor, I think we should develop some new verbs.

My list would start with the remarkably active verb *improvise*. Beyond the purely musical meaning, there is the suggestion of making something out of the materials at hand: here is the piano; here are hands to make it speak, ears with which to hear, and air all around to carry the sound. A child touching the keys for the first time improvises— she creates a sound that wasn't there before. The same child, a few years earlier, learned to speak this way—by trying out sounds, piecing them together, imitating the sounds she heard around her. In a very short time, she mastered a complex language, full of internal rules whose names she will not hear until school. Is music not a language? The Suzuki system begins with this simple premise but never reaches the higher implications inherent in improvisation. In spoken language, we constantly extemporize, rearrange words, invent new ones, build a sentence structure as we go. Jazz musicians do that in the language of music, and in a not-too-distant past, "classical" pianists did it too.

There is a world of activity in that verb *improvise*. Composition begins here. The most startling combinations of sounds are right under the fingers waiting to be released or found or conjured up. When we improvise, we bring the notion of *play* back to playing the piano. We welcome the element of surprise to a performance. When we improvise, we command the language as a speaker, not as a mere reciter. We *make* music, and when we play a piece from the standard repertoire, we are much more likely to bring it to life, to *animate* it. Pianists who learn to play spontaneously will *need* the piano in later life—it will be as necessary to them as their mother tongue.

Another verb I'd emphasize is *train*, as when an athlete (or a pianist) trains for life. Sports occupy an enormous place in our national psyche, and if training is good for the athlete, then I'm happy to borrow the word and use it in place of the word *practice*. Training suggests more levels of activity than we usually associate with practice—it is more than repetition. Training involves the mind and body: muscles are strengthened and coordinations are discovered and learned, all to achieve freedom in the athletic event itself. Training also suggests that one *centers* the mind and body, *focuses* the attention. Anyone who has practiced well knows it is the same thing, but so much mindless drill has taken place in the name of practicing that the very word is contaminated.

Another verb I'd use in telling what it is we do at the piano is *read*. Our eyes gather information from a text that we immediately translate into sound. We can do it silently, just as a child learns to read without moving her lips, or we can do it aloud, as a result of our understanding of the language and our physical *training*. I'd rather not call it *sight-reading*; again, there are too many unfortunate connotations. It is reading, just as you are reading this text without thinking about how you do it. Like all reading, it offers the opportunity to acquire knowledge—for aesthetic pleasure, for fun or profit, to pass the time, or to pass on knowledge to someone else. One cannot imagine a school system that skips over reading, nor a good reader at the piano who stays away from the instrument for years on end.

It doesn't take a genius to realize we *improvise* every time we make a casserole with leftovers from the fridge. We *train* whenever we learn a new skill, whether it be macramé or skydiving. We *read* everything from instructions on how to file an insurance claim to the plays of William Shakespeare. These verbs carry more meaning to our goal-oriented society than *play*, *practice*, or *perform*. If we are to make ourselves more than a peripheral part of that society, we have to be able to say what we *do* (active verb).

The trick, of course, is to live up to our advertising.

77

Why Music?

Out of the Woods

SEPTEMBER 1994

A disturbing, thought-provoking article in the most recent issue of *Chamber Music Magazine* by its editor, Philip Kennicott, begins with this simple statement: "Western classical music is nothing more—and certainly nothing less—than a pleasure."

In one candid declarative sentence Mr. Kennicott has clarified one of the dilemmas with which I have been wrestling in the woods—namely, why it is so difficult in this society to make a living anywhere in the vicinity of classical music. He goes on to shoot holes in several of my favorite fantasies, the first of which is torpedoed in the very next sentence: "While it is a pleasure with surprisingly broad appeal, it is not, as is so often claimed, a universal language."

Ouch. Yet if one gives up the illusion that humankind's happiness is imminent with the widespread appreciation of classical music, the situation makes a lot more sense. We live in a society in which pleasure is as cheap and readily available as the candy rack at the checkout line. We think of pleasure as something which should gratify quickly and efficiently, like jumping into a cool lake on a hot day or, more desperately, like drugs. It's no wonder no one wants to pay the classical piper—it takes too long to listen.

For that reason, I must disagree with Mr. Kennicott. Western classical music—indeed the art music of every culture—goes far beyond pleasure. There is much more at work here than mere enjoyment. If music were so enjoyable, people would be flocking to concert halls the world over!

It is astonishing that music is even a part of human existence. What role, after all, does it play in the grand scheme of things? Is it (or was it) necessary to our survival as a species? Is it a vestige of some long-forgotten, preverbal language? In short, Why music?

These are questions beyond the scope of a one-thousand-word essay, but I refer the curious reader, and Mr. Kennicott, to an excellent book that takes on these enormous issues: Anthony Storr's *Music and the Mind*. In examining the significance of music in human life, the author looks at music's origins and its purpose in a culture. His findings suggest that a good deal more than pleasure is involved here.

Storr's chapter one, titled "Origins and Collective Functions," entertains several notions, ranging from the idea that music began as an imitation of birdsong to Darwin's belief that song was originally a sexual invitation. In between are several persuasive arguments. I am particularly intrigued with the theory put forth by anthropologist Ellen Dissanayake, who thinks that "music originated in the ritualized verbal exchanges which go on between mothers and babies during the first year of life" (quoted in Storr).[1] As anyone with a child knows, this type of communication involves emotional expressiveness, not factual information. Dissanayake writes, "No matter how important lexico-grammatical meaning eventually becomes, the human brain is first organized or programmed to respond to emotional/intonational aspects of the human voice."[2] In other words, music could well be essential to our survival.

Since Kennicott picks on Western music, let's turn to the cradle of Western civilization, ancient Greece. Music was a pervasive part of that culture, so important that every freeborn citizen received instruction in singing and playing the lyre. "Music and poetry were inseparable," writes Storr. "The Greek word *melos* indicated both lyric poetry and the music to which a poem is set—it is the origin of our word 'melody.'"[3] In fact, what we would call ancient Greek poetry was something more than modern Western verse, which is primarily linguistic. "Here," writes Thrasybulos Georgiades in his book *Music and Language*, "the musical

---

1. Anthony Storr, *Music and the Mind* (New York: Ballantine Books, 1992), 8.
2. Storr, *Music and the Mind*, 9.
3. Storr, *Music and the Mind*, 14.

rhythm was contained within the language itself. The musical-rhythmic structure was completely determined by the language. There was no room for an independent musical-rhythmic setting; nothing could be added or changed."[4] In short, music and poetry were one.

This leads to an idea put forth by the psychoanalyst and accomplished amateur musician Anton Ehrenzweig, who is quoted by Storr:

> It is not unreasonable to speculate that speech and music have descended from a common origin in a primitive language which was neither speaking nor singing, but something of both. Later this primeval language would split into different branches; music would have retained the articulation mainly by pitch (scale) and duration (rhythm), while language chose the articulation mainly by tone colour (vowels and consonants). Language moreover happened to become the vehicle of rational thought and so underwent further influences. Music has become a symbolic language of the unconscious mind whose symbolism we shall never be able to fathom.[5]

This definition is a long way from music being "nothing more than a pleasure." It also suggests that the belief most musicians have of music as a universal language is not as far-fetched as Kennicott believes.

Perhaps the most distressing aspect of Kennicott's article, however, is the fact that he is a music lover who is deeply enmeshed in the musical scene. If that kind of statement can come from one of us, it's no wonder most Americans look on music as a frill and pay accordingly.

---

4. Storr, *Music and the Mind*, 15.

5. Storr, *Music and the Mind*, 16.

78

Reading Well

Out of the Woods

November 2000

There is no single way to read well, though there is a prime reason why we should read. Information is endlessly available to us: where shall we find wisdom?[1]

So begins Harold Bloom's latest book, *How to Read and Why*. Bloom is Sterling Professor of Humanities at Yale University and a former Charles Eliot Norton Professor at Harvard.[2] A MacArthur Prize fellow, his numerous books—including *Shakespeare: The Invention of the Human, The Anxiety of Influence*, and *The Western Canon* (in which he argues convincingly that certain books deserve axiomatic elevation and thus widespread study)—are evidence of a mind that has read, and continues to read, deeply. Although he is one of the most esteemed of present-day literary critics, his love of literature is contagiously vivid, suggesting the enthusiasm of the amateur and the passion of youth.

It matters, if individuals are to retain any capacity to form their own judgments and opinions, that they continue to read for themselves.[3]

As I stood in the bookstore reading those words, I wondered if this applied to musicians. Do we read music in the same way we read

---

1. Harold Bloom, *How to Read and Why* (New York: Touchstone, 2001), 19.

2. Bloom died in 2019, so there were many more books to come. His last two books were published in 2020: *The Power of the Reader's Mind over a Universe of Death* (672 pages) and *The Bright Book of Life* (544 pages).

3. Bloom, *How to Read and Why*, 21.

---

a literary text? Can we substitute the word *play* for the word *read?* Information, in the form of digital bits on compact discs representing the playing of Schnabel and Serkin and Solomon, is endlessly available to us. But is this the fount of wisdom?

I took the book home and have now read its opening chapters several times. We can debate the application to music, but creating the association raises some unsettling questions. Surely the goal of musicians is to find wisdom, to form our own judgments and opinions. According to Bloom, we must read—not books about Shakespeare, but the original texts themselves. We can enjoy watching Olivier's *King Lear,* but to really know the original, we must read it, and to know it still more deeply, we must read it again and again.

The parallel with music, I hope, is patently obvious: if we are to find the wisdom of the "Waldstein" Sonata, it can only be found by our direct involvement with the text. We can learn others' judgments and opinions by reading scholarly books and articles, and we can listen to recordings by everyone from Arrau to Zeltser, but it is not the same and, in the end, not as valuable as reading it ourselves. I believe this to be true for professional and amateur alike.

Bloom's concern is for the reading individual:

> *I turn to reading as a solitary praxis, rather than as an educational enterprise…Ultimately we read…in order to strengthen the self, and to learn its authentic interests. The pleasures of reading are selfish rather than social.*[4]

When was the last time you read through a piece for yourself? Both as performing and as teaching musicians, we usually think of ourselves as guides for others to learn or comprehend a composition. Our wisdom about a piece can be frozen at a certain level, whether it be that which can be absorbed by the student at hand or that which we can manage as we traverse the tightrope of public performance. Bloom views reading as a solitary pursuit, done away from the necessities of lesson

---

4. Bloom, *How to Read and Why,* 19.

preparation or the glare of the concert spotlight. It can strengthen the self and bring us to our authentic interests, to that which we uniquely value. It does not have to be about learning a piece and preparing it for performance; it can simply be about reading the piece.

Shakespeare speaks to as much of you as you can bring to him.[5]

Is that not also true of Mozart and Beethoven? Over a lifetime of coming to Bach, are you not constantly surprised by the newly discovered felicities that were there all along? It is not the score that has changed— it's the reader. We learn and grow over time, becoming more receptive to subtleties. However, if we never revisit that partita we played twenty years ago or ignore the other five in favor of the one we know, we remain locked in a self that never changes. Bach speaks to as much of you as you bring to him, or perhaps more accurately, Bach reads you more fully than you can read him. What matters is that you open yourself to a full reading and that you do so throughout the stages of a lifetime.

To read human sentiments in human language you must be able to read humanly, with all of you.[6]

Here is a sentence that some will resist translating to the musician's realm, but I find it fascinating. Surely music is a human language, although not everyone can read it. There are arguments as to the human sentiments found in some music. But can one doubt the humanity in Beethoven or Shostakovich? Then "to read humanly" is to bring your understanding of the human condition to the text. This surely is the case with the best music as much as it is in great plays, novels, or short stories. Bloom declares that it is one nature that writes and reads. We read to share in that nature.

---

5. Bloom, *How to Read and Why*, 28.
6. Bloom, *How to Read and Why*, 28.

You can read merely to pass the time, or you can read with an overt urgency, but eventually you will read against the clock.[7]

I've certainly done the first, and there have been times that the second was necessary. As we get older, the third becomes increasingly manifest. Our days are numbered, and we will leave this world without having read, touched, or played all the music we wanted to.

Yet there is some solace in the fact that we live amid such wealth. It is there for the taking. Wisdom awaits. We have only to pick up the score and read. The goal of several great pianists over the years was simply to learn one new page of music a day.

One could do worse.

7. Bloom, *How to Read and Why*, 21.

XIV

■ Politics and Our Profession

> The arts and sciences are essential to the prosperity of the state
> and to the ornament and happiness of human life. They have
> a primary claim to the encouragement of every lover of his
> country and mankind.
>
> —George Washington[1]

Musicians tend to be quiet people, apolitical for the most part, engaged in comparatively humble attempts to create beauty through their art. On the other hand, as mentioned earlier, our work requires us to take stands, to present firm, organic conceptions that confront the viewer/listener as worthy of their attention and reflection. In short, being an artist is not for weaklings.

The essays in this section were entreaties to the readership that music plays such an important part in our culture that it deserves the support of the government. These were political stances, and it was somewhat daring to submit these columns to a piano magazine. I felt it necessary, however, to use whatever soapbox I had to rouse fellow toilers in the musical vineyard to action.

Modern connotations of the word *politics* usually inspire a rolling of the eyes, but its origin is honest and unaffected. The root comes from the Greek word *polis*, or "city-state," and reflects the fact that humans are social animals whose lives are enhanced, indeed preserved, by living in communities. Aristotle's *Politics* states that the *polis* is the highest form of community. Politics, however, exist at every level: in the household,

---

1. Mark Bauerlein with Ellen Grantham, eds., *National Endowment for the Arts: A History, 1965–2008* (Washington, DC: National Endowment for the Arts, 2009), iv (epigraph).

in the neighborhood, in the place of work, and so on, up to the national and even international level.

Our nation is a *democracy*, another word born in the union of two Greek words: *demos* (people) and *kratos* (rule). Its deep meaning is powerfully evoked in Abraham Lincoln's immortal words: "that government, of the people, by the people, and for the people..."

When our elected representatives start to ignore some of the people, it's time to start making noise.

Why take on such a huge topic from the piano bench? Because this government of the people is ignoring—or trying to damage, intentionally or not—the community of artists.

There were glimmers of hope when Franklin Delano Roosevelt created the Works Progress Administration as part of the New Deal to employ out-of-work artists of all kinds. The Federal Music Project (FMP) lasted from 1935 to 1943 and gave employment to orchestral musicians and singers throughout the country. Music lessons were offered to underprivileged adults, and a music program for children was very popular. The project even led to the creation of new works for orchestra by such composers as Roy Harris and Aaron Copland.[2] The funding went not only to classical musicians but inspired the exploration and performance of indigenous music of all kinds: folk music, work songs, spirituals, Hispanic and Native American songs. This was, after all, the age of the "common man," so all varieties of music had support. Concerts were often free and open to a wide public. Music was accepted as a blessing for the spirit during the Great Depression.[3]

Still, there was political opposition to the New Deal, despite its benefits to the people, so much so that the FMP was eliminated in 1943. It was not until John F. Kennedy's administration that the arts again became something that engaged the attention of the Chief Executive. Robert Frost read his poem "The Gift Outright" at Kennedy's inauguration; also on the dais were the Abstract Expressionist painters

---

2. Kenneth Bindas, *All of This Music Belongs to the Nation: The WPA's Federal Music Project and American Society* (Knoxville: University of Tennessee Press, 2003).

3. Peter Gough, foreword by Peggy Seeger, *Sounds of the New Deal: The Federal Music Project in the West* (Chicago: University of Illinois Press, 2015).

Franz Kline and Mark Rothko.[4] In 1961, the Kennedys hosted an event that was notable in many ways: a concert in the East Room by the cellist Pablo Casals.

> In his opening remarks, President Kennedy said that it was intended not only as homage to Casals, but to Puerto Rico and its reforming governor, Luis Muñoz Marín. Second, President Kennedy pointed out that Casals, who was 84 when he performed in 1961, had also played in the White House for President Theodore Roosevelt in 1904. Finally, President Kennedy alluded to Casals's refusal to return to his native Catalonia, which was then under the dictatorship of Francisco Franco. The President closed his remarks with the words, "An artist must be a free man."[5]

Kennedy's influence led to the establishment of the National Endowment for the Arts in 1965 by President Lyndon Johnson. Kennedy once said, "The life of the arts, far from being an interruption, a distraction, in the life of a nation, is very close to the center of a nation's purpose...and is a test of the quality of a nation's civilization."[6]

The history of the Endowment echoes the political brouhahas of a government that simply isn't sure it should be funding anything as squishy as the arts. The period in which I was an NEA applicant was particularly volatile. For example, the number of grants awarded in 1995 was 4,000. In 1997, that number had declined to 1,100.[7] The Endowment's total budget hit its highest level in 1992 when Congress agreed to $176 million. (George H. W. Bush was still in the White House.) By 1998, that number had shrunk to $98 million.[8] The current budget (2022) of $167.5 million is basically the same as the

---

4. Bauerlein, *National Endowment for the Arts*, 5.

5. Bauerlein, *National Endowment for the Arts*, 5.

6. Bauerlein, *National Endowment for the Arts*, 9.

7. Bauerlein, *National Endowment for the Arts*, 124.

8. Bauerlein, *National Endowment for the Arts*, 123.

1985 congressional appropriation of $160 million, despite the change in the cost of living.

I applied in 1989 for a Solo Recitalist Fellowship, an award no longer given. (Awards to individuals are now verboten.) To my great surprise, I was promised $15,000 to support a piano solo recital series of three programs, each including a work of Aaron Copland. When the grant was later cut by 10 percent, I didn't really care. I'd survive by tightening my belt.

Then I became music director of the Skaneateles Festival in 1990, so for the first time, my community was larger than the music school where I taught. I had to reach an audience willing to pay for their seats. (My solo recitals were paid for by the presenting organizations where I played.) I also had to pay the musicians willing to play for minuscule sums, and somehow the festival had to balance its books so that a strict board of directors could sleep at night. Suddenly I became very interested in funding sources. This was about *my community* now.

My first sortie into protesting cuts to the National Endowment came in 1990 when I was asked to speak at a rally in North Carolina in support of the NEA. Organized by various performing organizations, including the Eastern Music Festival where I taught in the summer, the rally was held on the campus of Duke University in Durham. All the participating organizations had funding cuts that year. I told the story of how the House Un-American Affairs Committee, chaired by Senator Joseph McCarthy, scared a large portion of the public when it accused many prominent people of being Communists. Among those accused was Aaron Copland, the very composer whose works I would feature in my NEA-supported recitals.

The next step in my conversion to activism occurred in the early 1990s when the governor of New York State cut the budget of the NYSCA,[9] another predictable source of income for the Skaneateles Festival. While I respected Governor Mario Cuomo in many ways, I felt I had to raise my small voice in protest and wrote two letters over the

---

9. New York State Council on the Arts. Its current budget is $46.9 million. Interestingly, its budget in 1991 was $46.4 million, reflecting a cut of 7 percent followed by another cut of $3.6 million late in the year. So much for growth.

course of a year. The final words of the letter included in this collection still ring true—ultimately, one person is responsible, and that person's name is on the ballot. I hope those reading this value their power to vote.

The remaining essays are personal reports from the front. Government support for the arts in the United States will always be controversial. It seems so clear to me that the arts enhance life for all those who participate. If Germany can budget one billion euros just to "restart culture" after the COVID pandemic, surely the United States can do better. The NEA has survived, but its funding remains frozen at a level now four decades old. Given inflation, that means the NEA is dying a slow death—unless we, the people, do something about it.

79

Address to National Endowment for the Arts Rally

JUNE 21, 1990

I would like to tell the story of a highly respected, widely performed American composer who experienced a form of government censorship almost forty years ago. Three days before Dwight Eisenhower's inauguration as president in 1953, Aaron Copland learned through an article in the *New York Times* that his composition *Lincoln Portrait* had been removed from the official inaugural concert. It seems that a Republican congressman from Illinois, a certain Fred E. Busbey, had questioned Copland's patriotism in a speech to the House of Representatives. Never mind that Aaron Copland gave this country such cultural landmarks as *Appalachian Spring*, *Billy the Kid*, and *Fanfare for the Common Man*. Never mind that *Lincoln Portrait* is based on a narration that uses Lincoln's own words. Never mind that Copland had served, at the invitation of the Truman State Department, as an artistic ambassador to Latin America, the first composer to receive such an invitation.

Copland's problems were only beginning. On May 22, 1953, he received the following telegram: "You are hereby directed to appear before this committee on Monday May 25th at 2:30 p.m. room 357 Senate Office Building Washington DC. Signed Joe McCarthy Senate Permanent Subcommittee on Investigations." Like many other artists of that day, Copland faced questions, grilled on his political associations of twenty years earlier. He spent only two hours before McCarthy's committee, but the red-baiting had its effect. Universities cancelled Copland's upcoming lecture invitations; the Hollywood Bowl cancelled a Copland performance; even three years later, when TV personality Ed Sullivan broadcast a performance of *Lincoln Portrait* in honor of Lincoln's birthday, he did not credit the composer. As late as 1960, the Dallas Symphony received anonymous cards protesting a Copland concert.

Fast-forward to 1986: Copland was awarded the Congressional Gold Medal, which requires an act of Congress and is the highest civilian honor in the land.

Today, it seems that some of our senators and congressmen long for the good old days of the Red Menace. Lacking an appropriate target, they pick on artists instead, especially artists helped by the National Endowment for the Arts. They choose to overlook the thousands of grants that have been made to artists whose work has uplifted an eager public. They choose to overlook the fact that there has been an 81 percent increase in the number of artists making a go of it since the NEA's inception. They choose to ignore the fact that an organization like the Eastern Music Festival, with a yearly budget of $1.3 million, pumps $5.5 million into the local economy. They choose to ignore the fact that the NEA costs the average taxpayer less than sixty cents a year in a tax bill that can run to thousands of dollars.

In September, I will begin a recital tour supported by a Solo Recitalist Fellowship from the National Endowment for the Arts. Each recital, ironically enough, will include a major work by Aaron Copland. In another time, my application might have been refused on political grounds. If the NEA's opponents have their way, that time will be the 1990s, not the 1950s.

One hopes that those fighting the NEA go the way of Congressman Fred E. Busbey, to be heard of only in scholarly footnotes. More likely, they will go the way of Senator Joe McCarthy, remembered with shame by Americans everywhere, especially the Wisconsin voters who sent him to Washington.

To all of those who would make artists the scapegoats of the '90s, I suggest they read a chapter in a book they hold above all others— the Holy Bible. In Psalms 33, verse 3, we find "Sing unto him a new song; play skillfully with a loud sound!"

Thank you.

80

Dear Governor

The View from the Second Floor

July–August 1991

Dear Governor:

Last year, as you and the legislature argued over how our fair state would spend $51.2 billion over the next twelve months, I wrote a letter encouraging you to restore the proposed 20 percent cut in money for the arts. It seemed to me that your clever budget staff could find a way to lop off a measly $10 million (.0002 of the total budget) without reducing money to the arts by one-fifth.

That was a nervous time for artists. The National Endowment for the Arts was under attack, and it looked as though our nation's twenty-five-year experiment in public arts financing might die an early death. The NEA survived, but only to give grants based on populist criteria. The State of New York is now proposing a 56 percent cut in its arts council budget; California and Michigan are considering eliminating their arts budgets entirely. It's time to write to you again.

On the radio I've heard you explain the problem to simple folk like me: the state budget is just like my household budget. If I spend more than I take in, I will eventually go broke. I should therefore choose carefully how I spend money.

Governor, if I were strapped for cash, I would not spend money ripping up trees from the side of our rural road so that when it rains the water rushes down the valley to pollute what was once a perfectly clear stream with silt and farm runoff. Your crews have taken the better part of six months to do that and left many broken, bulldozed trees lying along the roadside. How much did that cost? How many other state roads received similar "beautification"?

If I were short of money, I'd be more likely to buy a book or concert ticket, something inexpensive that would give me a lift beyond the moment. Perhaps we have different values.

Many people assume that a thing has value if money is spent on it. If that is true, we can assume that bailing out savings and loan presidents is important. The federal government is heaping great mounds of money on reckless, greedy financiers while it claims there is not enough money for student loans.

Supporting the arts is apparently not important; when times get tough, you and most of your 49 colleagues want to cut the arts budget. From the marble steps of the statehouse, you proclaim in fiscally responsible tones how, to balance the budget, frills must be cut. The arts are elitist, you say; what we need are jobs, tax breaks for developers, and more prisons. We will all benefit by trimming the budget in this way, you say.

I disagree. The arts are for everyone. They provide us with one of our few remaining opportunities to experience beauty, to come into direct contact with "a shadow of the divine perfection" (Michelangelo), "the expression of one soul talking to another" (Ruskin), "the wine of life" (Jean Paul Richter).

The arts provide jobs, and not only to artists; the greater world of the arts encompasses bureaucrats, broom-pushers, and everything in between. When money to the arts is cut, the little guys are hurt too.

The arts even provide tax breaks because charitable giving to nonprofit organizations is still partially deductible. The wealthy might give more if the government encouraged active support of the arts.

As for prisons, it is my firm belief that we would not need as many if more children were taught an art. There is evidence that arts projects in tough neighborhoods keep kids out of trouble. Such school activities as band, orchestra, choir, and theater give students an appreciation for teamwork and artistic achievement that lasts a lifetime. Piano lessons teach discipline and an enjoyment of something beyond the cheap entertainment of television. Young people involved in art don't have time or inclination to steal cars.

If anything, Governor, the money you want to cut from the arts might have leveraged some of the greatest value per dollar in your entire budget. If you make another cut, my fear is not for art but for the people. A lot of folks stand to lose here.

Finally, I am not one to assume that it is the impersonal state making decisions about where to cut spending. Some one person is in charge up there, and ultimately you are that person. I don't care if it's your budget chief wanting to take the axe to the arts—you hired the guy. Next election I'll remember that someone deserves blame or credit for everything the government does. Your name is on the ballot.

81

It's an Election Out There

The View from the Second Floor

It's an election out there, and like most of the voting public, I find myself adrift in more questions than I can answer. My business has been hit hard from all directions. There's less disposable income, so people aren't going to concerts as often; their children are less likely to take piano lessons. Many of the wealthy keep their money at home instead of contributing to the local orchestra or school. The government has also cut back on assistance to education and the arts. I'd like to think my vote will count toward changing this gloomy situation.

If only music ranked higher in the competition for those disposable dollars. What could we do to make music more important in the scheme of things?

When I dream of a musical utopia, I imagine a society where a majority values great music as a necessity rather than a luxury. Music would be a part of this society's early education, and many children would learn to play an instrument. Later in life, they would also have ample occasions to play, perhaps in nonprofessional orchestras or amateur chamber music groups. They listen to music with the excitement of a participant, adept in the language, knowledgeable about its possibilities. Orchestras and other professional performing activities thrive, supported by listeners who attend concerts as the high point of their week. The elected officials of such a society allocate sizable amounts of tax revenues to the arts, knowing their constituents place a high value on the moral and spiritual rewards music brings to their lives.

Scoff at the idealism, if you will, but it would be a better world. People want meaning in their lives and yearn to believe in something larger than themselves. What better than a Brahms symphony? Children who learn to play the piano hone many skills that carry over into all aspects of their lives. The music keeps them busy, fosters pride in the work of their hands, and builds self-esteem. In such a society, the lives of professional musicians and teachers are obviously enhanced.

Effecting such a sea change would take nothing less than a redefinition of our education system, but that is already sorely needed. If our schools lack the resources to develop in our children an appreciation of humankind's finest accomplishments, where else will it happen?

At present it is laughable to hope that music and art have a place in the curriculum; school administrations in many cities are so short of funds that they must fight just to keep a roof over the students' heads. Read Jonathan Kozol's *Savage Inequalities* if you want to ruin your sleep for the next month. Imagine water pouring down the stairs of an inner-city school whenever it rains (a painfully true story related by Kozol), and then try to justify spending money on flutophones for fourth graders. Our astonishingly rich, ostensibly enlightened society has yet to figure out how to educate all our children in what it considers the basics.

If our nation is to throw its economic weight at a problem, let it be at education, and let basic education include the arts.

An aesthetic sense distinguishes man from the other animals; in evolving from the squalor and hardship of sheer survival, humans somehow developed a sense of the beautiful, an appreciation of the timeless. How tragic that at this supposedly advanced stage of our evolution, we do not include any significant degree of aesthetic instruction in our schools because there is not enough time and money.

The politicians are right: it *is* a question of values. On what should our elected government spend money? Answer that yourself, but as you do, remember that the entire budget of the National Endowment for the Arts is slightly less than the Defense Department's allocation for military bands. Look as well at the substantial cuts made in federally supported student loans in higher education.

Confucius puts it bluntly in the *Analects*: "If you would know if a people are well governed, and if its laws are good or bad, examine the music it practices."

82

The New Majority?

Out of the Woods

MARCH 1995

I write this as the new Congress begins its work on Capitol Hill, shaping once again (tongue firmly in cheek) a better future for us all. The self-proclaimed New Majority, elected on the promise of hope and change by the 39 percent of eligible voters who showed up at the polls, wants to slash spending and reconsider nearly every program currently funded by the American taxpayer.

High on the hit list is the National Endowment for the Arts, an agency that passes on about $123 million in grants to arts organizations throughout the country. The average taxpayer contributes about sixty cents annually to the NEA's budget.

Given a total Washington budget of $1.5 trillion, such a minuscule amount seems hardly worth fighting over, but there are other issues at hand here, as any friend of Jesse Helms will tell you.[1] First among these is the belief that the US government has no business funding the arts (the arts are for the elite who can afford to pay their own way, goes the theory), and second, that the NEA itself is a den of iniquity, passing on the taxpayer's hard-earned sixty cents to revolutionaries intent on bringing down the American way of life.

In all the high dudgeon inspired by this controversy, many citizens are not aware of how the NEA works. People are often surprised to learn that the agency's employees, even those appointed by the president, have no say in who receives a grant. Competition is fierce for the limited funding, and the average application form takes at least thirty hours to fill out. The actual grantors are panels of artists considered experts in their specialization, who meet in marathon sessions to read and discuss

---

1. Jesse Helms (1921–2008) was a deeply conservative senator from North Carolina who served for five terms, fighting civil rights, gay rights, foreign aid, and modern art.

each proposal. These panels then make their recommendations that the NEA executes. At least a year goes by from the time of application to disbursing money, most of which goes to organizations with very conservative boards of directors.

That's how it works. Having filled out my share of NEA applications, I can tell you there is nothing elite about it. In fact, organizations have a better chance of receiving funds if they can prove that they reach disadvantaged constituencies. Nor is the NEA particularly generous: the grants given to the chamber music festival I run amount to less than 5 percent of our annual budget, and there is no guarantee from year to year that our thirty hours of paperwork will pay off.

You may wonder, Why bother? Here the answer is simple and unambiguous: leverage. By law, all grants require matching funds to be raised at the local level; last year's $123 million in NEA grants brought $1.3 billion onto the nonprofit books of arts organizations everywhere. It is remarkable efficiency for one dollar to become eleven dollars. I doubt that the General Accounting Office could duplicate that anywhere else inside the Beltway.

So, before the axe descends, you may want to tell your Congressperson not to slash something that actually works. While you are at it, mention how much the arts invigorate the local economy. Last summer, 5,550 people came to the concerts given by our Skaneateles Festival, all of whom spent money at businesses in our town. Most estimates suggest that for every dollar spent by the arts organization, patrons spend another five dollars in the community on everything from parking to dinner and babysitters. Remember, too, that businesses prefer locating in communities that offer its employees quality-of-life enhancements like the arts. All this sounds a lot like hope and change to me.

Given the political leanings of this Congress, however, there will still be much hewing and crying over the "immoral" art previously supported by the taxpayer's money. At issue are roughly ten controversial cases spread over thirty years out of many thousands of grants.

It is curious that those who oppose government funding for the arts use the word *elite* pejoratively. If anything, the NEA has made the arts more inclusive and has instilled in those who can afford to give an urgency toward charity for the public good. The arts bring out the best in us; indeed, they help us discover and connect with whatever nobility dwells within humanity. We would do well to remember what makes us elite, but instead, a few on the extreme right use the word to sow division, and many reasonable minds are taken in. They declare much of art inaccessible to the majority and, thus, elitist or anticommunity. Moderates, anxious to be seen as defenders of the common man, fall in line as if choreographed. These charges are frighteningly reminiscent of those made by Stalin and his party lackeys against Dmitri Shostakovich. Our own version of the show trials may have already begun by the time you read this.

I regret the note of militancy in my tone, but I fear a quiet, reasonable voice may be lost in the din. Before the new Congress, in its haste to honor its Contract with America, eliminates the NEA, I hope it considers just how much will be lost.

83

"I'm Calling from the NEA"
Out of the Woods
JANUARY 1996

The phone call I've been dreading came in the middle of November. It was a woman's voice on my answering machine: "Mr. Weirich, please return my call as soon as possible. I'm calling from the National Endowment for the Arts."

I knew it had to do with the $5,000 grant promised to the Skaneateles Festival, the chamber music festival I've directed since 1990. Early last summer, our organization was one of a handful of music festivals accepted by the NEA into a two-year application cycle. Based on our 1995 application, the NEA and its peer-review panel deemed us worthy of a grant in 1996 without having to apply again. Instead of a fifty-six-page application in triplicate, all we had to submit was about eight pages assuring them we were still in business. It was too good to be true.

First thing Monday, I called the number. I won't try to reconstruct the conversation; the facts are clear enough.

We will not be getting our grant. In fact, none of the festivals approved for '96 will receive funding. The entire music festivals category has been cancelled. In October, the arts endowment's appropriation shrunk by 40 percent, as legislated by the congressional budget passed last summer.

There is more. To survive, the Endowment is laying off some ninety people, including my bearer of bad tidings. A reorganization is underway that will eliminate the separate programs for the various arts. For example, my chamber music festival will no longer compete for funding with other music festivals; instead, every arts organization—be it a dance company, regional theater, or the New York Philharmonic—will apply to one of four general areas: Creation and Presentation;

Education and Access; Heritage and Preservation; or Planning and Stabilization. Guidelines and new applications should be ready in early 1996. Organizations awarded funding through the new system will not receive any money until 1997.

My caller did not speculate on whether the Endowment would exist in 1997. There is nothing much she can do about it.

Nor is there much that I can say, but I keep trying. This is my fourth *Clavier* column since 1990 on government support for the arts. The last one drew a couple of irate letters suggesting that political issues have no place in a piano magazine. I disagree.

This magazine exists because a readership cares enough to buy it. If the number of readers falls below a certain point, the magazine will close. In the scheme of things, that readership is not large compared to that of the *National Enquirer*, for example, or even *Guns & Ammo*. *Clavier*'s readers love the piano and its music; they want the joy they have found at the piano to be passed on to future generations. They represent a culture with music at its center. Scientists speak of growing things in a culture; under the right circumstances, these things can be lifesaving. What are we growing in our culture?

Consider: The children of the next generation attend public schools in which music programs have been cut. They are barraged by mindless entertainment on television and at the movies. Their radios blast loud, violent music with lyrics about murder, mayhem, and a few other deadly sins. This, too, is a culture, and things grow in it.

Guess which culture has more money. Guess which culture is winning. Guess what magazine's future may be limited.

In the midst of all this, Congress decides that the government should not fund the arts. The money (a mere $60 million, a light lunch by Washington standards) is needed elsewhere; the artists are immoral and have misused the public's money.

The rumblings in previous years have been threatening, but now I am actually scared. We have turned a corner as a nation and are headed down a darkening street.

Speaking as someone trying to run a music festival, the loss of the $5,000 grant represents only 2 percent of our total annual budget. We will try to make that up by selling more tickets and through contributions from individuals, corporations, and foundations. The problem is every other nonprofit organization will be trying to make up their cuts too. Past supporters of musical organizations will receive frequent, urgent solicitations. At the same time, the nonprofit human services sector will have increased financial needs. Charitable people with limited money to give away will find themselves with difficult choices: Should I support the soup kitchen, my college, my church, or that cute summer music festival? A move toward a flat income tax, another of Congress's pet projects, could end the charitable tax deduction as we know it, driving several more nails into the nonprofit coffin. Contributions from corporations often come from marketing departments; decisions on which organizations to fund are based on the size and significance of the benefits that come back to the company. With increased competition for corporate funding from all sectors, businesses can be quite selective about who they help. Finding that $5,000 will not be easy.

Speaking as a citizen, I see the defunding of the National Endowment for the Arts as having graver consequences than our leaders may have considered. By withdrawing support for a culture in which beauty can grow, the other culture—the one thriving on greed, ignorance, and the lowest common denominator—will grow stronger. The dumbing down of America will continue. The example set by Congress tells the nation's people that the arts are not valuable enough to subsidize with government money (which is of course the people's money). So why on earth would you want to support the arts with the funds you have left over after you've paid your taxes?

I'm scared. It is an insidious action that will cause great damage if not checked. Watch your local arts organizations over the next year or two if you don't believe me. After all, for most people, art—like politics—is local.

XV

■ On Relevance

The very first *Winds of Change* column (see page 13) admitted my fear that classical music is not relevant in today's society. As I try to understand the role of classical music in modern America, I ask myself how does it (and with it, I) belong to *this* society. What is its contribution as well as mine? That same column quoted a Chinese proverb: "When the wind changes directions, there are those who build walls, and those who build windmills." The essays in this section consider potential construction blueprints for those power sources.

For better or worse, I've considered my career a calling, a way to contribute something good to the larger society. With or without me, classical music will live forever, but I'd like to see it matter more to more people. I'll not be content crafting swan songs to a noble yet superfluous pursuit.

In previous sections, I questioned music's sustainability in a culture wild for the Super Bowl. I documented the ups and downs of a musical career in academia as those zigzags threatened to derail normal life. My humid ruminations provided no soothing answer beyond T. S. Eliot's "For us, there is only the trying. The rest is not our business."[1]

Not exactly comforting.

The essays here date back to 1992. Starting innocently with a disquisition on the classical/pop divide, I move on to the glories and challenges of making music matter to a community and how a community can form around that music. The David and Goliath story (local piano recital versus the Super Bowl) follows, with questionable assertions of a TKO. Later essays invoke Simon and Garfunkel, silent movies, Al Pacino, and William Shakespeare. I'll look *anywhere* for answers. During my College Music Society presidency, I invited

---

1. T. S. Eliot, *Four Quartets* (New York: Harcourt, 1943), 31.

the esteemed composer Gunther Schuller to answer some of the "big questions" in a keynote address at the national meeting. Alas, he admitted he didn't have any good answers either. The final essay, one of my last for *Clavier Companion*, proposes the activist-artist, a more explicit version of the citizen-artist envisioned by Juilliard president Joseph Polisi.

The dictionary tells us that something is *relevant* when it has "significant and demonstrable bearing on the matter at hand."[2] The first question: What is the matter at hand? If it is relevant, it has value to the beholder. A question then follows: How is that value measured? How valuable is it? Can a case be made that classical music has value to a broader spectrum of the population than currently recognizes it? Is there a community of classical music lovers? How can more people be added to that group? How do you invite them in? Can that community have more ways to interact? Are there locked doors that keep people out? How do you open those doors, or how do you give new people a key to the space?[3]

Stay tuned!

2. *Webster's New Collegiate Dictionary* (1973), s.v. "relevant."

3. See the Maxine Greene quote in the final essay of this section (on page 370).

84

The Classical/Pop Divide
The View from the Second Floor
MARCH 1993

Last night I stood in the lobby of the local concert hall, anthropologically observing the throng of listeners milling about in search of friends or Diet Coke. For a while, I felt like a spy because—please don't tell—I was attending a pops concert.

I was there for a variety of reasons that went beyond the scientific or covert, one of which was I had a free ticket, but midway through intermission, several internal bells started going off. Their reverberations have found their way into this column.

First, a confession: I like a lot of Broadway music. Admitting that to serious musicians usually has the same effect as bad breath, so I've learned to keep quiet about such peccadilloes, at least until last night. Standing with my back to the lobby wall, scanning for and not finding faces I would recognize, the first bell sounded.

Is there a better melody anywhere than the song "Tonight" from *West Side Story*? Think of that instantly memorable first phrase, open intervals rising skyward in opposition to gently descending whole steps. How can one even attempt to describe it? That song generates a complete emotional response in almost every listener, and the fact that it resides in the world of popular music belittles it in no way.

That's when the second bell started chiming. It was more like an alarm, warning me away from the edge of the yawning chasm that exists between serious and popular music. I threaded my way back through music history, looking for the beginnings of the gulf, wondering if it has always been thus. It hasn't.

Once upon a time, there was folk music, and it found its way into "serious" music with ease. Schubert wrote ländler that could be mistaken for folk music; Tchaikovsky borrowed themes intact from the vast

---

reservoir of Russian folk music. We all know about Bartók. In our own backyard, we have Copland's ballets, Ives's symphonies, and Gershwin's *Porgy and Bess*.[1]

There is a sociological trend to consider as well. With the rise of the middle class in the nineteenth century, composers like Offenbach, Strauss (*père et fils*), and Sullivan filled the demand for a lighter vein of serious music. Gershwin, Kern, Rodgers, and Sondheim followed their lead into the twentieth century, producing music of real quality, which appeals to the many who find *Parsifal* and its ilk heavy going.

Starting in the 1950s and early '60s, though, the landmasses of these coexisting styles began a period of continental drift, and the planet hasn't been the same since. Serious composers wrote music of mechanistic objectivity and mathematical abstruseness. With artistic morals held high, they rallied around the banner bearing Milton Babbitt's immortal quote "Who cares if you listen?" and drove the serious music audience right out the door.[2] Those listeners can presently be found immersed in their umpteenth cycle of the "fifty greatest classical masterpieces," safe in the knowledge that they are partaking of the best.

Folk music simply fell into the sea in a landslide that left behind country music as an ersatz imitation of the real thing. Where once there was "Simple Gifts," we now had "Drop Kick Me, Jesus, through the Goalposts of Life." If I'm a snob on this issue, so be it.

It is on the isle of popular music, though, that the most seismic activity has occurred. Mountain ranges shift every couple of years. Blues, a folk art until torch singers borrowed it, evolved into rock 'n' roll, which further evolved into rock, which moved on to punk, heavy metal, music videos, and the rest—all in a forty-year period, and all to great commercial success. There are now "classic rock" radio stations that play only '50s and '60s pop music. For a while in the Washington, DC, area, I knew a station that specialized, for as long as it was hot, in reggae. The scene changes daily.

---

1. See Joseph Horowitz's *Dvorak's Prophecy*, released in 2021.
2. Ironically, Babbitt was Stephen Sondheim's composition teacher at Columbia.

Meanwhile, back in the lobby, I sucked on my ice and wondered who all these people were. More than anything, I wondered how it was that so many parallel audiences could exist, each listening to one kind of music and excluding the others. I kept thinking how close certain aspects of this pops material were to the traditional symphonic literature. If the melody of "Tonight" can move one, Tchaikovsky's *Romeo and Juliet* can't be too far away. There are pops orchestrations that recall Ravel at his most colorful. These worlds have much in common.

I wanted to get my hands on that audience. I wanted to sit them down and play some Schubert ländler for them and then some Rachmaninoff and Ravel. To make the point, I'd then have to play my own arrangements of tunes they know, even if it were from *Phantom of the Opera*.

Would that be so different from what nineteenth-century pianists did back in the days when piano recitals were popular?

85

Grassroots Music—
the Skaneateles Festival

The View from the Second Floor
NOVEMBER 1992

"Grass roots" has been a hot topic this political season. Classical music presentation is often called elitist, but I want to talk about a concert series that uses local performers, involves the community, and presents itself with few of the fancy trappings usually associated with concert life.

There is a lot of personal experience in this essay, since I've been involved with just such a grassroots organization, the Skaneateles Festival, for several years now. It has changed my attitude about many things, from audiences and repertoire to the reason concerts exist in our society.

The Skaneateles Festival was organized in 1980 as a chamber music series by a group that included one professional musician and three music lovers, all of whom resided in a small town (population two thousand) in central New York. The first season of eight concerts was planned in May and presented three months later in August, giving the proceedings a certain seat-of-the-pants quality that remains to this day. The musicians were all natives that year and were not all professional: talented amateurs mixed with the pros for performances of, among other things, a Bach Cantata, the *Trout Quintet*, and music by a local composer who also held down the piano part in anything requested of him. The concerts were given in the upstairs, hundred-seat lecture hall of the town library, a room with warm acoustics and even warmer August temperatures. Dress on both sides of the stage was casual. Tickets were inexpensive; performers' fees were concomitantly modest.

The organizers agreed that they would tear up their payment checks if the festival ran into the red. As it turned out, they needn't have worried—audiences poured into Library Hall and, when it was over, signed on for more. By 1984, things had progressed to such a point that the concerts were moved to a local church to accommodate larger audiences, and a general manager was hired to oversee the increasing number of organizational details. By 1987, an occasional concert was filled to overflowing, even in the larger venues. Thirteen years after its founding, the audience is still clamoring for more.

Since coming onto the scene in 1986, I've asked myself why the festival has been so successful. Many concert series in large cities are barely making ends meet. Audiences are dwindling everywhere. Why are they growing in Skaneateles?

The easiest answer is that Skaneateles had no concert series at all before 1980, and this one filled a vacuum. But how does a town of two thousand draw an average audience of 285 in an un-air-conditioned hall for fourteen August nights?

Strictly speaking, it doesn't. An audience survey shows that people come from as far away as Buffalo (three hours to the west). After thirteen years, word is out that the festival has something unique.

But how did word get around? The festival has only two paid staff members, both part-time. Marketing consists of one flyer sent out six weeks before the concerts begin. The festival is blessed, however, with a working board of directors, eighteen people who receive no payment for their work other than the satisfaction that they make it all possible. The board member in charge of press releases has a mailing list of 125 media organizations, and without recompense she gets the word out. There is a man on the board who dots every i and crosses every t when it comes to dealing with the musician's union. A retired businessman has served as treasurer for several years, and a local teacher sees to it that children under twelve are admitted to concerts for free.

Were it not for this volunteerism, the festival would not exist. It never occurred to me, as a performing musician cradled in the arms of academia, that ordinary people would go to this much trouble to have music presented in their hometown. Most of the musicians who come to the festival from out-of-town have this same reaction. I'm convinced that it's because we musicians are out of touch with the audience and with the people most responsible for putting on the concert. We complain when the audience is small, yet we often have little to do with anyone in the audience on a personal level. In the university, we open our doors to the masses with little more than a "Here we are; come absorb our *great art*" and expect everything else to take care of itself.

I realize that one of the things Skaneateles has done right is to encourage the audience to take ownership, to believe that it's *their* festival. Who else should it belong to? So many of the big performing organizations think their raison d'être is simply their own continuation, misinterpreting Liszt's famous quip *"Le concert, c'est moi!"* The concert exists only because it has an audience. We on the stage should remember that.

While we're at it, we might also remember that a great performance can take place anywhere and is worth just as much in a small town as it is in one of the "musical centers" of the nation. In fact, the small towns have the greater need. If Skaneateles can do it, so can hundreds, even thousands, of other towns. All it takes is a small group of catalysts— and a lot of help from their friends.

86

The Year of the Listener

Program Book Introduction

SKANEATELES FESTIVAL 1993

The 1993 season of the Skaneateles Festival is dedicated to you, the listener. We celebrated composers in 1991—without them we'd have no music. Last year performers were center stage—without them the composer's music might never come to life. And in this third year of our exploration of the concert experience, we arrive literally at the heart of the matter:

If there were no listeners, there would be no concert.

In this Year of the Listener, we musicians want to learn from you— why you come to concerts, what you hear, what you remember later. We also want to present things in such a way that you are the center of attention. For all of us, the Skaneateles Festival is something special, but this year the glory is entirely yours. I know of no audience anywhere that enjoys itself more. May this be the best year yet!

Amid this pleasure is a lot of active listening. Last winter during our benefit concert, I looked out from my seat at the piano to catch a cue from the violinist Laurie Smukler at a spot in the music when everything comes to rest on an expectant chord before springing ahead with renewed excitement. As I looked, my eyes were caught by the eyes of a listener who was looking at Laurie with the same intensity I felt at the moment. It was as if she were waiting for the cue herself, conscious of both the enjoyment we were feeling in the performance and of the musical joke Haydn had come up with almost two hundred years ago. *That's* listening!

One of the great things about listening is that you are in charge. If you want to revel in the heavenly sound of a string quintet and pay no attention at all to the melodies, you can. If you want to focus with your eyes on one player and let your ear sort out that player's line in the overall texture, that's fine too. You are, in a sense, your own composer.

And there is always more to hear, always another level of meaning to listen for. It's tremendously rewarding to hear from experienced listeners after a concert that they heard something new. And there is that eternally-sought-after revelation of a score in which every note seems to make sense from start to finish. It is difficult enough for the performers to achieve; when the audience has been there following every sound, the magic is boundless.

In preparing this season, I thought long and hard about the act of listening. When we listen to a speech, we take in verbal information, and if the speaker has anything to say, we can later tell our friends the subject of the speech. But after listening to a piece of music, it is much harder to describe what we have heard. Claude Lévi-Strauss put it this way: "Music is the only language with the contradictory attributes of being at once intelligible and untranslatable." It is a language unto itself and, as such, speaks of things we cannot speak about. I would go even further and say it is the only way left for us today to speak of the things that really matter.

A listener recently asked me, "If a performance happens in a forest and no one is there to hear it, does it make any sound?" I will let you answer. The music will always be there, in the mind and ear of the composer, perhaps in the living room of the performer, and thanks to technology, digitally encoded on little plastic discs. But for music to live as it was intended, and for its message to be felt, it requires a listener whose ear welcomes these untranslatable truths. The circle is finally completed.

Music is not about "I [the performer or composer] felt grief once." Rather it implores, "Let us all feel this grief together." It is not "I'm having a wonderful time" but "Let's enjoy this together." This is the listening experience, and it doesn't happen at home with your stereo. It happens in concert, where there is a joining of forces, a pooling of energies. It is social in the best sense.

So, please, join us many times during the Year of the Listener. And bring friends—it may be the nicest thing you've ever done for them.

87

The Goliath of Mass Culture
Out of the Woods
MARCH 1996

As I sit at my desk writing, most of America is celebrating Super Bowl Sunday. Estimates suggest that a hundred million people will watch at least part of the game. Thirty-second commercial spots are going for $1.2 million apiece. Each player in the game will receive a paycheck totaling significantly more than my annual salary. The figures stagger this meager pianist's imagination.

Earlier this week, I gave my first faculty solo recital at Syracuse University. About two hundred people came. They paid seven dollars apiece to hear a two-hour program. I received no fee for the performances, since faculty throughout the country truly "give" the recitals they play to the university community. These figures I can understand, like them or not.

I realize that comparing these two events is ridiculous; what interests me more is a look at the collision of cultures supporting both events. A concert will never achieve the mass appeal of a sporting event, the Three Tenors notwithstanding. Who wants to share the intimacy of a Debussy Prélude with one hundred thousand people? Still, those of us trying to survive in art music need to be more than a blip on the radar screen of the larger society. The Super Bowl makes a lot of a noise; 250 million of our fellow citizens know what it is. Try asking the next five people you meet at the mall what a Debussy Prélude is.

There are, of course, some enormous differences between watching a televised football game and going to a concert at a university. The Super Bowl viewer flips on the tube for free; the entire spectacle of clashing manhood, flashy halftime shows, cheerleaders, and all those glitzy ads cost the viewer nothing more than pennies for the electricity and maybe a few nickels for the cable bill. Our intrepid concertgoer, on the other hand, must go out of the house, journey miles through the dark, find parking in an unfamiliar location, perhaps pay for the parking, walk in the dark from the parking to the concert hall, and pay for a ticket.[1]

The Super Bowl viewer settles back in the Barcalounger, reaches for the popcorn fresh from the microwave, and slips into the game, talking about it, even cheering aloud, with friends and loved ones gathered in the warmth of the family room on Sunday, their day off. On the other hand, the resolute concertgoers attending my recital were out on a Tuesday night in January, temperature below freezing with occasional snow flurries. They sat in rows of hard-backed chairs, suitable for the Spanish Inquisition, and silently, formally observed my playing. They applauded at all the right times. They might have talked about the recital at intermission since there is not so much as a Coke machine in the building.

We could keep the comparison going, but it's getting more than a little depressing. Note, however, that we are talking about the process of viewing or listening, not about the content itself.

Attending a concert clearly requires effort on the part of the listeners. Once they are in the hall, there is significant mental exertion involved in following the musical train of thought laid down by composers as diverse as, in this case, Beethoven, Schumann, and Debussy. Getting that message isn't easy; not getting it means the listener has spent two hours in a state of boredom, whether they admit it or not. Those most likely to get it are those who have played the piano themselves. Millions of Americans, whether male or female, have at some time played football. No wonder half the country watched the Super Bowl. Concert presenters interested in audience development would do well to remember this simple fact: doing fosters familiarity.

Those others who "get it" have had help in learning how to follow the music. I doubt if there are many Americans who know *nothing* about the game of football. Even if they can't tell a quarterback from a goalpost, they still understand that the team that scores the most points wins. There is a quantifiable outcome. What's more, there is always someone

---

1. It is probably too early to know whether the streaming necessitated by the COVID-19 pandemic will have a long-term effect on concert life.

there to tell them more about the game, whether it be a friend, relative, or TV commentator. Most listeners to serious music aren't so fortunate. They deserve some help.

I am hopeful that a few of you reading this may have raised an eyebrow in pleasant surprise that two hundred people showed up for my recital. I was delighted but must report that it had nothing to do with my stellar reputation. Blame it instead on good old-fashioned American marketing. Even the Super Bowl advertises. At my own expense, I acquired a couple of local mailing lists and sent postcard invitations to nearly seven hundred addresses. I wrote a press release and sent it to three local newspapers. I went to the local classical FM station and did a short interview with the morning drive-time host, which was taped and aired more than once. As a result, at the very least, the people most likely to attend knew about the recital.

On the postcard, I made sure they knew the who-what-where-when of it all but also added that there was free parking at a particular location and a reception would follow the recital. When your competition is the remote control and free pizza delivery, most people need more enticement than "Great art—come and get it!"

Once the audience was there, I provided program notes. While there were probably very few first-time concertgoers, I wanted to be sure everyone in attendance had some kind of guide to what they would be hearing. On the other hand, I had no intention of condescendingly telling them what they should listen for. I am convinced that many people avoid concerts because they think, or are made to feel, that they don't know enough to understand the music. Program notes inadvertently add to the problem when the author writes about the modulation to the mediant, or the influence of Fauré on Debussy. There is plenty one can say without jargon, addressed to the heart of the listener, which is of course the destination of the music itself.

The rest of the concert was up to me. Whatever else the listener took home that night depended on my playing. It says a lot about a culture that something as esoteric as a piano recital can still exist surrounded by the noise of the Super Bowl. Something deeply meaningful takes place in terms of human interaction, without the roar of tens of thousands, without a clear winner.

For the performer, I think it is no exaggeration to say that one's entire life goes into the effort of playing, no matter what the objective outcome. Audience members witness that effort and respond according to their own sensibilities. Sometimes, taken together, the results can last a lifetime, far longer than a football score.

88

Hello, Chatter

Winds of Change

MARCH–APRIL 2012

"Hello chatter, my old friend."

So wrote *New York Times* columnist Maureen Dowd, who in calling attention to the new silent film *The Artist* last December 7, 2011, took on much more. (All indented lines below come from her column.)

> The sounds of silence are a dim recollection now, like mystery, privacy and paying attention to one thing—or one person— at a time.

My students will tell you that I insist they hear the silence before playing music. That I repeat myself on this point so often suggests they may already be immune to silence.

> As far back as half-a-century ago, the Swiss philosopher Max Picard warned: "Nothing has changed the nature of man so much as the loss of silence," once as natural as the sky and air.

During a student summer in Austria, I remember visiting an area in the Salzkammergut far from the noise of modern life. The inn in which our group stayed was nestled against the mountains on an *Alm*, or Alpine pasture. I walked alone from the inn out toward the horizon that promised a view of the valley below. The farther I walked, the quieter it became. When I reached the edge, I realized I could hear nothing but the wind. I also realized that this was the first time in my life that I had experienced true silence. No furnace blower, no jet overhead, no traffic noise, no voices. When an occasional cowbell clanked in the distance, its clarity, delimited by mountains and air and no other sound, was incredible.

> There will be fewer and fewer of what Virginia Woolf called "moments of being," intense sensations that stand apart from the "cotton wool of daily life."

In my best-of-all-possible worlds, music is a conduit to such experiences. I speak not of the music that is the soundtrack of modern experience (radio, TV, iPods, Muzak), but only of music that comes from silence and returns to it. Think of the opening of Mahler's First Symphony: that five octave A, hovering in space as it is played by the strings, is an evocation of the dawn's quiet, a primeval hush against which awakening birds announce their presence. Music that begins with a bang can be just as effective—Beethoven's Seventh Symphony whacks the listener upside the head with an A major chord played sforzando by full orchestra; the solo oboe is left holding the tonic pitch, turning it into a motive of four notes. Then whack! A sforzando E major chord, from which a clarinet continues the journey. The message: *Listen!* This is important—even if you've heard the piece before.

All great music requires silence to have meaning. Silence, in turn, is the sonic equivalent of zero. We understand "number" because we realize that there is also "nothing."

The catalyst for these ramblings was, of all things, a piano concerto competition. One after another, accomplished young pianists came onstage, sat down, and began their pieces. Keyed up to show their stuff, their performances came not so much from silence as from the last practice session or from the memory of all the recordings they had ever listened to. It was as if each concerto already existed as an omnipresent sound-world, like traffic on the freeway, that simply became audible when they played. And was it ever loud!

The pieces played were the usual suspects, with a preponderance of Russian Romantics. We've all heard these pieces many times before. Students want to play them because, alas, they tend to win the competitions and because all the other "good" students are playing them. They measure their value as pianists by the number of notes required per page. One wonders if these unfortunate, overused pieces can ever be heard afresh or whether their meaning is lost in the daily din to which they contribute. Today, the sound of your world will be honking horns, crying children, argumentative politicians, and interminable Rachmaninoff Seconds.

Yet even that hackneyed piece in a great performance emerges from silence. A quiet F minor chord in the solo piano, midrange, followed by a tolling low F, followed by a slightly different midrange chord and another low F. The progression continues, harmonies changing in each bar, but the top of each chord (C) and bottom (F) remain constant, everything growing in volume and intensity, until the eighth bar when three bass notes move us to a roiling pianistic sea of C minor and a heart-wrenching, long-lined melody played by the violins and violas in unison. It can be extraordinarily powerful. Or it can sound like the last hundred Rachmaninoff Seconds.

As teachers, we need to foster in our students an attitude of listening such that Maya Angelou's words in *Gather Together in My Name* would not need explanation: "Music was my refuge. I could crawl into the space between the notes and curl my back to loneliness." This lovely metaphor reminds one of a Schnabel witticism: "I don't think I handle the notes much differently from other pianists. But the pauses between the notes—ah, there is where the artistry lies." A respect—perhaps even reverence—for silence brings us, ironically, much closer to the sound. Music is the sum total of both.

While we're at it, let's de-commoditize the standard repertoire. Poor Beethoven, Chopin, Liszt, Rachmaninoff! Our focus on the same pieces year in and year out has created a Muzak of conservatory greatest hits that makes top-forties radio look adventurous. We owe these pieces an immense debt of gratitude—without them, we wouldn't have jobs. The least we can do is give them a break now and then.

89

Looking for Richard the Third

Winds of Change

OCTOBER 2009

Not long ago, I saw a documentary called *Looking for Richard.* The actor
Al Pacino released it in 1996; it centers on his attempt, as an American
actor, to come to terms with Shakespeare, in particular the play known
as *The Tragedy of Richard the Third.* Pacino had always wanted to
perform Richard, but as he quips early in the film, he didn't want it to be
"John Wayne does *Hamlet.*" His basic question was how to communicate
Shakespeare to a contemporary American audience.

I immediately saw connections between his dilemma and that of
any contemporary American musician trying to communicate Beethoven,
or Bach, or [name any serious composer of concert music dead or alive].

At least Pacino is famous. Within the first five minutes of the
documentary, we see him on the streets of New York talking to people
about Shakespeare. One hip young woman volunteers that she has
seen *Hamlet.*

"What did you think of it?" asks Pacino.

"It sucked."

He keeps trying. He asks a twentyish male, "Is there anything you
can think of in Shakespeare that makes you think that it's not close to
you or connected in any way?"

"Yeah, it's boring."

"Oh, man," I'm thinking as I watch it, "I can so relate to this."
And this is a *really famous movie star* in the same boat as [name your
favorite international concert artist who makes more in one concert than
you earn in six months]. Sure, a small audience of cognoscenti will come
to hear Big-Name Pianist play a serious concert. But I know in my bones
that if Big-Name Pianist were walking around Greenwich Village asking
hip young people what they think of the *Goldberg Variations*—well, let's

get real—he wouldn't even be recognized! The BNP never played Michael Corleone.

Pacino then summarizes his goal. "It's a dream of mine to communicate how I feel about Shakespeare to other people, communicate our passion for it, our understanding that we've come to, and in doing that, communicate a Shakespeare that is about how we feel and think today."

Once again, my inner bells go off. "Exactly," I think. The music we are passionate about, whether it was written three hundred years ago or last week, has everything to do with how we feel and think every day. But why is it so hard to communicate that? Why aren't there more people curious enough to listen? Pacino wonders the same thing about Shakespeare.

He asks high school students studying Shakespeare what they know about Richard III. He asks, "Humpback?" Blank faces. "One arm?" No reaction. "My horse, my horse, my kingdom for a horse." A vague recollection crosses a few faces.

Pacino then performs (thrillingly, by the way) the opening monologue: "Now is the winter of our discontent / made glorious summer by this sun of York." He asks what it means. No answer. He teases out a few meanings; he tells them what had just happened in English history prior to Richard's speech. What had been metaphorically a winter in Richard's eyes was now becoming a glorious summer thanks to the sun of York—oh, the son of York (Richard himself)! Faces start to show engagement. Pacino admits it's not easy: "The relationship between all these characters—who can keep it straight?"

Here's proof, if proof is needed at this late date, that audiences appreciate a musician who can talk to them about the music. My one quibble with Pacino: he made his audience feel their ignorance before he engaged them. When we talk to concert audiences, the last thing we should do is remind them how much more we know about music than they do.

Another problem: the language itself.

In a working session with other actors, Pacino says, "You can do something from Shakespeare, and you're feeling it or whatever you're doing—you love it—and you think you're communicating it, and the person you just said it to has not understood a word you said, and you can't believe they didn't get it."

Another actor suggests that Shakespeare used a lot of fancy words. But Pacino replies, "Excuse me, they're not fancy words. They're like poetry. It's hard to grab hold of some rap slang, too; it's hard to get hold of it until your ear gets tuned."

I loved that last phrase: tuning the ear; attuning one's consciousness; ramping up one's attention so as not to miss the good stuff. This may require repeated listening. I hit the rewind button more than once in this film.

Pacino also cites the intimidation factor American actors find in Shakespeare. "The problem—you approach it reverentially and you shouldn't. But we do, and we have a feeling, I think, of inferiority as to the way it's done by the British, their critics, their scholars."

Indeed. We revere the classical performance tradition and live in fear that the ghost of Schnabel will strike us down if our Beethoven veers too much from his recordings. Somehow, though, Pacino shows in the film that the role and the actor can merge. Eventually this famous Hollywood icon, born in the Bronx and known the world over, becomes a convincing, fascinating, hateful Richard III. Shakespeare's words find a voice that we believe. It doesn't matter that it happens to be Al Pacino saying the words.

Such a merging of role and actor takes courage. Later in the film, the actor Alec Baldwin puts it this way: "We're not here to get it right. If we get it right, it's a happy accident."

There were two more speeches in the film that I jotted down for their insight and poetry. One was spoken extemporaneously by the British actress Vanessa Redgrave about iambic pentameter (and American actors' fear thereof): "Shakespeare's poetry, his iambics, floated and descended through the pentameter of the soul, and it's the soul—if we like, the spirit—of real concrete people going through hell and sometimes moments of great achievement and joy. *That* is the pentameter you have to concentrate on, and should you find that reality, all the iambics will fall into place."

Read that more than once. Tune your ear. Think of it the next time you play Beethoven.

The other speaker was an anonymous street person who is seen early in the film and then is given the last word. When asked by Pacino what he thought of Shakespeare's words, he said, "Intelligence is hooked with language, and when we speak with no feeling, we get nothing out of our society. We should speak like Shakespeare. We should introduce Shakespeare into the academics—know why? Then the kids would have feelings. We have no feelings. It's why it's easy for us to get a gun and shoot each other—we don't feel for each other. But if we were taught to feel, we wouldn't be so violent."

Pacino: "And you think that Shakespeare helps us with that?"

Street person: "He did more than help us—he instructed us."

The street person's final words: "Everything are [*sic*] words and things, and we have no feeling in our words, and we say things to each other that don't mean anything. But if we felt what we said, we'd say less and we'd mean more."

90

Connecting Classical Music to Our Culture

Winds of Change

OCTOBER 2015

Something that never seems to change: the difficulty of connecting classical music to the rest of our culture.

Twelve years ago, the College Music Society invited a true musical polymath—composer, conductor, educator, publisher, author, and jazz musician Gunther Schuller—to discuss this very thing. He began his speech by citing the problems, bemoaning the isolation of serious music at every turn, and then said he had no idea what to do about it. This led to a lively discussion among the various attendees and quite a few sighs of frustration. One person suggested that if cable television can make a profit on food shows, surely classical music can find a way. To date, alas, we have not come up with anything like the Cooking Channel.

Music may be more a part of our culture than ever before, but classical music finds itself stashed away in the attic. One need only visit YouTube to discover that the number of hits for Lang Lang's "Emperor" Concerto[1] at 1,288,176 compares rather unfavorably to "Charlie Schmidt's Keyboard Cat!—THE ORIGINAL!" at 41,768,095. Yes, friends, *this* is our culture.

When we think about classical music culture, we think of concerts in fancy halls and recitals in school auditoria and churches. We also remember our own musical educations and how accustomed we are to this comfortable normalcy. Concert presentation methods are long established: a printed program of masterworks by dead white European males, the artist plays the works on the program in the announced order, and the performances sound pretty much like the last one of the

---

1. A popular Beethoven concerto played by one of the most popular pianists today.

same works. There is an audience for this kind of presentation, but it is small, aging, and conservative.

How do we change this? Do we even want to? Gunther Schuller didn't know, and neither do I. However, there are some things we might think about.

While the larger music world has few boundaries, classical music has a lot of them. An audience must sit still during the concert and remain quiet for a long time, and texting is not allowed. If you've attended a concert before, you probably know in advance the pieces you will hear. They likely sound a lot like you remembered. If attending for the first time, you might be surprised at how formal, even uninviting, the whole thing is. The artist could just as well be a cyborg, moving about the platform in silence and communicating with the audience through stiff body language. Maybe we should devise a friendlier delivery system.

The cooking shows introduce viewers to new or improved things to eat. We all need sustenance to stay alive. Classical music, however, is seen as a nonessential luxury, something in which those with the time and money can indulge. Can classical music be presented as something as nourishing as home-baked bread?

I think there is a lot of promise in home-baked concerts, which would be musical presentations in the home. The relaxed, personalized communication possible in a house concert offers great opportunity to bring new listeners to classical music. I do not suggest, however, a standard recital presented in the home. I envision an altogether different presentation—a party with good conversation, interesting people to meet (a mix of classical devotees and complete newbies), and a host or hostess who can steer the flow of the party to a subject that can be illustrated by a piece of music. Perhaps someone at the party has had a recent trip away from home. The hostess offers to play Beethoven's "Les adieux" Sonata and introduces the piece by telling some interesting things about the friendship of Beethoven and the Archduke Rudolph, how Napoleon was shelling Vienna in 1809 and the Archduke had to leave for his own safety while Beethoven remained. Encapsulated here are many deeply human experiences, and we can sense these qualities in the music. The performance, be it by the hostess or by an invited student as guest, emphasizes the communicative power of the music. The party can then continue after the music or explore other pieces that express something all the guests know about. The subject need not be too specific; we all know about beauty, or simplicity, or anxiety, or loss. We are so lucky to be involved with music that can speak to (and for) us in this way.

Concerts, then, are not about the talented performers who have gifts that many do not; they are about finding our common humanity through great music. They are not sporting events in which instrumental athletes conquer the unplayable. Nor are they mere entertainment, pretty tunes to relax you on an evening off. Good music has the power to sustain us. Let's never forget that.

91

The Activist-Artist

Winds of Change

MAY 2016

In the heat of this political season, the airwaves are full of talk about systems that don't work, about reform. I recently gave a political speech of sorts at the MTNA national conference, suggesting that those in our profession might benefit from reforming their approaches to music, leading to more activism as well as a strengthening of community.

In a nation that values economic growth, music education doesn't attract much attention. In the *Times* this morning, I read of a hedge fund manager who was moving from New Jersey to Florida. His incipient change of address meant that the entire budget of the state of New Jersey would face a major deficit simply because this man's income tax payments would disappear. That's wealth. I doubt that all our incomes put together would match his take-home pay. Talk about the 1 percent!

Just to survive, we need to become activists for our art. At every opportunity, we must demonstrate the importance of music and the value of learning to play an instrument. We can't be quiet providers of "extras," those life enhancers considered luxuries. If we think of our art as purely beautiful music, beautifully played in beautiful concert halls, attended by beautiful people in beautiful clothes, we are part of the problem. If all we do as teachers is coach a louder, faster, more perfect rendition of a familiar warhorse, we are living with our heads in the sand. It's time to realize that the role of art in society has slipped.

What is art's function in society? John Dewey (1859–1952) was an American philosopher, psychologist, and educational reformer, whose 1934 book *Art as Experience* submits that there is continuity between art and everyday life. Art is not a frill, a bauble with beautiful surfaces. Art is a transformation of the ordinary. When it has its greatest impact, it is different, unexpected. Art exists for human interaction; after all, humans make art for other humans, not to be judged as a "good performance" only but as a creation that makes you think in a new way.

Maxine Greene was a teacher and education theorist for fifty years at Teachers College, Columbia University, who promoted the arts as a fundamental learning tool for children. Her goal was not to produce hundreds of little musicians; she believed that children could learn things from studying the arts that they could not learn in other ways. I particularly like this statement (italics mine):

> Aesthetic experience requires *conscious participation in a work, a going out of energy*, an ability to notice what is there to be noticed in the play, the poem, the quartet. *Knowing "about," even in the most formal academic manner, is entirely different* from constituting a fictive world *imaginatively* and entering it *perceptually, affectively*, and *cognitively*.[1]

Many academics "know about" too much. We drown in esoteric details and hold to a petrified—yet acceptable (even required)—performance tradition. In other words, we perpetuate the way it has been done for the last fifty years. In order to break the mold, we must consciously participate in the work, indeed, re-create it. Only then do we have a chance of being the artist Dewey sought.

I am drawn to Greene's adverbs. *Perceptually* indicates that our immediate sensory perceptions are involved. We must listen with fresh ears to the directness of the sound, not be caught up in judging it for its correctness. *Affectively* suggests the presence of the emotions, that one understands the message of the composer with the heart, not the left brain. *Cognitively* tells us the brain is nevertheless still involved. We might sense the form of the composition as it is revealed with the passing of time. It requires attention to suppress the accepted "textbook" form to be swept along emotionally *and* mentally in the unfolding of the work, carried to its conclusion in excitement or repose, depending on the piece.

---

1. Maxine Greene, *Releasing the Imagination: Essays on Education, the Arts, and Social Change* (San Francisco: Jossey-Bass, 1995), 125.

Bronisław Huberman, the great violinist and founder during the Nazi era of the Palestine Symphony (later the Israel Philharmonic), said, "The true artist does not create art as an end in itself. He creates art for human beings. Humanity is the goal."

We are social animals; humanity requires community. Again Maxine Greene:

> [Community] has to be achieved by persons offered the space in which to discover what they recognize together and appreciate in common. It ought to be a space infused by the kind of imaginative awareness that enables those involved to imagine alternative possibilities for their own becoming and for the group's becoming.[2]

Art, in particular music, offers that space. We can imagine, through music, a better world. When the Palestine Symphony first played in 1936, the people who heard it not only could imagine a better world—they realized they lived in a world that wasn't Nazi Germany.

As much as music and teaching inhabit our lives, this is truly what we live for—to create a space infused by imaginative awareness. It allows us to hear someone utter "I have a dream," and change can occur.

---

2. Greene, *Releasing the Imagination*, 39.

XVI

■ The Next Chapter

In planning this book, I wanted to end on an optimistic note, something to suggest that life with the piano is still possible, even if you are not a star. That life, however, is likely to be very different from mine. Looking back, I wonder, as stated in the previous section, if people like me were part of the problem. Although I worried deeply that classical music lacked relevance to the larger society, I was focused on being a soloist; "making it" was the goal. While the definition of "it" changed over time, I was often blindered to the bigger responsibility of making music matter to a definable community.

If a tree falls in the forest and there is no one there to hear it, does it make a sound? What about music? Performers, faculty, and students work hard to make lots of sound, but is it heard in a forest that doesn't really value classical music? Many performers isolate themselves in like-minded communities, affiliated as they are with established schools or performing organizations. Within the walls of their world, these musicians study, practice, finesse details, and perform, usually for an audience of peers: the other faculty, their students, and the niche audience. It's time to get off that merry-go-round.

In parts 85 and 86 of the previous section, I wrote of the Skaneateles Festival, which presents chamber music in a small, upstate New York town during the last four weeks of the summer. Because of this organization, there are community residents who love classical music who never dreamed it would be such an important part of their lives. During the season designated "The Year of the Listener," following our first chamber orchestra concert, a man shared what might be my favorite audience reaction of all time. This was a guy who was not only a dyed-in-the-wool rock music fan, but he sang in a popular local band. He was attending one of our concerts for the first time because his son was playing the toy trumpet part in the *Toy Symphony*. What he said was "Man, that concert last Saturday really took my doors off!"

I love this metaphor. We usually use doors to keep things out. His doors had come down to let in a kind of music he hadn't expected to like. He opened his doors from the inside, but we can't always count on that. If you are on the outside, it takes a key to open the doors, preferably one that turns easily. What constitutes the key(s) we need?

Sometimes classical music insiders erect the doors themselves. Seldom do the cognoscenti offer keys to outsiders allowing them easy access. Some insiders even want to preserve their exclusivity. Tickets can be expensive. The program can be intimidating, presented in a stiff, formal manner. The rest of the audience can seem distant, even unfriendly to a stranger. The keyholes can be hard to find. No wonder classical music seems irrelevant.

Let's take a deeper dive into how that festival program was put together. We used local children who were far from prodigies to play the toy instrument parts. That brought in curious townies, as well as the children's families and friends. The program opened with the *Toy Symphony*, leaving everyone with a smile, but more-challenging listening lay ahead. While the evening ended with the popular *Serenade for Strings* by Tchaikovsky, it also included a beautiful but little-known oboe concerto by Vaughan Williams and an almost atonal piece for string orchestra, Irving Fine's *Serious Song* from 1955. When was the last time you heard that one? The location of the concert—outdoors on the grand old porch of a private home overlooking Skaneateles Lake— put the music in gracious, comfortable surroundings on a beautiful summer night. People would love to be there even without the music. Finally, we advertised the entire season as dedicated to the listeners, putting them at the center of attention. One Friday night in our indoor location, St. James' Episcopal Church, we programmed a quartet for clarinet and strings by Howard Boatwright, the retired chair of Syracuse University's music department (again the local touch). We learned that the concert took place on his birthday, so after the performance of his piece, we rolled in a birthday cake for people to celebrate with him and enjoy a snack at intermission. This kind of human engagement led to the festival's rapid growth. After only three years of this approach, attendance had more than doubled and fundraising tripled.

Sadly, I left the festival in 1999 to accept what I thought was a promotion. Despite nine years of deep immersion and satisfaction in bringing classical music to a delightful community, my appetite for more-tangible recognition led me to accept the teaching position in Missouri. The rewards were obvious: a good salary, a named endowed chair, tenure, the rank of full professor. A close friend, a founder of the festival, said, "You really don't have a choice." After a career of chasing success and recognition, the choice did seem obvious. Twenty-plus years later, I realize what I gave up.

If I had it all to do over again, I would add one more job to the musician's curriculum vitae. I think a serious musician today needs to be a community organizer. It's not enough to play beautifully, to teach persuasively, to write interesting program notes, to keep learning repertoire. You have to become a community organizer for classical music. You must roll up your sleeves and be the spark plug for a community who doesn't know it yet but will soon appreciate the joys of classical music. As the local advocate for this pleasure, you organize a group whose common goal is wanting more people to recognize its value to all. I was on my way to being such a community organizer in Skaneateles, but I still thought of myself as a performing musician and artistic director who used music to bring personal recognition. I still thought if I played beautifully enough, it would be sufficient.

If you research a community organizer's job description, you find that they are neighborhood mobilizers who conduct outreach and organize residents year-round, listening to and addressing the individual concerns of residents.

Start with the neighborhood—the people who live or work near you. They are the ones you should mobilize and invite to a concert or to your house for a little performance. I'm reminded of Warren, a missed opportunity. (See page 306.) It's pointless to offer a recital and not actively recruit attendees. How you plan those recitals makes a huge difference in how readily new attendees might enjoy it. A friendly stage presence helps. So does talking to the audience, as long as your comments assume neither too little nor too much prior knowledge. The music offered matters, of course; while a piece like Webern's Variations shows the performer's erudition, it may leave the audience cold. Earlier I admitted to playing it on a very intellectual program (see page 272); I would not do this again. I reasoned then that the program was intended for a specialized academic audience, and the Webern was less than seven minutes long, sandwiched between more standardized repertoire (if you can call the Copland Sonata and Beethoven's Op. 111 standardized!). It was also my response to the tragedy of 9/11. I now see this as wishful thinking on the part of someone trying to be an intellectual rather than a community organizer.

Your neighborhood is one of concentric circles: first, the people next door or nearby in the studio or school; then, there is the town, the state, and finally the nation. I am reminded of something I wrote earlier: all art, like politics, is local. (See page 344.) Art happens in spaces you inhabit. It happens between individuals—it can happen between two people or two thousand. Get to two before you try for more. It's difficult to change the world; you are much more likely to make a difference in your local community.

While extending the size of the musical audience is one goal, there is another community that exists wanting a larger audience. In my current hometown, there is a conservatory within a state university and another fine conservatory started by my former student Stanislav Ioudenitch at a private university. There are local teachers' groups connected to the Music Teachers National Association (MTNA) and the National Federation of Music Clubs (NFMC). There is a symphony orchestra, an opera company, a ballet troupe, and at least two high-quality chamber music presenting organizations, and recently a classical music FM station opened, joining one that broadcasts from fifty miles away. There are several smaller, independent orchestras working on limited budgets, as well as independent chamber groups (specializing in both Baroque and contemporary music, string quartets, other mixed groups). Each wants larger audiences. A friend at the new radio station told me that in a survey of the community, they found over forty organizations trying to bring classical music to more people. The larger organizations have staffs and offices; the smaller ones work overtime to reach whatever audience they can. Often, the attendees do not overlap; someone attending the symphony may not attend the Friends of Chamber Music. Both organizations, however, do parallel work to stay in existence.

Those workers in the field, arts administration people, are your other community. Those who want what you want, who share the goal of bringing relevant, classical music to a wider audience—they need a community organizer too. Echoing the soloist's mindset, however, the marketing manager of the opera company works only for the opera company, not for the community. I know of no city where arts groups' staffers cooperate.

Community organizers look outward, beyond the concerns of their private desires—the self-obsessed artiste doesn't belong here. It's a year-round effort—no seasonal breaks. You listen—you are receptive to what others tell you, even if it violates something you love. Your principal goal is to empower others in the group, to actualize their goals. Listening becomes an opportunity for dialogue; you aren't the prescriber-in-residence. You don't have to play the role of expert. This may be particularly difficult for teachers since they enjoy knowing more than their students. You need to address the concerns of the individuals with whom you interact. One solution does not necessarily work for everyone.

When you think about it, musicians have many of the characteristics needed to be good community organizers. They have spent years learning to listen. They are process-oriented—they can effectively organize learning a new piece or coordinate their sometimes-complex daily schedules. If they have taught, they likely can identify others' personal needs and sense the potential in those who will become part of the active community. Teachers readily establish and build working relationships with others.

What the music community organizer may find difficult is agitating for the cause. Classical music is so refined, so respectable, that the tendency is to shy away from anything too brazen or obvious. Yet think of the most powerful experiences you have had with classical music. After a recent recital in Kansas City, an acquaintance related his complete absorption in the experience, total acceptance of the music, and how tears welled up more than once. "Attending that concert was life changing," he said.

We should welcome such emotional release, in ourselves as well as others. Bringing this to a community of any size is a gift, worth whatever activism it takes.

* * *

Being an artist means: not numbering and counting,

but ripening like a tree...

—*Rainer Maria Rilke*

Acknowledgments

I wouldn't be a pianist today were it not for my third cousin, Stanley Sells, who was a year older than me when he showed me "Silent Night." Stanley became an excellent trumpet player, then found he had a remarkable tenor voice in college. His life changed enormously when he had to cancel a contract with an Italian opera house to help his father run the family business in Barnesville, Ohio, after his mother's sudden death. Family always matters. Great thanks to my grandparents Electa and Bert Weirich for giving us their old player piano, paving the way to my taking lessons. An aunt I never knew, Lola (1913–40), was the one who played that instrument in the old farmhouse; she must have been accomplished— in the bench were things like Chopin's B-flat Minor Scherzo and Liszt's Hungarian Rhapsody No. 2 in those old Century editions. Credit also goes to my father for his purchase of an Admiral high-fidelity console phonograph (in stylish walnut) at about the same time the piano arrived. He liked to lie down after work and listen to an Andre Kostelanetz LP, *Clair de lune*, which also contained "The Little Train of the Caipira" by Villa-Lobos. That one caught my ear, and before I knew it, I was a member of the Columbia Record Club. Thus began my musical education.

So much in life is the result of accidents, things you don't plan for, that nevertheless branch out into areas beyond your expectation. I think of performances that were over and done quickly but still resonate in my consciousness. At Oberlin, there was that "Charlie Rutlage" with Ben Bagby (he of *Beowulf* fame), or later stepping in to play the orchestral reduction of Stravinsky's Violin Concerto for Ron Copes (Juilliard Quartet) on a few days' notice. Most meaningful was the Conservatory's mounting of the Mozart Requiem immediately after the Kent State massacre. In three days' time, the chorus and orchestra rehearsed and traveled by bus to Washington, DC, performing the work at the National Cathedral under the direction of Robert Fountain. Mine was just one voice in the chorus, but that performance has had perhaps the most personal significance of any in my career.

A musician makes many friends throughout life; I have been lucky to have the kind with whom you can pick up after an absence of a decade or more and resume right where you left off. Each deserves acknowledgment for their roles in forming my outlook on life, but naming them here will require a second volume. Please forgive me, dear friends, but you know who you are.

Then there are the people with whom I had the honor and pleasure to perform chamber music. Violinist Hilary Hahn was only twelve years old when I first invited her to play in the Skaneateles Festival. It was her first "professional" engagement! About the same time, I was privileged to play with the great violinist Josef Gingold, then ninety years old, at the Eastern Music Festival. His inimitable way with a phrase continues to lilt in my heart.

I appreciate so much *Clavier*'s faith in me—publisher Jim Rohner and editors Barbara Kreader, Kingsley Day, and Judy Nelson were not only good wordsmiths but extremely patient, even forgiving, about deadlines. Pete Jutras lured me back to writing columns for *Clavier Companion* and upheld his promise to let me pen whatever I wanted. Now the Frances Clark Center has expanded into many modern media outlets, including something as old-fashioned as this book.

For inspiration and stamina, I am indebted to Martha Hilley, recent MTNA president, whose favorable mention of my old columns during the national convention's live stream in 2021 set me to work on this collection. Stuart Isacoff and Tim Page—both savvy, experienced writers on musical subjects—sent encouragement during difficult times. Mark Wait and E. L. Lancaster read sections as they appeared and offered suggestions. Albert Mendoza provided professional editorial assistance, from correcting errant syntax to preparing the book for publication. Nick Phillips and Chris Madden graciously accepted the thankless task of last-minute copy review. Jennifer Snow, the energetic spark plug behind the Frances Clark Center's recent renascence, supported the project from the start.

While I am solely to blame for the opinions espoused here, my students and their daily confrontations with the piano, its music, and the crazy culture in which we try to exist inspired many of the essays.

I dedicate this book to them. Having never force-fed these essays on them at the time, some may never have read any of my missals to the readership. Now that the statute of limitations has passed, I hope they happen upon this volume somewhere and recognize themselves.

No one has helped more than my wife Karen Kushner, who as a pianist and teacher herself was the sounding board I trusted most. She also proofread the entire text at least three times, spotting at a hundred paces such minutiae as errors between singular and plural possessives. She delicately pruned my sometimes-profuse verbiage with the care of the most sensitive grammatical gardener. I am forever in her debt.